A-level Study Guide

English Language

Revised and Updated

Alan Gardiner

REVISION express

Acknowledgements

I would like to thank the following for their help, advice and support during the writing of this book:

Caroline Wilkins (English Subject Officer, AQA-AEB); Robert Keeley (former student of Birkenhead Sixth Form College, whose essay on speech and writing is included in Chapter 2); Kevin Rogers (Head of English, Birkenhead Sixth Form College); Eleanor Wall; John Shuttleworth; Marian Murphy; Geoff Black and Stuart Wall (series editors).

The author and publishers are grateful to the following for permission to reproduce copyright material: Atlantic Syndication for Daily Mail masthead, Mirror Syndication International for Daily Mirror masthead, News International Syndication for The Sun masthead (p. 25); HMV UK Ltd for HMV recruitment advertisement (p. 74). In some instances we have been unable to trace the owners of copyright material, and we would appreciate any information that would enable us to do so.

Series Consultants: Geoff Black and Stuart Wall

Project Manager: Stuart Wall

Pearson Education Limited

Edinburgh Gate, Harlow

Essex CM20 2JE, England

and Associated Companies throughout the world

© Pearson Education Limited 2000, 2003

The right of Alan Gardiner to be identified as author of this work has been asserted by him in accordance with the Copyright, Designs and Patents Act 1988.

British Library Cataloguing in Publication Data

A catalogue entry for this title is available from the British Library.

ISBN 0-582-78412-3

First published 2000

Reprinted 2000, 2001

Updated 2003

Set by 35 in Univers, Cheltenham

Printed and bound in Great Britain by Ashford Colour Press, Gosport

Further Reading

This book aims to give you a comprehensive overview of the key topics studied in AS and A2 English Language. The books listed below will help you to explore some of these topics in greater depth. They might especially be of use if you are working on a piece of coursework, or if a particular aspect of the course interests you. Books marked with an asterisk (*) are especially recommended as books which are accessible to AS/A2 English Language students.

General
*Jean Aitchison *Linguistics: An Introduction* (Hodder & Stoughton)
Kim Ballard *The Frameworks of English* (Palgrave)
*David Crystal *Cambridge Encyclopedia of the English Language* (Cambridge University Press)
David Crystal *A Dictionary of Linguistics and Phonetics* (Blackwell)
*David Crystal *Rediscover Grammar* (Longman)
*Angela Goddard *Researching Language* (Folens Framework)
Grover Hudson *Essential Introductory Linguistics* (Blackwell)
*Howard Jackson and Peter Stockwell *An Introduction to the Nature and Functions of Language* (Stanley Thornes)
Tom McArthur *The Oxford Companion to the English Language* (Oxford University Press)
Sara Thorne *Mastering Advanced English Language* (Palgrave)
George Yule *The Study of Language* (Cambridge University Press)

Aspects of spoken and written language
Ronald Carter, Angela Goddard *et al. Working With Texts* (Routledge)
*David Crystal *Language and the Internet* (Cambridge University Press)
Dennis Freeborn *Style* (Macmillan)
Dennis Freeborn *Varieties of English* (Palgrave)
David Langford *Analysing Talk* (Palgrave)
David Lodge *The Art of Fiction* (Penguin)
Brian MacArthur (ed.) *The Penguin Book of Historic Speeches* (Penguin)
Brian MacArthur (ed.) *The Penguin Book of 20th Century Speeches* (Penguin)
Keith Waterhouse *Waterhouse on Newspaper Style* (Viking)

Social aspects of language
Deborah Cameron (ed.) *The Feminist Critique of Language* (Routledge)
Norman Fairclough *Language and Power* (Longman)
Norman Fairclough *New Labour, New Language?* (Routledge)
James Finn Garner *Politically Correct Bedtime Stories* (Souvenir Press)
Jonathon Green *The Cassell Dictionary of Slang* (Cassell)
John Honey *Does Accent Matter?* (Faber)
*Martin Montgomery *An Introduction to Language and Society* (Routledge)
Dale Spender *Man Made Language* (Rivers Oram Press)
Deborah Tannen *You Just Don't Understand: Women and Men in Conversation* (Virago Press)
*Linda Thomas and Shan Wareing *Language, Society and Power* (Routledge)
Peter Trudgill *Dialects* (Routledge)
Peter Trudgill *Sociolinguistics* (Penguin)
Clive Upton and J.D.A. Widdowson *An Atlas of English Dialects* (Oxford University Press)
Ronald Wardhaugh *An Introduction to Sociolinguistics* (Blackwell)

Language change
John Ayto *20th Century Words* (Oxford University Press)
Bill Bryson *Mother Tongue* (Penguin)
Andrew Dalby *Language in Danger* (Penguin)
Dennis Freeborn *From Old English to Standard English* (Palgrave)
Dick Leith *A Social History of English* (Routledge)
Tom McArthur *The Oxford Guide to World English* (Oxford University Press)

Language basics

This chapter explains some of the basic terminology involved in the study of English language. The examining boards call the terms and concepts covered here **linguistic frameworks**. This is because you will need to draw upon this knowledge throughout your course of study. As one of the syllabuses puts it, the linguistic frameworks are a toolkit for the analysis of language.

Much of this chapter is concerned with **grammar**. The first few sections, for example, look at **word classes** (also known as **parts of speech**) – nouns, verbs, adjectives and so on. Later sections relate to **lexis** (vocabulary), **semantics** (word meanings) and **phonology** (the role of sound in language).

Many students have difficulties with grammar, and if you find some aspects of it a struggle you are certainly not alone. A sensible approach is to try to master the simpler elements first. Get to know the word classes, and get into the habit of using this knowledge in your written work. Once you have a clear understanding of word classes, you will find it easier to grasp the essentials of phrases and clauses.

In the exam, you will not be tested directly on your knowledge of the terms contained in this chapter, but you will be expected to use them when you are analysing texts and writing essays. Unlike later chapters, this chapter does not therefore have practice exam questions. Instead, it has a number of exam 'warm-up' questions so that you can test your understanding of the topics covered. Good luck!

Topic checklist

○ AS ● A2

	AQA/A	AQA/B	EDEXCEL	OCR	WJEC
Word classes: nouns and adjectives	○●	○●	○●	○●	○●
Word classes: verbs and adverbs	○●	○●	○●	○●	○●
Word classes: other classes	○●	○●	○●	○●	○●
Phrases and clauses	○●	○●	○●	○●	○●
Sentences	○●	○●	○●	○●	○●
Word structure	○●	○●	○●	○●	○●
Words and meanings 1	○●	○●	○●	○●	○●
Words and meanings 2	○●	○●	○●	○●	○●
Phonology	○●	○●	○●	○●	○●
Cohesion	○●	○●	○●	○●	○●
Graphology	○●	○●	○●	○●	○●

Word classes: nouns and adjectives

The opening sections of this chapter are concerned with **word classes**. We group words into classes and categories according to the ways that they are used in sentences. There are eight major word classes:

nouns	adjectives	pronouns	prepositions
verbs	adverbs	conjunctions	determiners

In this first section, we look at **nouns** and **adjectives**.

Nouns

Nouns are often called 'naming words'. They are the names we give to people, places, objects, feelings, ideas, etc.

One way of identifying nouns is to remember that they are usually words that could be used in answer to the question 'What name do you give to this?' Another way is to see what happens when you put the word 'the' in front of it. If it is a noun, this can usually be done. Compare *the beautiful*, which doesn't make sense, and *the day*, which does. The word *day* is a noun, but *beautiful* isn't.

Here are some examples of nouns:

shoe	Rachel	dog	courage
sugar	air	boy	Glasgow

Types of noun

The main types of noun are shown in the diagram below.

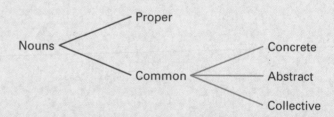

→ **Proper nouns** usually begin with a capital letter. They refer to specific people and places: *Paris, Andrew, Venus*.

→ **Common nouns** are less specific and refer to *types* of people, places, feelings, etc.: *city, man, planet, excitement*. Most nouns are common nouns, which can be subdivided further into concrete, abstract and collective nouns.

  → **Concrete nouns** refer to things that exist physically – things that we can see and feel: *computer, hand, house, tiger*.

  → **Abstract nouns** refer to things that do not exist physically – to feelings, ideas, qualities: *friendship, sadness, democracy*.

  → **Collective nouns** refer to groups of people, animals or objects: *team, family, flock*.

Nouns: number and possession

Nouns can be **singular** or **plural**. Most plural nouns end in –*s* (*books, bottles*, etc.) but some do not (e.g. *sheep, oxen, teeth*).

A noun has a **possessive** ending if an apostrophe, or an apostrophe followed by an *s*, is added to it to show that something 'belongs to' the

Action point

If you think you already know about nouns and adjectives, you could check your knowledge by trying the warm-up question on page 5.

Examiner's secrets

When you are analysing a spoken or written text you will be given credit for using the appropriate terminology, and you should try to get into the habit of referring to word classes.

Watch out!

You may have noticed that *Rachel* and *Glasgow* sound odd if you put 'the' in front of them – unfortunately there are exceptions to this rule!

Examiner's secrets

Many students know what nouns are but are hazy about different types of noun. Try to remember the types listed here.

Checkpoint 1

Writing that contains a large number of concrete nouns is often easier to understand than writing that contains a large number of abstract nouns. Try to explain why.

The jargon

Nouns which refer to individual, 'countable' items are known as **count nouns**: *trees, apples*. **Noncount nouns** have no plural form because what they refer to cannot be 'counted': *courage, rugby*.

noun. An apostrophe alone is added to plural words that already end in *s* ('the babies' toys'), otherwise an apostrophe followed by an *s* is added ('Sally's bag', 'men's magazines', 'Charles's bicycle').

Adjectives ●●●

Adjectives are 'describing words'. They are used to describe nouns:

a *beautiful* day   a *strange* feeling
a *boring* film   a *kind* person

Usually, as in the above example, they are placed in front of the noun they are describing, but sometimes they appear after it ('the day was beautiful'; 'the film was boring').

Comparatives and superlatives

Adjectives can be used to make comparisons:

a *hotter* day than yesterday   a *bigger* town
the *hottest* day of the year   the *biggest* town

Words such as *hotter* and *bigger* are known as **comparative adjectives** (or simply **comparatives**). Words such as *hottest* and *biggest* are **superlative adjectives** (or simply **superlatives**).

Most comparatives are formed by adding –*er* to the adjective, and most superlatives by adding –*est*. Comparatives can also be formed by putting *more* in front of the adjective ('more expensive') and superlatives by using *most* ('most expensive').

Don't forget

Adjectives are a type of modifier (see page 10).

Links

Superlatives are often found in advertisements (e.g. brightest, best). See pages 72–5.

Watch out!

A few adjectives are irregular and do not follow either of these patterns:
good – better – best
bad – worse – worst

Exam warm-up question   answer: page 26

Identify the word class to which the following belong by ticking the appropriate boxes (for some words tick more than one box). (10 min)

	Proper noun	Common noun	Concrete noun	Abstract noun	Collective noun	Adjective	Comparative	Superlative
mysterious								
swarm								
Abba								
marvellous								
further								
equality								
most wonderful								
Concorde								
sticky								
aeroplane								
more glamorous								
far								

Checkpoint 2

Two of these words can also be used as **verbs**. After studying the section on verbs (over the page) return to this exercise and see if you can spot them.

Word classes: verbs and adverbs

In this section, we look at two more word classes: **verbs** and **adverbs**.

Verbs

Verbs are often known as 'doing words', and it is certainly true that many verbs refer to physical actions:

jump   take   give   explode   throw

However, they can also refer to what might be called 'mental actions'. (*think*, *anticipate*) and to states:

→ The house *stands* on a hill.
→ That *seems* unfair.

One way to identify verbs is to remember that most sentences contain one or more verbs and that the verb(s) will usually tell you what the subject is doing or being.

You should also remember that *to be* is a verb, as are all its forms (*is*, *was*, *are*, *were*, etc.).

To be is an example of an **infinitive** (or 'base form') – the form from which all other forms of the verb are derived. All verbs have an infinitive, which always includes *to*: *to run*, *to walk*, *to decide*, etc.

Main and auxiliary verbs

The **main verb** in a clause or sentence is a single verb that expresses the main meaning. **Auxiliary verbs** (sometimes known as 'helping verbs') are verbs that are placed in front of main verbs:

I *must have been* thinking about something else.

Here there are three auxiliary verbs (in italics). The main verb is *thinking*. Auxiliary verbs are of two types: primary verbs and modal verbs.

There are only three **primary verbs**: *be*, *have* and *do*. Here are examples of these verbs used as auxiliaries:

(1) He *is* running   (2) *Have* you spent all your money?
(3) I *do* want to see you   (4) I *did* not go to school yesterday

These sentences illustrate some of the uses of auxiliary verbs. They can indicate when something happened (1), be used to construct questions (2), and add emphasis (3) and negatives (4). The three primary verbs are the only auxiliaries that can also act as main verbs:

She *is* tall   I *have* a new car   He *did* it

Modal auxiliaries are only ever used in conjunction with a main verb. They are:

can	will	shall	may	must
could	would	should	might	

Modal verbs can significantly alter the tone or meaning of something that is said or written. They might, for example, be used to make a request more polite:

Compare *Pass the salt* with *Can you pass the salt?* or *Would you pass the salt?*

The jargon

Verbs which refer to physical actions are called **dynamic verbs**. Verbs which refer to states or conditions (e.g. *She felt happy*) are called **stative verbs**.

Links

The term **subject** is explained on page 10.

Checkpoint 1

Do you know what a **split infinitive** is?

Watch out!

A sentence can have more than one main verb.

The jargon

Another distinction is between **transitive** and **intransitive** verbs. Transitive verbs have an object, intransitive verbs don't. The object of a verb is the object of the action – the person or thing that something is being done to. Some verbs can be used transitively or intransitively: *he was whistling* (intransitive – no object); *he was whistling a Beatles song* (transitive – the object is *a Beatles song*).

Checkpoint 2

Study the list of modal verbs and think of more ways in which their use might alter tone or meaning.

Tense

English has two tenses: the **present tense** and the **past tense**. The present tense can refer to an activity that is happening now but is not likely to last long:

I *am writing* a letter.

It can also refer to a more continuous state of affairs:

I seldom *write* letters.

Using the present tense can make a description of an event – such as a review of a pop concert – more vivid and immediate:

Lead singer Billy Glover *rushes* to the front of the stage and *reaches* out to the adoring audience.

Various constructions are used to refer to the future, the most common of which is adding the modal *will* or *shall* to the infinitive form of the verb ('I *will see* you tomorrow').

Active and passive

Verbs can be **active** or **passive**. If a verb is used actively, the person or thing performing the action is emphasized as the subject of the verb:

The minister *has issued* an apology.

If the passive voice is used, the emphasis shifts to the object of the verb (the person or thing to which something has been done). The order of the sentence is reversed:

An apology *has been issued* by the minister.

Using the passive form means that the agent responsible for the action (in this case, 'the Minister') can be left out completely:

An apology has been issued.

As this example shows, one of the reasons for using the passive voice may be to avoid drawing attention to the person responsible for an action.

Adverbs ●●●

Adverbs usually give us more information about verbs. They describe verbs in rather the same way that adjectives describe nouns. Many adverbs are formed by adding *–ly* to the ends of adjectives.

She ran *quickly*   He felt *better*   They left *immediately*

Exam warm-up question   answer: page 26

Identify all of the verbs in the following and state whether they are main verbs or auxiliary verbs.

I have been to the United States three times. I have a month's holiday in August and will be going again, though I may spend some time in Mexico as well. (5 min)

Examiner's secrets

Watch for texts in which the present tense has been used instead of the past and think about the effect that this has.

Examiner's secrets

Watch for the use of the passive voice in texts that you study. Consider what difference using the active voice would make.

Take note

Another effect of the passive voice can be to make the object seem powerless, a victim of whoever or whatever is performing the action: *The country was torn by war, devastated by drought and ravaged by famine.*

Take note

Adverbs can also modify adjectives ('*unbelievably* good') and other adverbs ('*remarkably* quickly').

Watch out!

Some words can be used as adjectives or adverbs; e.g. 'a *hard* question' (adjective); 'she worked *hard*' (adverb).

Word classes: other classes

This final section on word classes considers **pronouns, conjunctions, prepositions** and **determiners**.

Pronouns ●●●

Pronouns are words that take the place of nouns. Consider the following sentences:

> Wendy gave the address book to Stephen.
> *She*   gave   *it*   to *him*.

In the second sentence, the nouns have all been replaced by pronouns (shown in italics). There are seven main types of pronoun.

Personal pronouns   These replace the subject or the object of the sentence. *I* and *he* are examples of pronouns used to refer to the subject, *me* and *him* examples of pronouns that refer to the object:

> *I* drove *him* home.
> *He* thanked *me* for the lift.

Other personal pronouns are shown in the table below.

	Personal pronouns		Possessive pronouns		Reflexive pronouns	
	Singular	Plural	Singular	Plural	Singular	Plural
First person	I, me	we, us	mine	ours	myself	ourselves
Second person	you	you	yours	yours	yourself	yourself
Third person	he, she, it, him, her	they, them	his, hers, its	theirs	himself, herself, itself	themselves

Possessive pronouns   These show possession. Instead of saying 'This is Sarah's' we might say 'This is *hers*'. The table shows other possessive pronouns. Note that words such as *her, your* and *their* are determiners rather than pronouns because they *precede* nouns rather than take the place of them ('*her* purse').

Reflexive pronouns   These indicate that the object of a verb is the same as its subject: 'he congratulated *himself*'. They are easily recognized because they end in *-self* or *-selves* (see table).

Demonstrative pronouns   These are pronouns that have a sense of 'pointing' at something or someone: *this, that, these* (as used at the beginning of this sentence), *those*:

> Read her letter again. *That* gives you the answer.

Remember that pronouns take the place of nouns. If any of these four words is placed in front of a noun, it becomes a determiner (see below) rather than a pronoun:

> I hate *this* job.

Indefinite pronouns   These are pronouns that do not refer to specific persons or things. Examples include *someone, anything, no one, everything*.

Relative pronouns   These act as linking words in a sentence. They are like other pronouns in that they refer to nouns, and they are always placed immediately after the noun they refer to:

Checkpoint 1

Say whether the nouns in the first sentence are common nouns or proper nouns.

Examiner's secrets

If you identify a word not only as a pronoun but also as a particular type of pronoun you will gain extra credit.

Examiner's secrets

When you are analysing a text, think about the effect that the use of particular pronouns has. For example, use of the second person (*you*) is a way of directly addressing the audience; use of the first person plural (*we, our, us*) indicates that the writer or speaker is involving the audience and identifying with them.

A city *that* has many tourist attractions.

The relative pronouns are *who*, *whom* and *whose* (referring to people) and *which* and *that* (referring to things). *Who*, *whose* and *which* can also be used in a different way, as *interrogative pronouns*.

Interrogative pronouns These are used when asking a question. The interrogative pronouns are *who*, *whose*, *which* and *what*.

Who said that?
What do you want?

Conjunctions ●●●

Conjunctions (sometimes known as *connectives*) are 'joining words'. They join together the different parts of a sentence.

Coordinating conjunctions include the words *and*, *but* and *or*. They are used when the parts of the sentence to be joined are of equal value:

I went to the party *and* met Tony there.

Subordinating conjunctions connect a subordinate clause to a main clause. Examples include *because*, *although*, *unless*, *until*.

Prepositions ●●●

Prepositions usually indicate in some way how one thing is related to something else. Examples include prepositions relating to position (*at*, *on*, *opposite*), direction (*into*, *past*, *to*) and time (*before*, *during*, *after*).

A preposition shows the relationship between the noun that comes after it and something else in the sentence.

I spoke to the man *at* the reception desk.

Determiners ●●●

These words *precede* nouns and refer directly to them. The most common determiners are *the* (known as the **definite article**) and *a/an* (known as the **indefinite article**). Other determiners include **possessive determiners** (*my*, *our*, *your*, *his*, *her*, *its*, *their*) and **demonstrative determiners** (*this*, *that*, *these*, *those*). Note the difference between demonstrative determiners and demonstrative pronouns. Determiners precede nouns ('Hand me *that* pen'), pronouns *replace* nouns ('Hand me *that*'). Other determiners refer to quantity, either specifically (*one*, *two*, *three*, etc.) or more vaguely (*some*, *few*, *many*, etc.).

Links

Conjunctions play an important part in the **cohesion** of a text (see page 22).

The jargon

The term **connective** is also used more broadly, to refer not just to conjunctions but to any words or phrases that have a 'linking' function in a sentence.

Links

For more on **subordinate clauses**, see page 12.

Links

Short, compressed versions of sentences often omit determiners. Newspaper headlines (page 67) are an example of this.

Links

These sentences are examples of **dialect grammar**. See page 89. **Standard English** is discussed and defined on page 34.

Exam warm-up question	answer: page 26

Explain, with reference to appropriate terminology, how the grammar of these sentences differs from Standard English. (10 min)

1 Me and Fred went to the shop.

2 Give me them scissors.

3 Are youse coming?

4 I'm not involved so leave us out of it.

5 She left everything to my sister and I.

Phrases and clauses

So far we have looked at the forms and functions of individual words. In this section, we consider how words can be grouped together into **phrases** and **clauses**. To understand the difference between a phrase and a clause, it is first necessary to understand what a phrase is.

What are phrases?

A **phrase** is one or more words functioning as a unit in a sentence, usually containing a head word and accompanying modifiers.

→ **Head word** This is the main word in a phrase.
→ **Modifiers** These are words that describe the head word or give us more information about it. If they come before the head word they are known as **pre-modifiers**. If they come after the head word they are called **post-modifiers**.

Looking at different types of phrase will show more clearly what these terms mean.

Noun phrases

Links

Nouns and pronouns were defined earlier (see pages 4 and 8).
Adjectives were defined on page 5.

A **noun phrase** usually has a noun or pronoun as its head word. These are all noun phrases:

the beach   the sandy beach   the long, sandy beach
the beach nearby   the beach across the bay

In all of these examples the head word is *beach*. All have a pre-modifying determiner (*the*). Many noun phrases also have adjectives, which act as pre-modifiers. In two of the above examples, *sandy* and *long, sandy* are used in this way. The last two examples have post-modifiers (*nearby* and *across the bay*).

A noun phrase is not always a group of words. It can be a single noun or pronoun, without any modifiers. These two short sentences actually contain four noun phrases, shown in italics:

Squirrels eat *nuts*. *They* like *them*.

Verb phrases

Links

Verbs were explained on page 6.

A **verb phrase** usually contains a main verb (the head word) and any accompanying auxiliary verbs (such as *is*, *was*, *have*, etc.):

I *may see* him.   I *will see* him.   I *should have seen* him.

Watch out!

A verb phrase can be a single word: 'I *saw* him'.

Clauses

A **clause** usually contains both a verb phrase and other types of phrase. Clauses are made up of five **elements**, all of which are present in the following sentence:

My teacher | called | my project | a masterpiece | yesterday.

Checkpoint

Can you identify three noun phrases in this sentence?

1 The **subject** of a clause is the main person or thing that the clause is about ('My teacher'). It performs the action that is described, so it usually comes before the verb.
2 The **verb** ('called') is the second element.
3 The **object** ('my project') normally follows the verb and usually provides an answer to the question 'Who or what has something been done to?' In this case, it is 'my project' that has been called something.
4 The **complement** ('a masterpiece') gives more information about the subject or (as in this case) more information about the object.
5 The **adverbial** ('yesterday') is usually a kind of optional extra in a sentence. It normally provides information of the following kinds:

→ **Time** (when or how often something happened) 'I spoke to him *last week*.'
→ **Place** (where something happened) 'I spoke to him *at the bus stop*.'
→ **Manner** (how something happened) 'I spoke to him *quietly*.'

Adverbials can occupy different positions in a clause, although they are most often found at the end. It is also possible for a clause to contain more than one adverbial:

Last week I spoke to him *at the bus stop*.

Most clauses contain a subject and a verb. Whether or not the other elements are present will depend on the type of clause that is used (see below).

The elements that make up clauses can be combined in seven different ways. In the table below, S = subject, V = verb, O = object, C = complement, A = adverbial.

Clause types

S + V	She | fell
S + V + O	He | closed | the gate
S + V + O + O	Tom | gave | me | a screwdriver
S + V + C	They | were | hungry
S + V + O + C	I | found | the film | disturbing
S + V + A	She | smiled | broadly
S + V + O + A	I | caught | the train | yesterday

Watch out!

Clauses should usually have a verb, but you are also likely to encounter what are known as **verbless clauses**. Here it is usually possible to expand the clause so that the missing verb is supplied: for example, the newspaper headline *Owen Out For Six Weeks* can be expanded to *Owen Is Out For Six Weeks*. Verbless clauses are quite common in speech – e.g. someone buying a train ticket might say, '*Return to Camden Town, please.*'

Action point

Get used to these terms by making up clauses of your own.

Exam warm-up question   answer: page 26

Identify the clause elements (subject, verb, etc.) in each of the following sentences: (10 min)

1   My brother lent me his jacket.
2   He considered the verdict unjust.
3   The tree toppled.
4   The sea was rough.
5   The waves lashed the shore.
6   The audience cheered enthusiastically.
7   I ate the burger hungrily.

Sentences

This section considers sentence structure and looks at how sentences can be divided into types. Depending on their structure, sentences might be simple, compound or complex. Another way of describing sentences is to consider their purposes. Different purposes are served by sentences that are declarative, interrogative, imperative and exclamatory.

Simple sentences

A **simple sentence** contains only one clause. It includes a single main verb and a combination of some or all of the other clause elements (subject, object, complement, adverbial). The sentences in the table under the heading 'Clause types' on page 11 are all simple sentences.

Compound sentences

A **compound sentence** consists of two or more simple sentences joined together by one of the coordinating conjunctions *and*, *but* or *so*. Each clause in a compound sentence makes sense on its own, and each is of equal importance:

> Joe lived in Glasgow *and* his sister lived in London.
> The exam was difficult *but* he passed.
> You can jump in a taxi *or* you can wait for the bus.

Ellipsis occurs when part of a sentence is left out in order to avoid repetition. The last sentence above, for example, could be changed to:

> You can jump in a taxi or wait for the bus.

This is still considered a compound sentence, because if the missing element is restored, *you can wait for the bus* can stand on its own as a sentence.

Complex sentences

In a compound sentence, because both the clauses are of equal importance, they are both considered **main clauses**. In a **complex sentence**, one or more of the clauses is of lesser importance than the main clauses. These lesser clauses are called **subordinate clauses**. Unlike main clauses, a subordinate clause cannot stand on its own and make sense.

Subordinate clauses are especially likely to occur in long sentences. They can occupy the position of any of the elements in a main clause except the verb. This means that a subordinate clause might act as a subject, an object, a complement or an adverbial. One way of trying to identify subordinate clauses is to look for the subordinating conjunctions that often introduce subordinate clauses. These include such words as *because*, *when*, *after*, *although*, *as*, *except* and such expressions as *in order to*, *so that*, *as though* and *rather than*.

Examples of some of the most common types of subordinate clause are shown below.

→ **Clauses introduced by 'that'**

> I thought *that the journey was slow.*

Here the subordinate clause acts as the object of the sentence.

Links

For this section, you need to remember the work covered in the previous section, 'Phrases and clauses'.

Links

Conjunctions were defined on page 9.

Checkpoint

What grammatical terms would you use to describe the words that have been left out of this sentence?

The jargon

The term **ellipsis** is also used for sentences or grammatical constructions which are more obviously incomplete. Take the exchange *How old are you? – Nineteen.* Here *Nineteen* cannot stand alone as a sentence, but because of the preceding question we understand it to mean *I am nineteen.* Elliptical constructions are common in conversation, and in written texts are sometimes used for compression or for stylistic effect.

Watch out!

This is quite difficult.

- **Clauses introduced by a 'wh–' word**   These clauses are introduced by words such as *what, when, who, whether*.

  > He told me *what he wanted*.
  > She replied *when I wrote to her*.

- **Adverbial clauses**   These act as adverbials and usually explain when, where or why something happened. They are introduced by such conjunctions as *before*, *until*, *while*, *because* and *since*.

  > She left *before I arrived*.
  > She left *because it was late*.

- **Relative clauses**   These usually include the relative pronouns *who*, *whose*, *which* or *that*.

  > The hand *that rocks the cradle* rules the world.

The functions of sentences ●●●

Another way of classifying sentences is to identify their *functions*. If we look at sentences in this way, there are four types of sentence.

- **Declarative sentences** make statements. The usual order of these sentences is subject–verb–object.

  > I have read all of Shakespeare's tragedies.

  Information texts (such as leaflets or news reports), narrative texts and descriptive texts are likely to rely heavily on declarative sentences.

- **Interrogative sentences** ask questions:

  > Have you read any of Shakespeare's tragedies?

  In a written text, interrogative structures are often associated with a direct address to the reader. Advertisements, for example, sometimes try to involve the reader by asking questions. In speech, interrogative structures can be a way of making a command more polite ('Could you open the window?').

- **Imperative sentences** give instructions of some kind – orders, warnings, advice, invitations. They usually begin with the verb and omit the subject:

  > Read Shakespeare's *Hamlet* by next week.
  > Have a cup of cocoa and go to bed.

  Instructional texts usually include a large number of imperatives.

- **Exclamatory sentences** are emphatic sentences, which in writing are indicated by the use of an exclamation mark:

  > I've got to read *Hamlet* by next week!

The jargon

These four forms of sentence (declarative, interrogative, imperative, exclamatory) are also known as **moods**.

The jargon

Imperative sentences are sometimes termed **commands**.

Exam warm-up question   answer: page 26

Using appropriate terminology, write a paragraph explaining the kinds of sentences you might expect to find in a leaflet advising 7-year-olds on road safety. (15 min)

13

Word structure

The study of the structure of words is known as **morphology**. In this section, we consider the different elements that combine to form words. This involves looking at **morphemes** and at **prefixes** and **suffixes** (known collectively as **affixes**).

Morphemes ●●●

A **morpheme** is the smallest unit of language that expresses meaning or serves a grammatical function. It is always a letter or group of letters. Some morphemes are single words. Take the word *apple*, for instance. The meaning of *apple* is conveyed by the whole word. It cannot be broken down any further (i.e. we cannot say that it is made up of *ap + ple* or *app + le*). The word *apples*, however, has two morphemes: *apple*, which gives the main meaning of the word, and *s*, which tells us it is plural. Here are some more examples of words broken down into morphemes:

1	train	train
2	unfair	un + fair
3	hunters	hunt + er + s
4	truthfulness	true + th + ful + ness

Words that have more than one morpheme usually consist of a **root word** and one or more affixes. Affixes are the morphemes that have been added to the beginning or end of the word. An affix that appears at the beginning is a **prefix**. An affix that comes at the end is a suffix.

Free and bound morphemes ●●●

Free morphemes are morphemes that can stand alone as words. They are words whose structure cannot be broken down any further. Examples are *apple, train, orange, house*. **Bound morphemes** are morphemes that cannot stand alone. They have to be attached to other morphemes. Examples (taken from the words shown above) are *un–, –er, –s, –th, –ful, –ness*. These are all affixes.

Inflectional affixes ●●●

Inflectional affixes are used to indicate certain grammatical features, and in English they are always suffixes. Here are some of the purposes that inflectional affixes can have.

→ Indicating that a word is plural:

> Paper + *s* = papers
> Potato + *es* = potatoes
> Pony + *ies* = ponies

→ Indicating that a word is possessive:

> Henry + *'s* = Henry's (as in *Henry's briefcase*)

→ Indicating that a present tense verb is third person singular:

> walk + *s* = walks (as in *she walks*)
> go + *es* = goes (as in *he goes*)

Checkpoint 1

Make a list of some other words that have one, two, three or four morphemes.

The jargon

Another term for root is the **base form** of a word.

The jargon

Inflectional affixes are sometimes simply called **inflections**.

→ Indicating that a verb is in the past tense:

walk + *ed* = he walked

→ Indicating that an adjective is a comparative or superlative:

strong + *er* = stronger
strong + *est* = strongest

Derivational affixes

Derivational affixes are used to create new words. This can happen through the use of prefixes, suffixes or a combination of both.

Derivational suffixes usually change the word class of the word they are added to. For example, the verb *sing* becomes a noun if we add *–er* to it (*singer*). Here are some more examples of how suffixes are commonly used to change the word class of a word:

noun + *–ful* = adjective (e.g. *doubt* + *ful* = *doubtful*)
verb + *–ment* = noun (e.g. *agree* + *ment* = *agreement*)
adjective + *–en* = verb (e.g. *black* + *en* = *blacken*)
noun + *–en* = verb (e.g. *fright* + *en* = *frighten*)
verb + *–able* = adjective (e.g. *manage* + *able* = *manageable*)
adjective + *–ly* = adverb (e.g. *slow* + *ly* = *slowly*)

A small number of **derivational prefixes** act in a similar way and change the word class of the word they are added to. An example is *en–*, which can be added to the front of some nouns to form verbs (e.g. *en* + *circle* = *encircle*). However, most prefixes do not affect a word's class, although they usually do have a significant effect on *meaning*. Adding the prefix *un–* to words, for example, gives them an opposite meaning (e.g. *un* + *usual* = *unusual*). Some more examples of the meanings associated with particular prefixes are shown below:

Prefixes associated with size or extent – e.g. *under–* (*underweight*), *over–* (*overworked*).
Prefixes associated with quantity – e.g. *mono–* (*monotone*), *multi–* (*multicoloured*).
Prefixes associated with time – e.g. *pre–* (*prehistoric*), *post–* (*postwar*).

Some words contain both prefixes and suffixes. The word *unhappiness* (*un* + *happy* + *ness*) is an example of this.

Links

Affixation, discussed here, is one way that new words are created. Other types of word formation are described on pages 152–3.

Checkpoint 2

Add more examples of your own to the words shown here. This exercise is also a good way of checking your knowledge of word classes.

Watch out!

Some roots alter their spelling when affixes are added. The changed spelling of *happy* in *unhappiness* illustrates this.

Exam warm-up question   answer: page 26

Analyse the structure of the words shown below. For each word, identify the root and any prefixes or suffixes. Say whether the suffixes are inflectional or derivational. (15 min)

shamelessly	eaten	magical
unlikely	nonsensical	showing
teacher	passed	undesirable

Words and meanings 1

In the next two sections, we are concerned with **semantics** – the study of **meanings**. Initially, we look at two levels of meaning that words can have, **denotation** and **connotation**. Then we discuss some ways of grouping words according to their meaning: **lexical fields**; **hyponyms** and **hypernyms**; and **synonyms** and **antonyms**.

Denotation and connotation

Denotation refers to the straightforward, objective meaning of a word. It is the kind of meaning we might expect to find if we looked the word up in a dictionary. The word *winter*, for example, denotes the season between autumn and spring.

The **connotations** of a word are the *associations* that a word has – the emotions and attitudes that are aroused by it. For example, we might associate the word *winter* with dark evenings and cold, unpleasant weather.

Connotations can vary from individual to individual. Some people might look forward to winter and associate it with invigorating walks, roaring fires and Christmas. As this example shows, connotations can be *positive* or *negative*.

Connotations are very important to the study of English language. Writers choose their words carefully, and when you are analysing texts you need to think about the connotations of particular words. Imagine, for example, that one newspaper editorial describes a politician as *open-minded*, while another describes him as *indecisive*. They may be referring to the same aspect of the politician's character, but one description suggests it is a strength, the other a weakness.

Lexical fields

Lexis is another word for vocabulary. A **lexical field** is a group of words with associated meanings and uses. Computers, for example, have a lexical field that includes words such as the following:

> software, modem, mouse, cursor, monitor, keyboard,
> menu, file, document, upgrade, disk, memory.

In a text about computers, we might expect to find vocabulary drawn from this field. Such vocabulary can also be termed **field-specific lexis**.

Hyponyms and hypernyms

A **hyponym** is a word that is linked in meaning to, but more specific than, another word, known as a **hypernym**. Hypernyms are always more general than hyponyms, and a single hypernym will usually have several hyponyms. The word *flower* is a hypernym. Words referring to specific kinds of flower are hyponyms: *carnation*, *rose*, *daffodil* and so on. Here are some more examples:

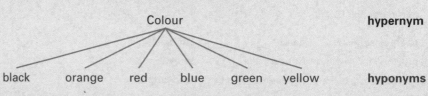

Colour — **hypernym**

black   orange   red   blue   green   yellow   **hyponyms**

Checkpoint 1

What are the connotations of the following words: *red, white, green*?

The jargon

Lexical fields are also known as **semantic fields**, and groups of words that are linked in meaning are sometimes known as **lexical sets**.

The jargon

Hypernyms are also known as **superordinates**.

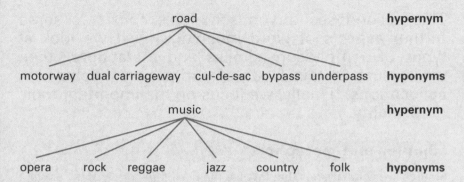

The same word can be a hypernym in one context and a hyponym in another. *Blue*, for example, is a hyponym of *colour* (see above) but is itself a hypernym in relation to words that identify different *kinds* of blue:

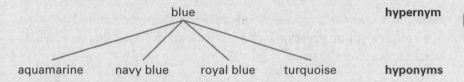

Synonyms ●●●

Synonyms are words that are *similar* in meaning. Here are some examples:

> begin – commence – start
> chat – conversation – talk
> assemble – gather – meet

We use the word 'synonym' quite loosely, because in fact there are very few true synonyms. That is, there are very few words whose meanings are absolutely identical in all contexts. *Fast*, *rapid* and *quick* are usually regarded as synonyms, but they are not completely interchangeable: we can refer to 'a fast car' but not to 'a rapid car'.

If you are analysing a spoken or written text, it can be helpful when looking at the vocabulary to consider what alternatives might have been used. Sometimes the lexical choice reflects regional variation (e.g. in different parts of the country a bread roll might be known as a *barm*, a *bap* or a *batch*). On other occasions, the choice might depend on the level of formality (e.g. compare the words *inebriated*, *drunk* and *legless*).

Antonyms ●●●

Antonyms are words whose meanings are in some way *opposite* to each other. Many antonyms are adjectives (e.g. *hot/cold*, *wet/dry*, *tall/short*, etc.), but antonyms can also belong to other word classes: e.g. verbs (*start/finish*), adverbs (*always/never*), nouns (*boy/girl*).

Checkpoint 2

Try to extend each example by adding more hyponyms.

Checkpoint 3

Could any of the other hyponyms listed previously also function as hypernyms?

The jargon

A word that has more than one meaning is said to be **polysemic**. For example, *clear* has different meanings in *The motorway was clear* and *His reasons were clear*. A related, broader term is **ambiguity**. An ambiguous word, expression or argument can be understood or interpreted in more than one way.

Links

There is more on levels of formality in the next section (page 19).

The jargon

The deliberate contrasting of opposite words or ideas in a text is known as **antithesis**.

Exam warm-up questions   answers: page 27

1   The following words are hypernyms: *furniture*, *stationery*, *clothing.* List four hyponyms for each word. (10 min)

2   Comment on the different connotations of the following words: *slim* and *thin*; *dry* and *arid*; *new*, *innovative* and *untried.* (10 min)

Words and meanings 2

This second section on semantics considers some further aspects of word meanings. First we look at types of comparison (**similes** and **metaphors**), then we discuss certain kinds of expression (**idioms** and **collocations**). Finally, we focus on the important topic of **formality**.

Similes and metaphors

Similes are comparisons that involve the use of *like* or *as*. Many are in everyday use:

as bold as brass	as slippery as an eel	tremble like a leaf
as cold as ice	swim like a fish	sleep like a log

Metaphors take the process of comparison a stage further and describe a person, object or situation as if it actually were something else. What is said is not literally true:

> The students sat there nervously as a *hail* of criticism *rained down* on their heads.

Like similes, metaphors are firmly embedded in our everyday language:

the road ahead	tied up	tread carefully
snowed under	laid back	borrowed time

We are so used to hearing and using these metaphors that we have effectively ceased to think of them as metaphors: we are no longer conscious of them as comparisons. Expressions to which this has happened are known as **dead metaphors** (itself a metaphor).

There are some especially common ways of forming metaphors. Many derive from parts of the body; for instance, *the eye of a storm*, *the foot of a cliff*, *the neck of a bottle* and expressions such as *on the face of it* and *face facts*. English also has many spatial metaphors, which describe mental and physical states in terms of physical movement and orientation. Usually 'up' corresponds to happiness and good health, 'down' to depression and sickness: *on top of the world*, *high spirits*, *looking up*, *under the weather*, *feeling low*, *the depths of despair*.

In the analysis of texts, unusual and original metaphors are especially worth commenting on. Explain what is conveyed by the comparison: how is the writer's perception of the thing being described made sharper, clearer or more powerful by comparing it to something else? If the writer builds on the original comparison, sustaining it over a considerable portion of the text, it becomes an **extended metaphor**.

Idioms

An **idiom** is an expression whose meaning cannot be understood from the meanings of the individual words that make up the expression. Foreign learners of the language have particular difficulties with idioms because the literal meaning of the words bears no apparent relation to the meaning that the words have when they are grouped together: *face the music*, *put a sock in it*, *out of hand* and so on.

Watch out!

Remember the difference between similes and metaphors.

Checkpoint 1

Try to think of more **dead metaphors**.

The jargon

Personification is a kind of metaphor in which something that is not human is described as if it were, as in the blues lyric *The sky is crying, tears rolling down the streets.*

Collocations

Groups (usually pairs) of words that are commonly found alongside each other are known as **collocations**. Some words have a restricted collocational range – e.g. the word *spick* is rarely used other than as part of the expression *spick and span*. Other words have no collocational restrictions (e.g. *the*, *after*, *of*). Then there are words with a large but not unlimited range of collocations. The word *long* is an example. Its collocations include many expressions to do with time (*a long day*, *a long week*, etc.) and many others to do with physical distance (*a long way*, *a long road*). When you are analysing texts, look for unusual collocations – does the writer put together words that are not usually linked?

Levels of formality

Informal language is language that is relaxed, familiar and conversational. At the opposite end of the spectrum is **formal language**, which has a more serious, distant and impersonal tone. There are different degrees or levels of formality. Each of the expressions below, for example, might be said to occupy a different level of formality.

suffering from chronic fatigue   FORMAL
very tired
shattered
knackered   INFORMAL

As in the above example, the key indicators of how formal or informal a text is will often be the vocabulary. Grammar can also be important: formal texts sometimes employ lengthy, elaborately constructed sentences, while informal language is associated more with short (perhaps grammatically incomplete) sentences.

If you are writing about a text and want to describe it as 'formal' or 'informal', try to develop this observation by asking yourself such questions as:

→ Where exactly is the formality/informality evident?
→ Is the same level of formality present throughout the text?
→ Why has this level of formality been chosen by the writer, and what effect does it have?

In your own writing, consider the nature of the task and the identity of your audience and try to adopt an appropriate degree of formality.

Checkpoint 2

How many collocations can you think of for the word *line*?

The jargon

An **oxymoron** is an expression in which words of contradictory or opposite meaning have been collocated – e.g. *bitter sweet*.

Checkpoint 3

Can you think of any more sets of expressions corresponding to different levels of formality?

Watch out!

A single text may move between different levels of formality. For example, it might be generally formal but also contain *some* informality.

Examiner's secrets

For these tasks you need to adopt different levels of formality. The key things to consider are *genre* and *audience*.

Exam question   answer: page 27

Imagine that as part of an exchange scheme you are spending a term at an American high school. Your head teacher has asked you to write a report of your experiences suitable for inclusion in your school's annual review, which is presented to the board of governors. Write the report, then write a letter to a friend, also about your experiences at the high school. (60 min)

Phonology

The study of the sounds of speech is known as **phonetics**. The study of the patterns and systems of sounds in particular languages is known as **phonology**. This section explains some key terms of relevance to the sounds of English and provides a list of the symbols used in the International Phonetic Alphabet.

Phonemes

A **phoneme** is the smallest unit of sound in a language. When a phoneme is replaced by another phoneme, a new word can be formed. The word *bat*, for example, has three phonemes: *b – a – t*. If we change the first phoneme we could make the words *pat* or *cat*. Changing the second phoneme could make *bet* or *bit*, and changing the third phoneme can create *ban* or *bag*.

Syllables

Phonemes combine together to form **syllables**. A syllable is a single unit of speech or a subdivision of a word and usually has a structure of consonant + vowel + consonant. The consonant element in this structure may include one or more consonants: *string*, for example, is a syllable made up of *str + i + ng*. Some syllables have only a single consonant element: *and*, *so*, *the*.

Words of one syllable are termed **monosyllabic**; words of more than one syllable are **polysyllabic**. Examples of polysyllabic words are: *plea-sure* and *ma-gic* (two syllables); *af-ter-wards* and *im-por-tant* (three syllables); *en-ter-tain-ment* and *un-de-ci-ded* (four syllables).

Prosody

Non-verbal aspects of speech such as *tone*, *intonation* and *stress* are known as **prosodic** or **suprasegmental** features.

Onomatopoeia

Onomatopoeia occurs when the sound of a word echoes its meaning: *splash*, *buzz*, *crash* and *thump* are onomatopoeic. Such words are also described as *echoic*.

Alliteration

Alliteration is when two or more words begin with the same sound: *crisp, crunchy cornflakes*. It is often used in newspaper headlines and in advertising because it can help to make a phrase catchy and memorable.

Rhyme

Rhyme occurs when words have similar endings. We especially associate rhyme with poetry, but it can occur in other contexts. As with alliteration, it is a common device in advertising (*Beanz Meanz Heinz*).

Watch out!

Make sure you understand the difference between phonemes and syllables.

Watch out!

Although all words with more than one syllable are technically **polysyllabic**, the term tends only to be used when words have three or more syllables. Extensive use of polysyllabic lexis is usually a feature of more complex or more formal texts.

Links

Prosody is discussed more fully on pages 60–1.

Examiner's secrets

Always try to explain the *effect* that these devices have when you are analysing texts.

Assonance

Assonance occurs when the vowel sounds in the middle of two or more words are similar: Kw*i*k F*i*t. If vowel sounds clash with each other, producing a discordant effect, this is known as **dissonance**.

The International Phonetic Alphabet

The **International Phonetic Alphabet** (**IPA**) is a set of symbols used by linguists to transcribe sounds. Many dictionaries use the IPA to show how a word should be pronounced. The IPA is designed to cover the sounds of all the world's languages. The symbols relevant to English are shown in the table below. In some cases, the symbol is an ordinary letter, but in others different sorts of symbols are used. Examples of words including the sounds are given, but note that in each case the table assumes that the words are pronounced with a southern English/RP accent. If you have a regional accent, your pronunciation of particular words may differ from that shown.

Consonants			*Short vowels*	
p	–	p<u>i</u>p	ɪ	f<u>i</u>t
b	–	<u>b</u>i<u>b</u>	ɛ	l<u>e</u>t
t	–	<u>t</u>ell	æ	b<u>a</u>t
d	–	<u>d</u>eck	ɒ	d<u>o</u>g
k	–	<u>c</u>ow	ʌ	sh<u>u</u>t
g	–	<u>g</u>et	ʊ	p<u>u</u>t
f	–	<u>f</u>it	ə	lett<u>er</u>
v	–	<u>v</u>an		
θ	–	<u>th</u>ick		*Long vowels*
ð	–	<u>th</u>ough		
s	–	<u>s</u>ip	iː	cr<u>ea</u>m
z	–	<u>z</u>ap	ɜː	f<u>ir</u>m
ʃ	–	<u>sh</u>ip	ɑː	c<u>ar</u>d
ʒ	–	mea<u>s</u>ure	ɔː	b<u>or</u>n
h	–	<u>h</u>at	uː	b<u>oo</u>t
tʃ	–	<u>ch</u>ip		
dʒ	–	<u>j</u>u<u>dge</u>		*Diphthongs*
m	–	<u>m</u>oat		
n	–	ma<u>n</u>	aɪ	r<u>i</u>ce
ŋ	–	si<u>ng</u>	ɛɪ	b<u>ai</u>t
l	–	<u>l</u>et	ɔɪ	b<u>oy</u>
r	–	<u>r</u>eef	əʊ	n<u>o</u>te
w	–	<u>w</u>ait	aʊ	t<u>ow</u>n
j	–	<u>y</u>et	ʊə	p<u>oor</u>
			ɪə	cl<u>ear</u>
			ɛə	ch<u>air</u>

Syllabus check

Not all syllabuses require you to have knowledge of the IPA. You should check with your teacher. Students sometimes make use of it if they study regional accents for their coursework.

The jargon

Diphthongs are a combination of two vowel sounds; the speaker starts with one sound and slides towards another.

Exam warm-up questions   answers: page 27

1   Give the IPA symbols for the *vowel* sounds in the following words: loose, court, head, hook, guard, here, flood, house. (10 min)

2   Give the IPA symbols for the *consonant* sounds at the *beginning* of these words: this, Thursday, shout, church, germ, yacht, psychology, cat. (10 min)

Cohesion

Don't forget

The more cohesion a text contains, the more tightly structured it is likely to be. For this reason, cohesion is especially important in texts that present complex information or a carefully developed argument.

Cohesion refers to the techniques and devices used to connect different parts of a text with each other. There are two main kinds of cohesion: grammatical, involving the use of sentence structure and the grammatical functions of words, and lexical, involving the use of word meanings.

Types of cohesion

Halliday and Hasan (1976) identify the following types of cohesion:

→ **Grammatical cohesion**, including *reference*, *identification*, *ellipsis* and *conjunction*.
→ **Lexical cohesion**, including *repetition* and *collocation*.

Grammatical cohesion

Reference

Reference often involves the use of third person pronouns (*he*, *she*, *it*, *they*), as in the following example:

> My great-grandfather was an Irishman. *He* was born in Dublin in 1875.

Here the word *he* is a cohesive link because it refers back to *great-grandfather*. Demonstrative pronouns (*this*, *that*) can be used in a similar way:

Checkpoint 1

What other words act as cohesive links in this example?

> He couldn't manage it on his own, but he knew there was no one who would help him. *That* was the problem he faced.

As this example illustrates, a single word can refer not only to another word but sometimes to whole clauses or sentences. When a word refers *back* to something or somebody that has already been mentioned, this is known as an **anaphoric reference**. References *forward* are known as **cataphoric references**.

Example

In this sentence, *following* is a **cataphoric reference**: He gave the following reasons for his decision.

Identification

This is the use of determiners such as *the*, *this* and *that* to indicate that a noun has previously been mentioned. When a noun is first used, it is often preceded by the indefinite article (*a*), but later references will use *the*:

Links

Determiners were defined on page 9.

> *A* ship appeared on the horizon. When Paul and Laura arrived with their ice creams, I pointed *the* ship out to them.

Ellipsis

Ellipsis occurs when elements are omitted from a sentence. This becomes a cohesive device if an earlier part of the text enables us to supply the missing elements:

> Beer cans littered the floor, the television had been kicked in and graffiti were sprayed over the walls. A bit of a mess.

Because of the information contained in the first sentence, we understand that the second, incomplete, sentence means (*The room was in*) *a bit of a mess.*

Conjunction

This refers to the use of conjunctions and conjunctive adverbs as cohesive devices. Words used in this way include *and*, *but*, *because*, *however*, *therefore*, *then*, *although* and so on. These words (also known as **connectives**) link together parts of a text and indicate the relationship between them; e.g. if a sentence begins with *But*, what follows will in some way contrast with, or qualify, what has gone before:

> The prime minister promised that the economy would soon recover. *But* it has not done so.

Lexical cohesion

Repetition

At its simplest, this involves the straightforward repetition of a single word. This has a cohesive effect because it forms a link between different sentences:

> I have great *news* to announce. I know it is *news* you have all been longing to hear.

Sometimes, however, the word itself is not repeated. Instead, a *synonym* is used:

> He *rapidly* gathered up the broken fragments of the vase and hid them under the sofa. He acted *quickly* because he did not want Mrs Hughes to discover what he had done.

Collocation

This refers to the tendency for certain words to occur together. This can apply to short expressions (e.g. the adjective *terraced* collocates with the noun *house*) but also to longer stretches of text. A review of a play, for instance, might be expected to include words such as *actor*, *director*, *audience*, *cast* and *performance*. Collocation is cohesive because it involves the use of words that, because of their meaning, are already linked in the reader's mind.

Exam warm-up question answer: pages 27–8

List and explain the cohesive devices present in the following text:

> Ninety per cent of the world's languages may be in danger. Around 6,000 languages are currently spoken in the world. Of these, half are moribund in that they are no longer learned by the new generation of speakers. A further 2,500 are in a danger zone, in that they have fewer than a hundred thousand speakers. This leaves around 600, a mere ten per cent of the current total, as likely survivors a century from now. Of course, languages inevitably split, just as Latin eventually split into the various Romance languages. So some new languages may emerge. But the diversity will be much reduced. The splendiferous bouquet of current languages will be whittled down to a small posy with only a few different flowers. (25 min)

(Source: Jean Aitchison, *The Language Web*, CUP, 1997)

The jargon

Lexical cohesion is cohesion achieved through word meanings rather than grammatical structure.

Checkpoint 2

Which other words act as cohesive links in this example?

Links

Words associated with the same topic are also known as **field-specific lexis**. See page 16.

Examiner's secrets

It is a good idea to have in your mind a checklist of the main cohesive devices – reference, conjunction and so on – and to see which of these is present in the text.

Grapology

"It is no good having a youthful font, like Hansel, and then writing in a really traditional, pompous style. That is like saying something with an opposite facial expression"

Diane Simpson, Institute of Graphologists

The **graphological features** of a text are its visual aspects – typeface, layout and so on. Although your main focus should be the language of texts, graphological features should not be ignored. Try to explain the effects that they have and how they relate to the written part of the text.

Layout and overall presentation

When you are examining graphological features, you should initially consider the general **layout** and overall presentation. Here are some questions you can ask:

→ Is there a lot of dense text, or is the text broken up – if so, how? Are parts of the text separated from the rest by the use of such devices as boxed sections and speech bubbles? Is there a reason for this?

→ Which part of the text immediately catches the eye? Does the design of the text encourage you to read particular parts of it first?

→ Is any use made of **juxtaposition**? This means placing words, ideas and pieces of information next to each other. Newspaper editors, for example, take care over the arrangement of stories on a page. Stories that are linked, or that contrast with each other, might be juxtaposed.

→ Does the text adopt the layout conventions of another **genre**? An advertisement, for example, could take the form of a letter, a recipe or a comic strip.

Typeface

Several different techniques are associated with the **typeface** used for the written text:

→ The *size* of words and individual letters can be important – most obviously, larger lettering used to give prominence to certain words.

> The new Sonnex hearing aid is so small you'll hardly notice it's there.

→ Use of upper and lower case letters. Upper case letters may be used for individual words to add emphasis or to reflect meaning in some way:

> If you haven't seen a Dreamland bed before, you're in for a BIG surprise.

→ Sometimes in advertisements, only lower case letters are used, often in an attempt to appear stylish and unconventional.

→ Use of such devices as bold face, italics and underlining, usually to highlight parts of the text.

→ Different typefaces have different connotations, and newspapers, business organizations and advertising agencies take great care when choosing typefaces. The mastheads of *The Daily Telegraph* and the *Daily Mail*, for example, have a conservative, traditional look, while those of *The Sun* and *The Mirror* are bolder and brasher.

Reproduced courtesy of The Sun/NI Syndication, Daily Mail/Atlantic Syndication, Daily Mirror/Mirror Syndication International.

Other examples are typefaces that are chosen because they appear elegant, sophisticated, zany or unconventional. Some typefaces resemble handwriting and are used because they appear more personal than those that are more obviously machine-produced.

→ Individual letters may be used as symbols. The letter X, for instance, can be used to indicate that something is incorrect or for adults only, and it is also used to represent kisses. In recent years, the letter k has come to be used as a modern, up-to-date symbol for one thousand (as in Y2k for the year 2000 or salary: £25k).

→ Deviant spelling is especially associated with trade names: *Kwik-Fit, Kwik Save, Ansafone.* The intention is to create words that are memorable because they are different and to evoke a sense of vitality and modernity. Sometimes companies create entirely new words for their products. McDonalds has established its own vocabulary: *Egg McMuffin, Filet-O-Fish, Big Mac* and so on. The idea is to encourage brand loyalty – you can buy a hamburger anywhere, but there's only one place you can get a Big Mac.

→ Other visual symbols such as asterisks, bullet points, arrows, etc. These may be used to organize, or draw attention to, points of a text.

Illustrations ●●●

Illustrations can take the form of photographs, cartoons, drawings, diagrams, etc. As a student of language, your main concern will usually be the *relationship* between the illustrations and the written text. What messages are conveyed by the illustrations, and how do they reinforce what is said in the written text? Alternatively, is there a contrast between the two? Look for captions beneath photographs – these are usually intended to influence the reader's response to the visual image.

Exam warm-up question answer: page 28

Comment on the appropriateness (or otherwise) of the following typefaces: (10 min)

Summer Soccer School

Hi-Tech Solutions

Spooky Stories

Rapid Repairs

Funeral Parlour!

Assertiveness Training

Checkpoint 1

Explain more fully why the typefaces used in these mastheads are appropriate to the newspapers on which they appear.

Checkpoint 2

Can you think of any other letters that have symbolic meanings of this kind?

Watch out!

Avoid vague comments such as 'The illustrations make the text easy to look at.' Be more specific about what the illustrations achieve.

Answers
Language basics

Word classes: nouns and adjectives

Checkpoints

1 If writing has a large number of concrete nouns, readers are usually able to imagine the physical reality of what is being described – the writing refers to solid, tangible objects. The reality described in writing with a large number of abstract nouns is less definite. The writing is more likely to be about ideas, concepts, qualities, feelings – making more demands upon the reader's intellect and imagination.

2 The words that can also be used as verbs are *swarm* and *further*.

Exam warm-up question

mysterious – adjective. *swarm* – collective noun, concrete noun, common noun. *Abba* – proper noun. *marvellous* – adjective. *further* – adjective, comparative. *equality* – abstract noun, common noun. *most wonderful* – adjective, superlative. *Concorde* – proper noun. *sticky* – adjective. *aeroplane* – common noun, concrete noun. *more glamorous* – adjective, comparative. *far* – adjective.

Word classes: verbs and adverbs

Checkpoints

1 A split infinitive occurs when there is a word between *to* and the verb: 'to boldly go where no man has gone before'. This has traditionally been regarded as incorrect grammar, although in some sentences it is unavoidable.

2 Here are a few more examples of sentences where modal verbs alter tone or meaning:
1 I can see you on Thursday / I will see you on Thursday / I must see you on Thursday.
2 Could you go now? / Must you go now?

Exam warm-up question

The verbs are: have been (auxiliary verb + main verb); have (main verb); will be going (auxiliary verb + auxiliary verb + main verb); may spend (auxiliary verb + main verb).

Word classes: other classes

Exam warm-up question

1 Standard grammar would use the first person singular pronoun *I* instead of *Me*. Also the order would be reversed ('Fred and I').

2 Standard grammar would use the demonstrative determiner *those* instead of *them*.

3 *Youse* is a regional dialect form of the second personal plural pronoun *you*.

4 Standard grammar would use the first person singular pronoun *me* instead of the first person plural *us*.

5 Standard grammar would use the first person singular pronoun *me* instead of *I*.

Phrases and clauses

Checkpoint

The three noun phrases are: *My teacher, my project, a masterpiece.*

Exam warm-up question

1 S + V + O + O (My brother | lent | me | his jacket.)
2 S + V + O + C (He | considered | the verdict | unjust.)
3 S + V (The tree | toppled.)
4 S + V + C (The sea | was | rough.)
5 S + V + O (The waves | lashed | the shore.)
6 S + V + A (The audience | cheered | enthusiastically.)
7 S + V + O + A (I | ate | the burger | hungrily.)

Sentences

Checkpoint

The subject and auxiliary verb ('you can') have been omitted.

Exam warm-up question

Sentences are likely to be mostly simple or compound. Imperative sentences (giving instructions) may be present, and there may also be exclamatory sentences (used for emphasis) and interrogative sentences (involving readers by addressing them directly and asking them questions).

Word structure

Checkpoints

1 One morpheme: *agree.* Two morphemes: *dis* + *agree.* Three morphemes: *dis* + *agree* + *ment.* Four morphemes: *dis* + *agree* + *ment* + *s.*

2 Noun + *en* = verb: *height* + *en* = *heighten.* Verb + *able* = adjective: *wash* + *able* = *washable.* Adjective + *ly* = adverb: *narrow* + *ly* = *narrowly.*

Exam warm-up question

Word	Root	Prefix	Inflection	Derivational suffix
shamelessly	shame			less + ly
unlikely	like	un		ly
teacher	teach			er
eaten	eat		en	
nonsensical	sense	non		ical
passed	pass		ed	
magical	magic			al
showing	show		ing	
undesirable	desire	un		able

Words and meanings 1

Checkpoints

1 *Red* can be associated with danger, passion, anger, radicalism; *white* with purity, fear; *green* with jealousy, inexperience, the environment.

2 Additional hyponyms: colour – *purple*, *brown*; road – *highway*, *toll road*; music – *classical*, *blues*, *ragtime*.

3 *Rose* can be a hypernym, as there are many different types of rose. Similarly, the music genres listed could each be broken down into different sub-genres: *rock* can be a hypernym, with *punk rock*, *heavy metal*, *indie*, *rock 'n' roll*, etc. as hyponyms.

Exam warm-up questions

1 Furniture: *table*, *desk*, *sofa*, *chair*, etc.
Stationery: *envelope*, *paper*, *file*, *folder*, etc.
Clothing: *trousers*, *dress*, *jumper*, *shirt*, etc.

2 *Slim* implies fit and attractive, *thin* implies underweight. *Dry* is more neutral than *arid*, which has similar connotations to *barren*. *Innovative* has the most positive connotations, *untried* the most negative.

Words and meanings 2

Checkpoints

1 A few additional examples of dead metaphors: *lend a hand*, *on your side*, *open-minded*, *iron will*.

2 *Line up*, *on the line*, *a hard line*, *next in line*, *draw the line*, *toe the line*, *in line for*, *in line with*, *line of fire*, etc.

3 Another example: *deceased*, *dead*, *six feet under*.

Exam question

Clearly the report needs to be more formal, not just in its language but also in its arrangement and presentation. Use is likely to be made of headed sections, and there should be a clear introduction and conclusion. The tone may be impersonal (not written in the first person).

Texts A and B below are extracts from a specimen answer. In each case, the beginning of the text is shown.

Text A
INTRODUCTION
Ten pupils from the school, accompanied by Mrs Bowhill, attended Winchester High School in New York for eight weeks of the autumn term. The visit was arranged by the organization Education Exchange. At the request of the head teacher, this report offers an assessment of the trip.
ACCOMMODATION
Pupils stayed with families of Winchester High School pupils. All pupils were made to feel very welcome. It was also felt that staying at family homes rather than at a hotel or hostel gave pupils a valuable insight into American life. All of the families were very willing to show their guests around New York. These outings were enjoyable and informative and supplemented the official sightseeing programme.
Text B
Dear Ali,
  Hi! how are you? Sorry it's taken me so long to write, but the weeks have gone by so fast. I really like NY. We've been here nearly a whole term and I still feel like I'm a character in some kind of American soap. I'm living in an apartment with this really cool family. I share a room with Lauren, who's the same age as us. We go to school together and I go to most classes with her and generally 'hang out' as they say over

here. The ten of us who are on the school exchange have made loads of friends. At first we all stuck together, but the families have been really good about taking us on trips and out for meals. We're all going ice skating in Times Square on Saturday and then to see a show in the evening. Sort of a goodbye bash I guess.
Commentary
Contrasting linguistic features of these two texts include:

- Text A is more formally structured, with headings and numbered sections.
- Text A is more factual; e.g. the school is named and the duration of the trip is precisely stated ('eight weeks'). Text B is vague: 'nearly a whole term'.
- Text B is much more personal. Its opening sentence has a phatic function: 'Hi! how are you?' The text addresses the reader directly and there is extensive use of first person pronouns (*I*, *we*, *us*). Text A is impersonal, making more use of passive constructions ('These outings were enjoyable', 'It was also felt').
- Text A uses more formal vocabulary – e.g. 'accompanied by', 'At the request of', 'supplemented'. The vocabulary of Text B is more colloquial and conversational – e.g. 'NY', 'really cool', 'loads of'.
- Text B includes a grammatically incomplete sentence ('Sort of a goodbye bash I guess').

Phonology

Exam warm-up questions

1 loose /uː/   court /oː/   head /e/   hook /ʊ/
guard /aː/   here /iə/   flood /ʌ/   house /aʊ/

2 this /ð/   Thursday /θ/   shout /ʃ/   church /tʃ/
germ /dʒ/   yacht /j/   psychology /s/   cat /k/

Cohesion

Checkpoints

1 The pronouns *he* (used three times), *his* and *him* are anaphoric references, as the identity of the person would presumably have been given in an earlier part of the text. Similarly, the pronoun *it* must refer to something explained more fully earlier.

2 Again the pronoun *he* (used four times) is an anaphoric reference. The determiner *the* in 'the vase' is an example of identification. There is further anaphoric reference in 'what he had done', which refers back to an earlier action.

Exam warm-up question

Anaphoric references include *these* (at the beginning of the third sentence), which refers back to 'Around 6,000 languages'; *they* (in the third and fourth sentences), which refers back to 'half' and 'A further 2,500' respectively; *This* (at the beginning of the fourth sentence), which refers broadly to the languages that are left after those previously mentioned are discounted; *the current total*, which refers back to 'Around 6,000 languages'.

Conjunction is evident in the use of connecting words and expressions: 'in that', 'A further', 'Of course', 'just as', 'So', 'But'.

All of the above are examples of grammatical cohesion. There is also lexical cohesion in the form of repetition and collocation. Words that are repeated include *language* (which occurs six times); *the world* (twice); *danger* (twice); *speakers* (twice); *split* (twice): *current* (twice, and the text also includes the word *currently*). Collocation is seen in the link between *languages* and *speakers*. There is further collocation in the last sentence because of the plant metaphor that is employed: *bouquet – posy – flowers*.

Graphology

Checkpoints

1 The *Daily Mail* and *The Daily Telegraph* both draw large numbers of their readers from the middle and upper classes and also from older age groups. In addition, both newspapers are politically to the right of centre and in the past have usually supported the Conservative Party. It is therefore appropriate that these newspapers should have a typeface that suggests conservatism and tradition rather than one that appears youthful and up to date.

The mastheads of *The Sun* and *The Mirror* opt for a more direct, no-nonsense approach. As tabloid newspapers, their readership is more working-class (the *Daily Mail* is also a tabloid but is what is known as an 'upmarket tabloid' or 'middle market' newspaper). It also has a higher percentage of younger readers. Like the newspapers themselves, the mastheads evoke less sense of heritage and tradition.

2 The letter *A* is symbolic of excellence (as in *grade A*). *B* suggests second best (*B movie*). Repetition of the letter *Z* symbolizes sleep (*zzz*).

Exam warm-up question

The faces are generally appropriate, except that for 'Hi-Tech Solution', which is inappropriately old-fashioned, and that for 'Funeral Parlour', which is inappropriately quirky and lively.

Speech and writing: essential concepts

This short chapter can be seen as an introduction to the chapters that follow on spoken and written language. Here, some of the essential concepts underpinning the study of speech and writing are outlined. First, the main differences between the two modes are discussed, along with the strengths and weaknesses of each. The different ways that different sets of people use language are then considered (this is sometimes known as *user-related variation*). In particular, we focus on **dialects** (which usually refer to *regional* varieties of speech), **sociolects** (the language of *social groups*) and **idiolects** (the language of *individuals* – each of us has his or her own idiolect, because no two people use language in exactly the same way). A separate section looks at **Standard English**, which is different from other dialects because it has more prestige and is generally recognized as the standard national variety. The same section also considers **Received Pronunciation**. Finally, the section on **register** is concerned with *use-related variation*: the ways that different situations cause users to employ different varieties.

Exam themes

→ Characteristics of speech and writing.

→ User-related variation.

→ Use-related variation.

Topic checklist

○ AS ● A2	AQA/A	AQA/B	EDEXCEL	OCR	WJE
Differences between speech and writing	○●	○●	○●	○●	○●
Dialects, sociolects and idiolects	○●	○●	○●	○●	○●
Standard English and Received Pronunciation	○●	○●	○●	○●	○●
Register	○●	○●	○●	○●	○●

Differences between speech and writing

This section looks at the main differences between speech and writing, and at the strengths and weaknesses of each as a mode of communication.

Status of speech and writing

We learn to speak before we learn to write, and speech is a naturally acquired skill, whereas we have to be *taught* to read and write. For these reasons, linguists sometimes refer to the *primacy* of speech. Inability to read and write is certainly a social disadvantage, but inability to speak is a more fundamental deprivation.

Despite this, writing has traditionally been regarded as more prestigious than speech. For many centuries, literacy was confined to an elite and was therefore a mark of social superiority. Written communication also tends to be more permanent (see below) and is often seen as more meaningful and more important: in business transactions, written undertakings are generally favoured over verbal agreements.

During the 20th century, however, there has been a growing recognition of the value of spoken English. This is partly because speech is central to a number of technological developments (telephone, radio, television, film). At the same time, near-universal literacy has meant that the ability to read and write is no longer confined to a minority of the population.

Permanence

One of the most fundamental differences between speech and writing is that writing is generally more permanent. The vast majority of speech is *transient* (short-lived) – the only exceptions are utterances that are recorded.

Writing can be preserved for years, even centuries. For this reason, writing is often used to provide a permanent record of events, decisions, agreements, etc. Even a quickly scribbled note has more permanence than most speech: the receiver may decide to read it twice to check particular details, or keep it as a reminder to do something.

Relationships: speaker, writer and audience

Writing is less restricted by time and space. A written message can be left for someone to read the next day, or sent to someone in another location. The permanence of writing means that the same text can be read at different times by many different people. Readers can also absorb a text at their own pace, looking over it as much as they wish.

However, writers are usually physically separated from their audiences. Speakers and audiences are usually present simultaneously, and audiences can be addressed directly. This means that the speaker receives instant feedback and can amend what is being said accordingly. If a teacher is explaining something to a class, for example, and their body language makes it obvious that the class is bored or confused, he or she can adopt a different approach. Writers may also receive feedback, but it is likely to be less immediate (e.g. a reply to a letter).

Checkpoint 1

Can you think of any other evidence to support the argument that society has in the past considered writing to be more prestigious than speech?

Example

Within education, there has been an increasing emphasis on the importance of speech (e.g. the speaking and listening component in GCSE English).

Checkpoint 2

Can you think how developments in technology have eroded some of the differences referred to here?

Structure and style

Writing is generally more structured than speech. It is organized into sentences and paragraphs (and, in the case of longer texts, may employ sections or chapters). Spoken language is more loosely structured and often includes digressions and repetitions. Most of the grammatical constructions used in speech are also found in writing, but most speech does not take the form of neatly formed sentences.

Because most speech is spontaneous and unplanned, we have to make up what we say as we go along. Inevitably there are hesitations, false starts and mistakes. A writer is able to take time over the composition of a text and can re-draft if necessary.

The vocabulary of speech is generally more informal. Colloquial expressions and slang are more likely to occur in speech than in writing.

Speech can be accompanied and reinforced by body language (gestures, etc.) and by prosodic features such as tone, pitch and stress. Devices such as exclamation marks, underlining, etc. are a graphic equivalent of prosodic features, but the human voice is much more expressive.

Speech and writing influence each other

Written language affects spoken language. In particular, the growth of literacy has encouraged the development of standardized varieties of speech and partly explains the disappearance of much regional dialect vocabulary.

At the same time, most new words enter the language through speech. If they begin to be used in writing, it is usually an indication that they have achieved a degree of permanence.

New technology means that some of the old divisions between speech and writing are disappearing. Email messages, for example, often have characteristics traditionally associated with speech.

Speech versus writing

As should be clear from the above outline of the differences between speech and writing, each mode has its advantages and disadvantages. The question of which is superior is in any case rather artificial, as in practice we rarely have to make a choice. If we meet some friends in the street, we inevitably speak to them; if we want to remember a recipe heard on the radio, we inevitably write it down. Each mode is appropriate to different situations. We especially favour speech for the purposes of social interaction. Writing is suited to the expression of complex ideas and is preferable when a permanent record is required.

Don't forget

Non-standard grammar (e.g. the use of double negatives) is more common in speech than in writing.

Links

The structure, grammar and vocabulary of written texts and spoken utterances are explored more fully in Chapters 3 and 4.

Links

Non-verbal communication, including body language and prosodic features, is discussed on pages 58–61.

Examiner's secrets

When you are faced with a text to analyse in the exam, an important question to ask is, 'What *type* of text is it?' Is it spoken or written? A common failing in the analysis of spoken texts is for students to show little awareness that what they are analysing was intended to be *heard* rather than read. Similarly, if you are given a writing task that involves the production of a spoken text, you must use language that is appropriate to speech.

Exam question   answer: pages 38–9

Writing has traditionally been regarded as superior to speech. What are your views? (45 min)

Dialects, sociolects and idiolects

This section looks at some of the methods that linguists use to classify varieties of English according to the people who use them.

Dialects ●●●

Dialect is a term used for a form of a language with distinct features of vocabulary, grammar and pronunciation. Any single language can usually be subdivided into a number of different dialects. They are called dialects rather than languages because they are mutually intelligible versions of the same language (in other words, the speakers of one dialect can, broadly speaking, understand the speakers of another dialect).

The term is most commonly used to refer to **regional** dialects – that is, different varieties of a language spoken in different geographical regions. In the case of English, these include the Yorkshire dialect, the Cockney dialect and so on.

As dialect refers to vocabulary, grammar and pronunciation, it is a broader term than **accent**, which refers only to pronunciation. To avoid confusion between the two, 'dialect' is sometimes used to refer only to vocabulary and grammar. If we use 'dialect' in this way, it is possible to say that – in theory, at least – the same dialect can be spoken with any accent. This is especially true of Standard English (see below), which is indeed spoken by people with many different accents.

Often one of the dialects of a language will come to be accepted as the 'standard' variety. This means that it has more social prestige than other dialects, is more generally accepted and is the dialect usually favoured in education, government and written communication. In Britain, this 'prestige' variety is known as **Standard English**, originally a dialect spoken in south-east England.

Although 'dialect' usually refers to regional differences in language use, the concept can be extended to include other types of difference: other terms used by linguists include social dialects (or sociolects – see below), occupational dialects and class dialects.

Sociolects ●●●

A **sociolect** is a variety of language associated with a particular social group. Examples of social groups that might be said to have their own distinctive styles of language use include those based on socio-economic status, age, occupation and gender.

Socio-economic status

The relationship between language and social class has been the subject of many investigations. Certainly, there is much evidence to confirm that members of different social classes use language in different ways. In Britain, there is a higher incidence of regional features in the speech of people from lower social classes. In other words, speakers from higher social classes are more likely to use Standard English forms, and their speech will tend to be closer to Received Pronunciation.

"You can spot an Irishman or a Yorkshire man by his brogue. I can place any man within six miles. I can place him within two miles in London. Sometimes within two streets"

Henry Higgins, a character in *Pygmalion* by G. B. Shaw

The jargon

A distinction is also sometimes made between urban dialects (found in cities) and rural dialects (spoken in country districts).

Links

Standard English is discussed more fully in the next section (pages 34–5).

Checkpoint 1

Lect (from *dialect*) is often combined with a prefix (as in *sociolect*). Do you know what is meant by *acrolect*, *basilect* and *genderlect*?

Links

The relationship between language and social class is discussed on pages 92–3.

Age

Probably the most notable difference here is between the speech of teenagers and the speech of older members of the same community. Teenagers have a large and ever-changing lexicon of slang words and expressions. This vocabulary serves to strengthen their identity as a social group and separates them from the world of adults.

Occupation

Any trade or profession – second-hand car dealers, lawyers, accountants, doctors, builders, estate agents, etc. – will have its own specialist vocabulary. In part, this will be made up of technical terms associated with the particular occupation (**jargon**), but it will probably also include **slang** – informal vocabulary used between members of the same occupation, either because it is humorous or because it is shorter and more economical than the Standard English equivalent. As with the language of teenagers, the effect of having a distinctive sociolect is to reinforce the exclusivity of the group.

Gender

This refers to the possibility that men and women use language in different ways. Research suggests that women tend to use more prestige forms: their vocabulary and grammar are closer to Standard English, and their accents are closer to Received Pronunciation. Other research has examined how men and women behave in conversational interaction. It appears that women are more cooperative and are more likely to offer encouragement and sympathetic feedback. Men tend to be more competitive: more assertive in their speech and more inclined to interrupt.

Idiolects ●●●

An **idiolect** is the language use of a single individual. No two people use language in exactly the same way. Every individual's linguistic style is a unique combination of social, regional, educational and other influences. The most obvious difference is in the physical quality of people's voices, but individuals also have words and expressions that they habitually use and grammatical constructions that they especially favour.

Dialects in speech and writing

Differences of dialect are usually associated with spoken rather than written English. However, dialect features can also be found in written texts. **Dialect literature** includes novels, plays and poems which deliberately imitate spoken dialects. An example is Irvine Welsh's novel *Trainspotting*, where the narrative style reflects the Glaswegian dialect of the central characters.

Links

Occupational dialects are also discussed on pages 96–7.

Checkpoint 2

Can you explain the difference between jargon and slang?

Links

Differences in the way men and women use language are discussed on pages 54–5 and 94–5.

Checkpoint 3

Individuals are sometimes said to have 'a language repertoire'. What does this mean?

Examiner's secrets

The emphasis here is on speakers rather than situations. Don't be sidetracked into talking about how the same people use varying forms of English for different situations. Concentrate instead on an explanation of how and why different speakers use different varieties of English.

Exam question   answer: page 39

'The form of a language will vary according to who is using it'. Discuss this assertion with reference to spoken English. (45 min)

Standard English and Received Pronunciation

> *"We may define the Standard English of an English-speaking country as a minority variety (identified chiefly by its vocabulary, grammar and orthography) which carries most prestige and is most widely understood"*
>
> David Crystal

Standard English and **Received Pronunciation** occupy unique positions among English dialects and accents: Standard English is the most prestigious dialect and Received Pronunciation the most prestigious accent.

Standard English

What is Standard English?
Consider the following pairs of sentences:

> I give it to me nan.
> I gave it to my grandmother.

> We'll get it sorted this after.
> We'll sort it out this afternoon.

In each case, the second sentence in the pair is Standard English, while the first is not. There are differences of both vocabulary (e.g. *after* instead of *afternoon*) and grammar (e.g. *give* instead of *gave*).

It is difficult to give an exact definition of Standard English, but in the *Cambridge Encyclopedia of the English Language* (1995), David Crystal identifies five key characteristics:

1 It is not regionally based. People from all parts of the country can and do use Standard English.
2 Standard English has distinctive features of grammar, vocabulary and orthography (spelling), but *not* of pronunciation. This is because Standard English can be spoken with any accent.
3 It is the most prestigious variety of English, associated with people of high social status.
4 It is the variety of English promoted by educational institutions and is used extensively in government, law and the mass media. It is the form of English that is most widely understood.
5 Standard English is the variety that is commonly used in printed texts. However, only a minority (e.g. radio or television newsreaders) use it when they speak. People are more likely to speak a regional variety, or a variety that combines standard and regional features.

Origins of Standard English
Standard English has its origins in the East Midland dialect. This was spoken during the Middle Ages over a large area of southern England, including London, Oxford and Cambridge. When William Caxton set up England's first printing press in 1476, he decided to follow the spelling conventions of this dialect and to use it when he published English-language translations of foreign texts. The development of a standard variety of English, with its own principles of grammar, vocabulary and spelling, continued apace during the 18th century, when many dictionaries and books on grammar were published. The most important dictionary was that compiled by Dr Samuel

---

Take note

Standard English is also the form of English that is taught to those learning English as a foreign language.

Checkpoint 1

Can you explain why Standard English is the variety used by newsreaders?

> *"Tongues, like governments, have a natural tendency to degeneration: we have long preserved our constitution, let us make some struggle for our language"*
>
> Dr Johnson, preface to *A Dictionary of the English Language*

Johnson in 1755. Johnson's dictionary promoted the standardization of word meanings and spellings, while the work of grammarians such as Robert Lowth established grammatical 'rules' that are still with us today.

Attitudes towards Standard English

Standard English is regarded by many as the most 'correct' form of English and is the variety that children are taught to write. Complaints about sloppy or incorrect use of the language usually refer to deviations from Standard English. Linguists, however, are careful not to describe particular varieties of English as 'good' or 'bad', or as 'better' or 'worse' than other varieties. They prefer to note the differences between the varieties and the appropriateness of varieties to particular situations.

Received Pronunciation

What is Received Pronunciation?

Received Pronunciation (or **RP**) is the accent associated with middle- and upper-class speakers of the language. It is also sometimes known as 'BBC English' (because in the past it was the usual accent of announcers on national television and radio), 'public school English' or 'Oxford English'. It is a regionless accent because it does not indicate a speaker's regional origin. However, it does suggest the social class to which he or she is likely to belong.

Origins of RP

RP is thought to have evolved from an accent spoken at the royal court and by members of the aristocracy in the late Middle Ages. The accent was associated with London and the south-east and came to be regarded as superior to the accents spoken in other parts of the country and by members of other social classes. In the 19th and early 20th centuries, it was the accent favoured in public schools and among high-ranking military officers and civil servants. When Britain's political power was at its height, it was known as 'the voice of empire'.

RP today

It has been estimated that only about 3% of the population now speak pure RP. However, many more speak what is known as **modified RP**. This is an RP accent with regional features, and it is spoken by people whose original regional accent has shifted closer to RP. Social attitudes have changed, and people in positions of power and influence are no longer expected to have pure RP accents. On national television and radio, a wider variety of accents is now heard, though newsreaders still usually have RP or modified RP accents.

Exam question   answer: pages 39–40

'Standard English and Received Pronunciation are the unchanging cornerstones of correct English'. Discuss. (45 min)

Take note

In the 19th and 20th centuries, universal education and the spread of literacy encouraged the acceptance of a variety of English that was nationally recognized and understood by all.

Checkpoint 2

Give examples of situations where regional dialects are appropriate.

Watch out!

Like other accents, RP changes over time. Linguists have compared the speech of the Queen, Prince Charles and the late Princess Diana in order to show this.

Take note

RP is a socially prestigious accent, associated with high social status and with such institutions as public schools, the Church, the legal profession and the House of Lords.

Example

When radio broadcasting began in the 1920s, it was the accent of BBC presenters and newsreaders.

Example

The speech of the former Conservative leader William Hague has obvious elements of a Yorkshire accent.

Examiner's secrets

You may well want to challenge this statement! Don't be afraid to question assertions made in examination questions, provided you have evidence to support your answer.

Register

Take note

We are likely to use several different registers each day: one kind of language with friends; another when speaking to strangers; another when writing a formal letter or an essay. As these examples indicate, registers can be spoken or written.

Links

Vocabulary especially associated with a particular topic is known as **field-specific lexis**. See page 16.

Links

Levels of formality are also discussed on page 19.

Links

In an earlier section, we looked at some of the many differences between speech and writing (pages 30–1).

Checkpoint 1

Add more written and spoken modes to these lists.

In the section 'Dialects, Sociolects and Idiolects' (pages 32–3), we looked at how different groups of people use language in different ways. In this section, we consider how different situations cause different varieties of language to be used. A variety of language appropriate to a particular situation is known as a **register**.

Influences on register

Michael Halliday identified three main influences on the variety of language that we use in a given situation: **field**, **manner** and **mode**.

Field

This refers to the topic or subject that we are writing or talking about. The field of discourse is likely to have an especially strong influence on the vocabulary that is used. A magazine article on the current music scene, for example, is likely to include words linked to popular music: *CDs*, *albums*, *singles*, *artists*, *bands*, *fans*, *charts*.

Manner

This refers to the relationship that exists between the participants (i.e. between speaker or writer and audience). We adjust the language that we use according to the people we are addressing and the relationship that we have with them. We might speak respectfully to someone in authority (e.g. an employer or a college principal), casually to friends, politely to strangers at a bus stop, and so on. Situations such as these require us to adopt different **levels of formality** – one of the main ways we are usually able to distinguish between different registers.

Mode

The main distinction here is between written and spoken modes. A letter cancelling an appointment will not use exactly the same language as a telephone call with the same purpose. However, we can also subdivide these modes further. Writing uses many different formats: letters, reports, newspapers, magazines, leaflets, essays, novels, biographies, etc. The language of each of these has its own conventions and characteristics. Similarly, speech can take the form of casual conversation, interviews, meetings, public speeches and so on.

How registers differ

In considering the linguistic differences between registers, we can focus on three main aspects of language use: **lexis** (vocabulary), **grammar** and **phonology**.

Lexis

The appropriate register in any given situation employs suitable vocabulary. If two people are having a conversation about computers, for example, and both possess specialist knowledge of the subject, the use of complex technical vocabulary would be appropriate. If the same language was used when speaking to a child, however, it would mean than an inappropriate register was being used. Some registers have their own distinctive vocabulary. **Journalese**, for instance, is a term for vocabulary especially associated with newspapers.

Grammar

Sentence length and structure can be one way of identifying different written registers. Long, complex sentences might be appropriate in an academic essay but would be inappropriate in a children's storybook. Long sentences with a large number of subordinate clauses are also a characteristic of the register found in legal documents. Such texts have a number of other distinctive grammatical features, such as the repetition of words and the use of passive constructions ('shall be paid', 'is to be paid'). Ellipsis (the omission of grammatical elements) is a feature of some registers (e.g. newspaper headlines).

Phonology

Of most relevance here is the pronunciation of words in spoken English. Researchers have found that in more formal situations our speech moves closer to Received Pronunciation. Trudgill's research in Norwich (1983), for example, found that people who were asked to read aloud were more likely to pronounce the *–ing* ending in words such as *fishing* and *swimming*. In more relaxed situations, there was a greater tendency to say *fishin'* and *swimmin'*.

Shortened pronunciations of words occur more frequently in informal speech situations than in more formal contexts. An example is the use of **contractions**, the shortening of auxiliary verbs in such expressions as *I've* (for *I have*), *don't*, *it's* and so on. Such contractions also occur in writing, but they are less common than in speech and again less common in formal texts than informal texts. Crystal and David (1969) found the following average occurrence of possible contractions per thousand words in the settings shown:

Television conversation between friends	59.9%
Telephone conversation with strangers	48.8%
Interviews	25.4%
Broadcasts	21.5%
Romantic fiction	19.0%
Academic writing	0.1%
Official documents	0.0%

Importance of register

If you are analysing a text, consider how context and situation have influenced the language that is used. When writing your own texts, take care to employ a register that is appropriate.

Exam question answer: page 40

Discuss with examples why and how speakers use different registers in different situations. (45 min)

Example

Journalese includes words such as *shock, horror, soar, plunge, blast, blaze, row* and *fury*.

Checkpoint 2

Do you know (or can you guess) the meanings of *commercialese, computerese, legalese* and *officialese*?

Links

Trudgill's research is discussed more fully on page 93.

Take note

Each of these situations requires a different register. The varying frequency of contractions occurs because some registers are written while others are spoken, and because the registers have different levels of formality.

Examiner's secrets

Note the reference to speakers – you do not have to discuss written registers.

Answers
Speech and writing: essential concepts

Differences between speech and writing

Checkpoints

1 Official records have traditionally been in written form. Certificates (e.g. those relating to births, marriages and deaths) are considered precious and important. The minutes of meetings are always in writing. Laws, and rules and regulations of many different kinds, are usually set down in writing.

2 The existence of answerphones, voicemail services, etc. means that recorded messages can be heard at any time. Spoken messages can be filmed or taped for future reference. The speed of email means that feedback can be almost instantaneous, and exchanges of email messages can have much of the spontaneity and immediacy of conversation.

Exam question

Here is one student's answer to this question: Traditionally, writing has often been considered the superior mode: for hundreds of years, when the majority of people were illiterate, to be able to write marked one out as a member of the upper-class social elite, and this has cemented writing's connection with education and knowledge. Certainly, writing has a considerable number of advantages over speech. However, in recent years the benefits of speech have been recognized, partly through the development of technology such as the telephone, television and radio, and this mode of communication is now rated much more highly – for example, by GCSE examining boards, which now consider 'speaking and listening' to be an important component of the English examination. Writing is not, in fact, superior to speech – it is simply that the two modes each have their own uses and are appropriate to different situations.

In certain situations, writing would seem to be the superior mode. A key advantage of writing over speech is that it is permanent rather than transient (notwithstanding technological developments in the last century, which have made it possible to record speech). A piece of writing may survive for centuries and be read by many different people, in many different times and places. Further suggestions that writing is superior to speech come from the fact that the reader has a number of advantages over the listener. The reader is able to digest the written information at their own pace, and to return to the written text to refresh their memory (I will use 'they' and 'their' to avoid sexism), check their understanding and so on. Much of speech tends to be transient, and while the listener may often ask the speaker to repeat what they have said, in speech there is a greater risk of information being misunderstood, misheard or even missed altogether. The reader also has other benefits when compared with the listener. For example, most writing tends to be in Standard English. In speech, a regional accent and/or dialect may distract the listener from what is being said, lead to lack of intelligibility or cause the speaker to encounter prejudice. The reader of Standard English encounters no

social difficulties. There is also an argument that the reader absorbs a message more quickly than the listener: the average reading speed is around three hundred words per minute, while that of speaking (and therefore listening) is, at most, one hundred and seventy-five words per minute. As far as the receiver is concerned, therefore, writing may often seem to be the superior mode.

The writer may also be seen to have several advantages over the speaker. A writer's audience does not have to be present when they write – a writer and potentially (e.g. with novels), thousands of readers may be separated by vast distances in time and space. A writer is also usually in a far stronger position to plan what they wish to say, and can devise an easily followed structure for their writing (e.g. via paragraphing and, in books, separate chapters) while being able to re-draft their work until they are satisfied. Spoken English is generally spontaneous, comes from the lips in long, complex, often disjointed constructions, and cannot be retracted once spoken. A final advantage of writing is that it is most suitable for recording long, complex pieces of information (again, books are the best example) – a piece of speech generally has to be shorter and more concise.

In more informal situations, however, and especially when a social tool is required for building personal relationships with others, speech is without doubt the superior mode. A social situation, such as a party, where everyone had to communicate in writing is unthinkable. The speaker does have various advantages over the writer, and these may often have been ignored by those in the past who have considered writing to be superior. A speaker, for example, usually has the benefit of instant feedback from their audience and may modify their speech accordingly, e.g. by speaking more slowly if their audience requests it. A speech may be geared towards a particular context, for example by the use of deictic expressions such as 'this one', 'over there' etc. In writing, all such references have to be incorporated into the actual text, a more complex process. The speaker may give additional emphasis to what they say via the simultaneous use of non-verbal communication – body language (hand gestures, facial expressions, eye contact, etc.), non-verbal aspects of speech (pace, volume, tone, stress, rhythm, etc.) and appearance (e.g. choice of clothing). While the writer may use such techniques as bold print, italics, etc. to add emphasis, the human body is more expressive. Speech may also include regional accents/dialects, and while these may also have their disadvantages (see earlier), they emphasize the individuality of the speaker and may lead to greater empathy on the part of the receiver, particularly if the receiver is of the same geographical or social origin or simply likes the 'sound' of the accent. While reading may be faster than listening, speaking is actually quicker than writing (a maximum of one hundred and seventy-five w.p.m. for speech versus a maximum of twenty-five for writing). There is therefore a case for arguing that speech is the speedier mode. A final point about speech is that it is often responsible for introducing neologisms into the language, and therefore for keeping English 'alive' via a wide and varied possible lexis. All of these examples surely show that in some ways, and in certain, sometimes more informal, social situations, speech may be the superior mode.

It may thus be seen that, although the social and educated elites have often considered writing to be the superior mode, neither mode is truly superior to the other, since each has its own advantages and disadvantages, and the two are appropriate to completely different situations.

Dialects, sociolects and idiolects

Checkpoints

1 *Acrolect* – The most prestigious variety of a language. In the case of English, this would be Standard English spoken with an RP accent.
Basilect – The least prestigious variety of a language.
Genderlect – A way of using language that is strongly associated with either men or women.

2 The difference between jargon and slang is discussed on page III. There is not always a clear distinction between the two, but in general terms jargon would be acceptable in formal situations whereas slang would not. Slang is informal and also has a subversive, irreverent edge that jargon lacks.

3 A language repertoire is the range of language varieties used by an individual. Most of us have command of many different spoken and written styles: we use different registers (see page 36) in different situations.

Exam question

This is a question about user-related variation. An answer would explain that people can be grouped together in a variety of ways; the groups that a person belongs to will influence his or her language use. One of the main groupings is based on regional origin: people from the same region of the country will tend to exhibit similarities in their use of language. Other groups that have an important influence on language use include those based on social class, age, occupation and gender. In answering the question, you should include examples of language use that reflect the influence of these factors (e.g. to demonstrate that people of different ages use language differently, you might refer to examples of teenage slang). It would also be relevant to mention idiolect – the idea that no two people are exactly alike in their use of language.

Standard English and Received Pronunciation

Checkpoints

1 One reason is that it is a variety that can be understood by everyone. Another is that it is the most prestigious variety and has connotations of authority and intelligence.

2 Regional dialects might be appropriate in less formal situations, especially when the participants in an interaction are from the same region. Use of the local dialect would strengthen feelings of group membership and solidarity.

Exam question

Before attempting a response to this question, it would be advisable to break the question down into its constituent parts and determine what each part actually means.

First, we might note that the question is about Standard English *and* Received Pronunciation. These are not the same thing (the first is a dialect and is associated with certain features of grammar and vocabulary, the second is an accent), and it would probably be better to discuss them separately.

Second, they are both said to be *unchanging*. Given that language generally is in a continuous state of change, this is an assertion you may want to challenge.

Third, Standard English and Received Pronunciation are said to be 'cornerstones of correct English', implying that they are superior to other dialects and accents. This view will again need to be examined critically and not simply accepted at face value.

Before addressing these issues, however, it would be a good idea to define Standard English and RP (defining the terms of a question is often an appropriate way to begin an answer). The answer might then focus initially on Standard English. Can Standard English be described as 'unchanging'? It is certainly fair to say that Standard English is less subject to change than other dialects, because as the nationally recognized 'standard' version of the language, its conventions of grammar, spelling and so on are laid down in books of correct usage and taught to children and foreign learners. Nevertheless, these conventions can and do change over time. Rules such as that which forbids ending a sentence with a preposition now seem old-fashioned and are frequently broken. Is Standard English a 'cornerstone' of correct English? It is undoubtedly more prestigious than other dialects and is regarded within education and wider contexts as the most 'correct' variety. However, linguists are generally reluctant to consider it intrinsically superior to other varieties and prefer to see Standard English and other varieties as *different*. The answer could then consider RP. This is not an unchanging accent. Old newsreels confirm that there are noticeable differences between the RP accent of 40 or 50 years ago and that heard today. Linguists have observed that the speech of different generations of the royal family reflects this change. Is it a 'cornerstone of correct English'? As with Standard English, it is an accent that is socially prestigious but is not intrinsically superior to other accents.

Provided that the speaker can be understood and is using a recognized pronunciation, there are no real grounds for considering one pronunciation of a word more 'correct' than any other.

Register

Checkpoints

1 Additional examples of written formats include legal documents, instructions, poems, playscripts.

Other examples of spoken forms include radio and television broadcasts, sermons, presentations, telephone conversations.

2 These terms are all usually pejorative:

Commercialese – language associated with business and commerce. Especially refers to expressions that are excessively formal and elaborate (e.g. 'We are in receipt of' instead of 'We have received').

Computerese – language associated with the world of computers. Usually implies language that is heavily reliant on jargon.

Legalese – language used by the legal profession, especially when it contains an excessive amount of legal terminology.

Officialese – the language of bureaucracy and officialdom. Usually applied to language that is pompous and pedantic.

Exam question

The key words here are 'why' and 'how'. The reasons for different registers can largely be explained with reference to differences of field, manner and mode and the way these require adjustments in the language that people use. A discussion of how registers are used can be illustrated by examples of differences in lexis, grammar and phonology.

Language in use: spoken language

The analysis of spoken English features prominently in the specifications for both AS and A2 English Language. The main differences between speech and writing were outlined in the previous chapter (pages 30–1). Here, we examine in more detail the distinctive features of speech. **Spoken language** comes in many forms, including news broadcasts, sports commentaries and public speeches. The most important of these forms is conversation, and much of this chapter is taken up with this topic: how conversations are structured; gender differences in conversational behaviour; and the major theories concerning how conversation works. We also consider **non-verbal communication**, an important additional element in conversational interaction.

Exam themes

→ Characteristics of speech.

→ Conversation.

→ Non-verbal communication.

Topic checklist

O AS ● A2	AQA/A	AQA/B	EDEXCEL	OCR	WJE
Spoken language: types, functions and influences	O●	O●	O●	O●	O●
Features of spontaneous speech	O●	O●	O●	O●	O●
Structure of conversations 1	O●	O●	O●	O●	O●
Structure of conversations 2	O●	O●	O●	O●	O●
Conversation theory 1	O●	O●	O●	O●	O●
Conversation theory 2	O●	O●	O●	O●	O●
Gender and conversational behaviour	O●	O●	O●	O●	O●
Specimen texts	O●	O●	O●	O●	O●
Non-verbal communication 1	O●	O●	O●	O●	O●
Non-verbal communication 2	O●	O●	O●	O●	O●

Spoken language: types, functions and influences

In this introductory section on spoken language, we consider some of the main types and functions of **spoken English**. We also look at some of the key influences on the kind of language that a speaker uses. When you are analysing a passage of spoken English, it is a good idea to begin by asking yourself three basic questions: What type of spoken language is it? What are its purposes or functions? What factors are likely to have influenced the kind of language that is present?

Types of spoken language

There are many different types of spoken English. The most basic distinction is that between **monologue** and **dialogue**.

A monologue is a single speaker addressing one or more listeners. Examples of monologue include lectures, speeches, commentaries (e.g. radio or television sports commentary), sermons, recitations.

A dialogue involves interaction: there are two or more people, who are both speakers and listeners. Examples of dialogue include informal conversations, interviews, meetings, debates, telephone conversations.

Functions of spoken language

Spoken language can also serve a variety of functions. The terms that linguists use for some of these functions are shown below. Note that a single utterance can sometimes have more than one function.

→ **Referential** Utterances that provide information are said to have a referential function (e.g. 'The train leaves at half past twelve and arrives in London just after three o'clock').

→ **Expressive** Utterances are said to have an expressive function if they express the speaker's feelings (e.g. 'I'm really looking forward to Alison's party').

→ **Transactional** Verbal exchanges in which the main emphasis is on getting something done are described as transactional. An example would be a motorist stopping to ask a passer-by for directions.

→ **Interactional** Interactional exchanges differ from transactional exchanges in that the main emphasis is on the social relationship between the participants. An example would be two friends who have not seen each other for a long time meeting by chance and having a long chat with each other.

→ **Phatic** Phatic communication (or **phatic communion**, as it is formally known) is the technical term for 'small talk'. Utterances such as 'Hello' or 'Isn't it a lovely day?' are phatic. Conversations, especially with strangers, often begin with phatic exchanges. Although phatic utterances are devoid of serious content, they play an important role in establishing and maintaining social relationships.

Checkpoint 1

Try to think of more examples of monologue and dialogue.

Take note

Another important distinction when considering types of spoken English is between **prepared** and **spontaneous** speech.

Action point

Watch an episode of your favourite soap and look for examples of each type of function.

Checkpoint 2

Explain why conversations with strangers might begin with phatic exchanges.

Influences on spoken language ●●●

The two main influences on the kind of language that speakers might use are **speaker identity** and **context**.

Speaker identity
The following aspects of a speaker's identity may influence the language that he or she uses: regional origin; socio-economic status (social class); occupation; gender; ethnic identity; age; group membership (e.g. membership of a gang).

Context
Context is a broad term referring to many different aspects of the *situation* in which speech occurs. Some of the most important of these aspects are listed below.

→ **Audience** The person(s) being addressed and the speaker's relationship with them is often considered to be the most important influence on how language is used. Differences of status can have a significant impact; they may, for example, mean that one speaker is more dominant in the interaction than another, and they can also influence the forms of address used between speakers (i.e. how speakers refer to each other). The relationship of the speakers may result in **convergence** or **divergence**. Convergence occurs when a speaker's style of speech moves closer to that of another person in order to reduce the social distance between them. Divergence is the opposite: styles of speech move further apart, increasing social distance.

→ **Setting** The *formality* of the setting is especially important. The language used at a casual social gathering (e.g. a party) would be different from that heard at a committee meeting or a job interview.

→ **Topic** The subject that is being talked about is especially likely to influence the vocabulary that is used. A conversation about politics, for example, may contain a fair amount of **field-specific lexis**: 'right-wing', 'left-wing', 'election', 'Parliament', 'MPs', 'policies' and so on.

→ **Purpose** Some of the most common functions of spoken language were outlined opposite. Different kinds of language might be expected, for example, if a conversation was transactional or interactional.

Links

The ways in which speakers are influenced by these factors are discussed in the section 'Social aspects of language' (pages 85–116).

Links

The influence of differences in status is discussed on pages 102–3. For more on convergence and divergence, see page 50.

The jargon

Field-specific lexis is vocabulary associated with a particular topic or field. See page 16.

Exam warm-up questions   answers: page 62

1   Illustrate the following functions of spoken language by making up one utterance for each: referential; expressive; transactional; interactional; phatic. (15 min)

2   For each of the following aspects of context, describe a situation in which the aspect concerned would be likely to have a significant influence on language use: audience; setting; topic; purpose. (15 min)

Features of spontaneous speech

This section lists some features of spoken language that make it different from written language. Most of these differences arise because speech is usually more informal and more spontaneous than writing. However, there are some situations where spoken language is formal and carefully planned (presentations, for example), in which case the differences are likely to be much less marked.

Lexis ●●●

→ **Vocabulary** is often less formal than in written texts. Colloquial expressions may be present (e.g. 'I gave my mate a tenner for it'). Slang is generally found in speech rather than writing. Informality is also evident in the use of contractions (*can't*, *we've*, *it's*, etc.)

→ **Phatic expressions** are generally found only in speech: 'hello', 'pleased to meet you', 'how's things?' etc.

→ **Deictic expressions** may be used (see below).

Deictic expressions ●●●

These are expressions that cannot be understood unless the context of the utterance is known.

Examples are the pronouns *I*, *me*, *mine*, *you* and *your*. The specific referential meaning of these words (i.e. the identity of the persons referred to) varies according to who is speaking (or writing) and who is being addressed.

Other frequently used deictic expressions relate to time: *now*, *then*, *yesterday*, *tomorrow*, *next week*; and to place: *here*, *there*, *these*, *those*.

Deictic expressions are found in both speech and writing, but they are especially common in speech. A single utterance can contain several:

I'll speak to *you* about *this tomorrow* – *my* train's *here now*.

Grammar ●●●

Spontaneous speech is not arranged into neatly separated sentences. The structure is much looser, and it can be difficult to determine where one construction ends and another begins. Grammatical features specifically associated with speech include the following:

→ **Interrupted constructions** One construction is abandoned in favour of another:

I think you could have – you should have told me.

These are also known as false starts (see 'Non-fluency features' opposite).

→ **Disjointed constructions** such as the following, which would not be found in writing:

He knows about computers – how to fix them.

→ **Incomplete constructions** These are incomplete because words or grammatical elements are missing:

Seen Tom recently? (not 'Have you seen Tom recently?')

Checkpoint 1

Can you think of any types of written text that might also have some of these features?

Checkpoint 2

Make up another sentence containing three or more examples of deixis.

Watch out!

Transcripts of speech are often unpunctuated. Instead of referring to 'sentences', it is better to refer to **utterances** or **constructions**.

The jargon

Another term for an incomplete construction is **ellipsis**.

→ **Non-standard grammar** This reflects the informality of speech:

We was half an hour late.   I don't know nothing about it.

Non-fluency features ●●●

This is a broad term referring to a range of features that might interrupt the flow of a person's speech. They occur naturally when a person is speaking spontaneously.

→ **Fillers** Words and expressions that have little meaning but are often inserted into everyday speech. Examples include 'you know', 'like', 'sort of', 'I mean'. Although they usually add nothing to the content of an utterance, they nevertheless serve important functions:
  → They may give the speaker time to think.
  → They can soften the force of a statement, lessening its bluntness.
  → They can be a way of involving the listener.
→ **Filled pauses** These are hesitations such as 'um' and 'er'. If a pause is silent, it is termed an *unvoiced pause*.
→ **Repetitions** Either of single words, or of several words at a time.
→ **False starts** Changing from one grammatical construction to another before the initial construction has been completed (see 'Interrupted constructions' opposite).

Discourse structure ●●●

In the same way that individual utterances are not made up of neat grammatical sentences, longer stretches of speech are not organized into paragraphs. Transcripts of spoken English can appear rambling, disorganized and repetitive. There may be **digressions** – deviations from the main theme or topic – and ideas or information may not be presented in a logical sequence. Note though that in certain respects informal conversation does usually follow predictable patterns. This will be discussed in the next two sections (pages 46–9).

Exam question   answer: page 62

In the transcript below the speaker is talking about a Paul McCartney concert at the Cavern Club in Liverpool in 1999. The concert was broadcast on the internet and on a giant screen in a Liverpool park. In what ways is the language used typical of spoken English? (45 min) (.) = a brief pause

it was a waste of time (.) complete waste of time (.) first off we tried to get him on the internet but it came up you know server down server busy (.) anyway we thought we'd go to Liverpool it was only about quarter past twenty past eight it started on the internet at eight but I didn't think he'd be on stage then (.) anyway it was on a big screen in Liverpool (.) you know Chavasse Park (.) by the (.) the Albert Dock so we got there really quick (.) anyway (.) we were just walking across it's only across the road we were walking along and I could hear him singing 'Party' (.) I said when he was on the telly that was his last number anyway next thing all these people were streaming towards us we kept going cos we could still hear the crowd you know (.) anyway we got there and on the screen was this shot just an empty stage (.) great picture and everything (.) people were still hanging about but after a couple of minutes we gave up

Watch out!

Non-fluency features are inevitable in spoken language. Do not dismiss them as 'bad' or 'incorrect' English.

The jargon

The term **discourse** refers here to a complete text, such as a newspaper article, an advertisement or a transcript of spontaneous speech.

Watch out!

A transcript may appear to make little sense on first reading. Be patient and try again.

Take note

This transcript includes pauses but omits other prosodic features such as stress and intonation (see page 60). If these are indicated on a transcript you are analysing it is important to comment on them.

Examiner's secrets

One way of answering this question would be to look back over the headings used in this section and organize your own points in a similar way.

Structure of conversations 1

Although we do not usually think of informal conversation as a structured activity, much of it follows predictable patterns, and the participants in a conversation do usually adhere to a number of rules and conventions. In the next two sections, we shall be examining the structure of conversations, looking initially at how conversations begin and at the underlying principles of turn taking.

Openings ●●●

Most interactions begin with an **opening sequence**, which eases people into the conversation.

→ Most common are exchanges of greetings: 'Hello', 'Hi', 'How do you do?' etc.

→ Many greetings refer to the time of day ('Good morning', 'Good afternoon', etc.) or enquire after the other person's health ('How are you today?'). Such enquiries are not usually taken literally, and people will generally say 'Fine' or 'OK' regardless of how they are feeling.

→ Greetings between friends are likely to be informal and may involve established rituals (e.g. hand slapping).

→ Opening sequences between strangers often involve some kind of self-identification ('Hello, I'm Mike Dobson. Nice to meet you').

→ The topic of the conversation may be initiated in some way. For example, in a shop a customer might ask an assistant, 'Excuse me, can you tell me more about this computer?' An utterance such as this (indicating the topic of the conversation) is known as a **topic marker**.

→ Context is an important influence on how a conversation opens. Formal settings (e.g. interviews) are obviously associated with more formal openings. Some situations have their own traditional opening sequences. Telephone conversations, for example, usually begin with an exchange of 'Hellos'. If you stop a stranger in the street to ask the time, you are quite likely to begin the enquiry with 'Excuse me'.

Turn taking ●●●

One of the most important features of conversation is that we take turns at speaking. Generally, we manage this with great efficiency; if we didn't, conversation would be chaotic: full of interruptions, simultaneous speech and awkward silences. It has been estimated that only about 5% of conversation consists of overlapping speech, while the average gap between utterances is only a few tenths of a second. In other words, we are very accurate judges of the precise moments when it is appropriate for us to contribute to a conversation. This is because, despite its informality and spontaneity, conversation has its own rules and conventions, which speakers follow even though for the most part they are not consciously aware of them. We are also sensitive to a range of verbal and non-verbal cues, which signal that a speaker is reaching the end of an utterance, or that a listener wishes to speak.

Checkpoint 1

What term (apart from **greetings**) can be used to refer to expressions such as 'Good morning' and 'Nice to meet you'?

Watch out!

If you are given a transcript to analyse, it may only form *part* of a conversation, so the opening sequence may be omitted.

Examiner's secrets

When you are analysing a transcript of conversation, look at the turn-taking behaviour of individual speakers. For example, one speaker might have a greater tendency to interrupt.

How turn taking works ●●●

In formal situations, turn taking is often easier because it is managed more explicitly. In committee meetings, for example, the chairperson may invite individual members to speak. In job interviews, conversation follows a clear question-and-answer pattern.

In informal conversation, turn taking is also sometimes quite explicit. Direct questions are an obvious invitation to speak, as are **tag questions** (questions attached to the ends of statements – e.g. 'We're going to be late, aren't we?'). Another explicit way of indicating that you want someone to speak is to mention their name (e.g. 'Pauline knows about that' or 'Laura was there – she'll tell you what happened').

Usually, however, the cues are more subtle. One indication that an utterance is at an end is that the grammatical construction involved will be completed (the equivalent of a sentence coming to an end). Another, more obvious, verbal cue is when the speaker makes a concluding statement such as 'That was that' or 'I haven't spoken to her since'.

When speakers approach the end of an utterance their voice begins to fall, and it appears that listeners unconsciously sense this. Also, the last syllable spoken may be more drawn out.

Eye movements are an important non-verbal cue. We usually look at another person more when we are listening than when we are speaking, but when we near the end of an utterance we will often look up at the other person's eyes.

Listeners also have ways of indicating that they wish to speak. There may be an increase in body tension, and they may lean forward. Rapid head nods can be a sign of impatience (conveying the message, 'Yes, yes, you don't need to say any more').

Speakers have ways of prolonging their turn when they do not want to give way to others who wish to speak. They may avoid eye contact or extend constructions by continually adding words such as 'and' or 'but'. If a speaker continues for too long, or a listener decides to speak anyway, an **interruption** can occur. The speaker usually responds to this either by stopping (giving up the floor) or by continuing, but more loudly.

Differences in status can influence turn taking. In some situations (e.g. a football manager giving a half-time team talk), the person of superior status holds the floor and others are expected to listen. In other situations the roles can be reversed, and the lower-status person does most of the talking (e.g. a speeding motorist trying to explain his behaviour to a police officer). High-status persons are also more likely to interrupt.

Some research suggests that turn taking may also be influenced by gender. For example, it has been found that women tend to ask more questions, while men are more likely to interrupt (see 'Gender and conversational behaviour', pages 54–5).

The jargon

In conversational analysis, the person who is speaking is said to be **holding the floor**.

Checkpoint 2

Can you think of any other body movements that might indicate that a speaker has finished, or that a listener wishes to speak?

Links

The influence of status on language use is discussed more fully in the section 'Language and power' (pages 102–3).

Examiner's secrets

The theories of conversation discussed on pages 50–3 are also relevant to this question.

Exam question   answer: page 62

Would you agree that most conversations are cooperative rather than competitive? Give reasons for your answer. (45 min)

Structure of conversations 2

In this second section on conversational structure, we consider some other features of conversations: adjacency pairs; the ways in which topics are introduced and changed; repairs; and standard ways of closing a conversation.

Adjacency pairs

Adjacency pairs are two-part exchanges that follow a predictable pattern. A question followed by an answer is an example of an adjacency pair:

What's the time?   Ten past three.

Adjacency pairs help to structure a conversation, and a typical conversation will have a large number of them. Other examples are greeting + greeting, summons + answer ('Dad!' – 'Yes?'), apology + acceptance ('Sorry' – 'That's ok'), invitation + acceptance or refusal. The progress of a conversation is likely to be disrupted if the pattern of an adjacency pair is violated (e.g. if a question does not receive a reply).

Three-part exchanges can also occur, with the second speaker's response generating a further utterance from the first speaker. Teacher–pupil interaction often has this pattern.

Teacher: Who wrote *Trainspotting*?
Pupil: Irvine Welsh.
Teacher: That's right.

Topics

The **topic** of a conversation (what is being talked about) also helps to give it coherence and structure. Generally, utterances will be relevant to the current topic or will attempt to initiate new topics.

In more formal situations (e.g. a business meeting), there may be a predetermined topic or set of topics, which the participants discuss in a systematic way. In informal interactions, however, conversation will often drift from topic to topic.

Introducing new topics can be a sign of conversational dominance and may reflect the speaker's superior status (e.g. a teacher deciding the content of a lesson). Correspondingly, unsuccessful attempts to initiate new topics can show that the speaker occupies a subordinate position.

Changes of topic are know as **topic shifts**, and utterances that initiate them are termed **topic shifters**. Examples of expressions conventionally used to signal a change of topic are 'by the way', 'incidentally', 'something else has been bothering me', etc.

If a conversation returns to an earlier topic, this is known as a **topic loop**.

Repairs

A **repair** resolves a problem that has arisen in a conversation. The simplest kind of repair occurs when speakers make a mistake and correct themselves:

Checkpoint 1

Try to think of more examples of common adjacency pairs.

Links

Research suggests that women are more likely than men to attempt to initiate new topics but are less likely to be successful. The possible reasons for this are discussed on pages 54–5.

The jargon

As explained on page 46, an utterance indicating the topic at the beginning of a conversation is known as a **topic marker**.

We ended up on the North Circular (.) the A6 (.) I mean the A406.

The repair can also be carried out by another speaker:

We ended up on the North Circular (.) the A6 (.)
You mean the A406.

Other examples of situations requiring repairs are when a listener has not heard something and asks for it to be repeated, or has not understood something and requests clarification.

Feedback

Another convention of conversation is that those being addressed give **feedback** to the speaker to show that they are listening. Failure to give such feedback can be very disconcerting for the speaker – e.g. someone speaking on the telephone soon begins to feel uncomfortable if there is complete silence at the other end of the line. Feedback can take various forms:

→ Verbal responses such as 'Absolutely', 'I know', 'Really?' etc.
→ Back-channel noises: sighs, gasps and other expressive noises such as 'mm', 'uh huh', etc.
→ Non-verbal responses such as nodding, smiling, making eye contact, etc. Such feedback is usually positive and supportive, but it can also register disagreement, boredom or inattention.
→ As with other aspects of conversational behaviour, the amount of feedback given can vary between speakers. If you are analysing a transcript, look for the kind of feedback that is given and also see if there are differences in the responses of individual speakers.

Ways of closing a conversation

Just as there are standard ways of opening a conversation, so there are conventional **closing sequences**, which prevent a conversation ending abruptly or unexpectedly.

Often the last words spoken are a ritual exchange of farewells (e.g. 'Goodbye', 'So long'), but these are usually preceded by **pre-closing signals** – ways of indicating that a conversation is reaching its end.

Often the topic of the conversation is concluded in some way. There might be some kind of summing-up of what has been agreed, or a remark such as 'I think that's it', 'I think we've covered everything', etc.

The participants may speak of meeting again. On some occasions this is meant literally ('I'll call for you at seven then'), but often such remarks are essentially phatic ('See you soon', 'We'll have to meet for a drink sometime', etc.) Other phatic expressions such as 'Nice talking to you', 'Look after yourself', etc. are also common.

There are also non-verbal pre-closing signals such as starting to turn away, collecting together belongings, rising from one's seat, etc.

Checkpoint 2

Why might repairs carried out by another speaker have a negative impact upon the conversation as a whole?

Links

Research also suggests that women tend to give more feedback (especially positive feedback) than men. See pages 54–5.

Checkpoint 3

Formal situations often have firmly established closing sequences. Try to think of examples.

Exam question   answer: page 62

'The conduct of a conversation is governed by a set of unspoken rules and conventions'. Discuss. (45 min)

Conversation theory 1

In the next two sections, we look at some important conversation theories that have been developed to explain the ways that people behave in conversation. Initially we look at accommodation theory and Grice's cooperative principle.

Accommodation theory

Accommodation theory was developed by Howard Giles and others in the 1970s. It suggests that we adjust our speech to 'accommodate' the person we are addressing. This may result in convergence or divergence.

Convergence (which is more common) occurs when we move our speech closer to that of the other person. **Divergence** occurs when people's speech styles move further apart.

Convergence has the effect of decreasing the social distance between people. An RP speaker, for instance, may tone down his accent when in the company of working-class speakers because he is afraid his accent will set him apart. This is termed **downward convergence**. On the other hand, a man with a strong regional accent who is being interviewed for a job by an RP speaker may attempt to eliminate some of the regional features from his speech and move it closer to RP. This is **upward convergence**. Research suggests that status is an important influence on accommodation, and that someone of subordinate status is more likely to converge towards a superior than the other way round.

If both participants in a conversation converge towards each other, **mutual convergence** occurs.

An example of convergence was investigated by Coupland (1984), who studied the speech of a woman who worked in a Cardiff travel agency. He found that her pronunciation of certain sounds varied according to the social background of her customers, and that her speech tended to mirror that of her clients.

Divergence has the effect of emphasizing the differences between people. Two supporters of rival football teams engaged in an argument, for example, may unconsciously exaggerate their respective regional accents as a way of asserting regional loyalty and identity.

The cooperative principle

As explained in the earlier sections on the structure of conversations (pages 46–9), a conversation 'works' because the participants abide by certain rules and conventions. H. P. Grice (1975) saw cooperation between the participants as the fundamental principle underlying conversation. He argued that conversations proceed on the assumption that those taking part have common goals and agreed ways of achieving these goals. He called this assumption the **cooperative principle**.

The four maxims

Grice developed his idea of the cooperative principle by identifying four specific **maxims** (rules or principles), which he said participants in a conversation usually follow.

Links

Accommodation theory has relevance to the study of accents and dialects (pages 86–9) and language and social class (pages 92–3).

The jargon

Audience design theory is a related theory. It suggests that the primary influence on the language we use is our audience.

Examiner's secrets

If you are analysing a transcript of conversation, you can look for examples of the participants following, or flouting, Grice's maxims.

1 **The maxim of quantity**   In making a contribution to a conversation, you should say neither more nor less than is required. If I ask a stranger the way to the nearest post office and he simply says, 'It's not far', he is clearly not telling me enough. On the other hand, he will be telling me too much if he tells me the names of the twenty shops I will pass on the way.

2 **The maxim of relevance**   What you say should be relevant to the ongoing context of the conversation. If a group of friends are having a conversation and one of them repeatedly returns to a topic exhausted several minutes previously, this will obviously have a disruptive effect on the conversation.

3 **The maxim of manner**   You should avoid ambiguity and obscurity and be orderly in your utterances. If the stranger giving directions to the post office presented the information in a confusing sequence, he would be violating this maxim.

4 **The maxim of quality**   You should also be truthful and not say anything that you suspect to be false.

Flouting the maxims

When these principles are not abided by, the maxims are said to be **flouted**.

Many remarks used in everyday conversation show that we are conscious of these maxims and try to excuse ourselves if we think we are in danger of flouting them: 'I'll try not to speak for too long', 'I know this may not seem relevant', 'I'm sorry if I'm not explaining this very clearly', etc.

Flouting of the maxims can lead to conversational difficulties and breakdown. Other participants may show their dissatisfaction by insisting that speakers answer the question or 'get to the point'. People who consistently flout the maxims are often described in a negative way (e.g. as windbags, shifty customers, liars).

However, in some situations speakers may appear to be flouting the maxims but in fact be cooperating at a deeper level. If the stranger who was asked the way to the post office replied 'It's Sunday today', this would not on the face of it be an answer to the question. In reality, however, he is being cooperative, because what he means is 'It's Sunday today, so the post office will be closed'. To understand how the maxims are being observed by speakers, we often need to read between the lines and look at what is implied rather than what is stated. Grice called information conveyed in this way *implicature*.

Another example of conversational implicature would be a teacher saying to a class of students, 'I hear a lot of talking'. The students would obviously understand the implication of what the teacher had said – that they were being asked to quieten down.

> *"Make your conversational contribution such as is required, at the stage at which it occurs, by the accepted purpose or direction of the talk exchange in which you are engaged"*
>
> H. P. Grice

Checkpoint

Try to think of more everyday remarks that show awareness of the maxims.

Examiner's secrets

The theories outlined in the next section (pages 52–3) could also be brought into an answer to this question.

Exam question   answer: page 63

With reference to relevant theory, discuss some of the ways that the participants in a conversation are sensitive to others' needs. (45 min)

Conversation theory 2

In this second section on conversation theory, we look at the role that politeness plays in conversation, considering face theory, positive and negative politeness, and Lakoff's politeness principle.

Links

Research suggests that women are more attentive to the face needs of others than men. See pages 54–5.

Links

Forms of address are discussed more fully on pages 102–3.

Links

Turn taking was discussed on page 46.

Face

In any interaction, we present a particular image of ourselves to others. We may, for example, present ourselves as a good friend in one context and as a knowledgeable student or teacher in another. Irving Goffman (1955) called the image that we present **face**. In everyday speech, we use the word in a similar way when we speak of 'losing face' or 'saving face'.

As we have seen in previous sections of this chapter, conversation is a cooperative activity, and one aspect of this cooperation is that we generally accept the face that others offer to us.

On rare occasions, we may reject the face that someone presents to us: we may accuse them of insincerity, for example, or mock them for pretending to be more knowledgeable than they really are. If something is said or done that challenges or rejects another's face, this is termed a **face-threatening act**. An example would be bluntly telling somebody 'You don't know what you're talking about' or turning your back on someone who is speaking to you. More often, however, we will keep our reservations to ourselves and behave as if we accept the other person's face. Psychologists argue that this kind of tactfulness is partly motivated by self-interest: we respect others' faces in the hope that they will respect ours in return.

Face-work often has the aim of maintaining the **status** of participants. This might be the status that they have within a particular conversation or, more generally, the status that they have in society. People in a lower-status position tend to be more attentive to the face needs of those in a higher-status position than *vice versa*. They show this by using language that is respectful and deferential.

Politeness

Having regard for another person's face is an important aspect of **politeness**, a broad term for the sensitivity that we show to others in conversation. Examples of politeness include:

→ Using appropriate forms of address.
→ Speaking to others in a way that is appropriate to the social relationship you have with them.
→ Speaking with a degree of formality appropriate to the occasion.
→ Understanding the conventions of language associated with particular situations (e.g. accepting or refusing an invitation, beginning and ending a conversation).
→ Understanding the conventions of turn taking.

Positive and negative politeness

Brown and Levinson (1987) have developed Goffman's ideas and speak of face needs being met by positive and negative politeness.

Positive politeness is demonstrated when we show people that they are liked and admired. We may pay them compliments, take an interest in their well-being, make it obvious that we enjoy their company and so on. If the manager of a company invites a subordinate to address her by her first name ('Call me Barbara'), this is an expression of positive politeness because it is a gesture of friendship and an attempt to reduce the social distance between them.

Negative politeness is shown when we avoid intruding on others' lives, taking care not to impose our presence on them or pry into their personal affairs. Negative politeness results in language that is indirect, apologetic and respectful. Saying 'Excuse me' before asking a stranger the time is an example of negative politeness, because you are showing that you understand the stranger has a right to expect to be left alone. If a subordinate addresses a superior as 'Sir' or 'Mr Jones', this is also negative politeness, because the subordinate is respecting Mr Jones's status and is not seeking to reduce the social distance between them.

Brown and Levinson's research suggests that particular societies and cultures may place greater emphasis on one or other of these forms of politeness. Britain, for example, has been identified as a culture that stresses negative politeness.

The politeness principle ●●●

Robin Lakoff (1973) argued that much conversational interaction is governed by what she called the **politeness principle**. She defined this further by specifying three rules or maxims that speakers usually observe:

→ **Don't impose**   This is similar to the concept of negative politeness explained above. It is illustrated by such expressions as:

> I'm sorry to bother you.
> Could you possibly?
> I know it's asking a lot.

→ **Give options**   We avoid forcing the other person into a corner. Examples of expressions that demonstrate this maxim are:

> It's entirely up to you.
> I won't be offended if you don't want to.
> Do you want to go first?

→ **Make your receiver feel good**   We say things that flatter others and show that they are appreciated. Again, there are many utterances in everyday use that illustrate this:

> What would I have done without you?
> I'd really appreciate your advice on this.

Checkpoint 1

Would you agree that Britain is a society in which negative politeness is especially important?

Checkpoint 2

Try to think of an additional example for each maxim.

Exam question   answer: page 63

With reference to appropriate theory and relevant examples, explain some of the ways in which the participants in a conversation show politeness. (45 min)

Gender and conversational behaviour

An important aspect of the study of conversation is the question of **gender differences** in conversational behaviour. In this section, we summarize some of the research findings relevant to this topic and also outline the main theories that have attempted to explain these differences.

Who talks more?

It is a common assumption that women talk more than men, but research (e.g. Fishman 1990) has consistently suggested that in mixed-sex interactions at least, the *opposite* is in fact the case. In mixed-sex conversations, the average amount of time for which a man will speak has been found to be approximately twice as great as the average time for which a woman will speak.

Conversational support

Women tend to be more **supportive** in their conversational behaviour than men. In essence, women's approach to conversation tends to be **cooperative**, whereas men's approach tends to be **competitive**. Specifically, women tend to:

→ Ask more questions (showing interest in what other speakers think, and encouraging them to participate).
→ Give more supportive feedback when listening (e.g. through back-channel noises such as 'mm' and through expressions of agreement and understanding such as 'Yes', 'I know', etc.).
→ Pay more compliments.
→ Initiate more topics of conversation.
→ Make more effort to bring others into the conversation.
→ Use 'you' and 'we' more often (i.e. they address others more and involve them more in what is being said).
→ Develop the ideas of previous speakers more than men do.

In contrast, men are more likely to:

→ Interrupt (see below).
→ Express disagreement.
→ Ignore the other person's utterances.
→ Show reluctance to pursue topics initiated by others.

Interruptions

Many researchers have found that men are more likely to **interrupt** than women.

American researchers Zimmerman and West (1975) taped informal conversations between students in coffee bars, shops and other public places. In same-sex exchanges, they found that interruptions were generally quite evenly distributed between the participants. In mixed-sex interactions, however, they found a dramatic imbalance: 96% of the interruptions were from men, and only 4% from women.

Links

Other differences in male and female language use are considered on pages 94–5, much of which is relevant to this section.

Watch out!

Don't assume that all men and women are the same! Researchers have identified trends and tendencies, but many individual men and women do not conform to the expected pattern.

Example

Studies of classroom talk have also found that boys talk more in front of the whole class than do girls.

Checkpoint 1

How else might the asking of questions be interpreted? (See the discussion of 'dominance' theory opposite.)

Example

In conversations analysed by Fishman (1978), 62% of topics were introduced by women.

Analysis of conversations in other contexts has confirmed both that men are responsible for most of the interruptions and that women speakers are more likely to be interrupted than male speakers.

In studies of parent–child interactions, fathers have done most of the interrupting, and daughters have been interrupted more than sons, by both their fathers and mothers.

Studies of women in business organizations have found that women are interrupted less when they are managers than when they are subordinates, but that overall they are still interrupted more than men.

Topics of conversation ●●●

As well as investigating how men and women talk, researchers have also studied what they talk about. Here there is some support for the stereotyped notions of gender differences. Put simply, women tend to talk about 'feelings' and men tend to talk about 'things'. Women's conversation is often focused on personal experiences, relationships and problems. The topics of male conversation tend to be more concrete, relating to information, facts, objects and activities: sport, cars, computers, home improvements and possessions are popular subjects.

Explanations of the differences ●●●

Two main explanations are offered for these differences in conversational behaviour. Some theories are based on the idea of **dominance**, while others are based on the idea of **difference**.

Dominance

This approach argues that because women occupy a less powerful position in society than men, their conversational behaviour is less assertive and less confident. Men are dominant within society, so it is not surprising that they tend to dominate mixed-sex conversations. Women are said to be used to male dominance, and as a result of social conditioning will often be polite and respectful when speaking to men.

Difference

This approach focuses more on differences in male and female attitudes and values, differences that are said to be inculcated from childhood, when we form, and are influenced by, single-sex peer groups. Studies of children's play have found that in boys' games there is more emphasis on competition and confrontation, while girls' games are more cooperative. In adulthood, women's talk often focuses on personal feelings and problems (see earlier), and this helps to explain why their approach to conversation is more sympathetic and supportive.

Check the net

There is a language and gender website with useful information and resources related to language and gender studies: www.english.tamu.edu/pers/fac/bucholtz/lng/

Checkpoint 2

In your experience, are the observations that researchers have made about gender differences in conversational behaviour accurate? (Male and female conversational behaviour is an interesting topic for a language investigation.)

Example

Robin Lakoff (1975) argues that because of their social position, women are more tentative than men in their speech, evident for example in their use of indirect expressions such as 'would you mind?' and 'could you possibly?' and of tag questions (questions added to the ends of statements – e.g. 'isn't it?').

Watch out!

These two approaches are not incompatible – e.g. the 'dominance' approach could explain why men dominate mixed-sex interactions, and the 'difference' approach could account for women's conversational behaviour being more supportive.

Exam question   answer: page 63

What evidence is there to support the argument that men and women behave very differently in conversation? How do theorists account for such differences? (45 min)

Specimen texts

Aspects of the conversations you might look at include:

Structure
→ How the conversation begins, develops and ends
→ How topics are introduced and changed
→ Adjacency pairs

Language
→ Vocabulary
→ Grammar
→ Non-fluency features

Interaction
→ Dominance (Is one speaker dominant? How is this evident?)
→ Supportive or competitive conversational behaviour
→ How the conversational behaviour supports or contradicts relevant theory (e.g. relating to gender differences in conversational behaviour)

Exam questions

answers: pages 63–4

The following conversations were recorded at a sixth-form college. Write an analysis of each conversation, paying close attention to the following:

→ the structure of the conversation;
→ the language used by the participants;
→ the way the participants interact with each other.

You can analyse each transcript separately and do not need to compare them with each other. Spend about 45 minutes on each analysis.

(.) = a brief pause   <u>underlined text</u> = interruptions/overlapping speech

Text A ●●●

<u>A teacher and a student (both male) are discussing an essay</u>:

TEACHER: so this essay (.) I thought this was better than your last essay (.) you know <u>the</u>

STUDENT: <u>the</u> analysis one

TEACHER: yeh the analysis one (.) you wrote more for this one and there was a bit more depth to it as well (.) did you find it easier or did you (.) you know (.) approach it differently

STUDENT: I spent more time on it (.) I thought it was more interesting than <u>the other</u>

TEACHER: <u>yeh a lot</u> of you seemed to prefer this one (.) I think it was (.) it gave you the chance to write about the local accent (.) you had some good [turns the pages of the essay and points to a paragraph] (.) see this here (.) I thought that was a really good paragraph (.) what you say here about prejudice and stereotyping (.) you explain it really well (.) and there's good good examples

STUDENT: I thought that bit might've sounded a bit biased

TEACHER: no because you say you're from Merseyside so you're (.) you know (.) up front about it (.) and the main thing is you've got evidence for what you say (.) I believe you anyway [laughs] (.) I thought the only weak bit was the end [turns to last page and points to the last section] (.) see this last sentence (.) if you read it – read it now (.) it ends very suddenly doesn't it

STUDENT: yeh (.) I didn't just want to repeat what <u>I'd already</u>

TEACHER: <u>no I know</u> what you mean (.) but it's still a bit abrupt (.) you could bring it back to the question again (.) whenever it says anything like (.) you know how far do you agree or do you agree make sure it's clear where you stand

STUDENT: yeh

Text B ●●●

<u>Two students are having an informal conversation</u>:

WENDY: we went out in Becky's car last night
STEPHEN: has Becky got a car now
WENDY: it's her mum's (.) we went to Stairways

STEPHEN: I've seen her (.) red Escort
WENDY: no that's her brother's (.) Mondeo (.) anyway Stairways was crap
STEPHEN: when's she taking her test
WENDY: dunno (.) where'd you go
STEPHEN: didn't she take it once already
WENDY: no (.) she's <u>sent off</u>
STEPHEN: <u>I remember</u> her failing
WENDY: no (.) she would've told me (.) so what d'you do
STEPHEN: went for a drink with Andy (.) Halfway House
WENDY: I'm going there tonight
STEPHEN: Becky told me she failed on her 3-point turn (.) she's failed I know she has
WENDY: Rory's going up the Halfway House (.) you should come
STEPHEN: what's Rory (.) is he still working at Dixon's
WENDY: yeh

Text C ●●●

<u>This was recorded at a student union sub-committee meeting. Kate is chairing the meeting</u>:

KATE: o.k. (.) now the next item on the agenda is the study areas (.) Carla I think you (.) yeh Carla's going to talk on this
CARLA: right well what everyone seems to think is there's not enough (.) the college should have should have more
SARAH: where they going to put them
CARLA: there must be somewhere (.) there always seems to be empty classrooms <u>when you</u>
SARAH: <u>that's only</u> at lunchtimes (.) didn't the Principal say there was no free classrooms so they couldn't (.)
KATE: do you really think we need more anyway (.) do you know anyone who studies in them (.) <u>they just</u>
CARLA: <u>that's the point</u> (.) people use 'em for social areas (.) having drinks (.) they need proper study places
KATE: what's to stop them taking drinks in there as well
CARLA: we need social areas AND study areas
KATE: you can study in the library (.) that's where <u>all the</u>
CARLA: <u>oh yeh</u> with all that noise going on (.) it's since they knocked that wall down
KATE: yeh but that's made the study area bigger (.) you can't complain there's not enough study rooms and they've just made one just for studying
CARLA: I still think we need more smaller rooms spread round round the college (.) the library's too big (.) too noisy (.) who works in there you can't (.)

Non-verbal communication 1

Non-verbal communication (NVC) is a broad term that refers to all the ways in which one individual might communicate with another, excluding the actual words that the individual uses. It includes not only **body language** (gestures, facial expressions and so on) but also **appearance** and **non-verbal aspects of speech**, such as pitch and intonation.

Functions of NVC

Social psychologists have identified five main functions of NVC:

→ **Accompanying speech** We use NVC to support and reinforce what we are saying – e.g. using gestures as we speak.
→ **Replacing speech** Sometimes NVC takes the place of speech – e.g. waving, giving a thumbs-up sign.
→ **Betraying attitudes and feelings** In some situations, our NVC may contradict what we are saying. For example, a person unexpectedly meeting an acquaintance she has been trying to avoid might feel obliged to say she is pleased to see her, but her facial expression might hint at the truth. In these situations, NVC suggests to others what we are really thinking and feeling. When NVC reveals how we feel without our wishing or intending it to, this is known as *leakage*.
→ **Self-presentation** NVC contributes to the way that we choose to present ourselves to others (e.g. wearing a suit to an interview).
→ **Social rituals** NVC often plays a part in these – e.g. when people meet they will often shake hands.

Types of NVC

NVC can be said to consist of three main aspects:

→ **Body language** The communication of meaning through body movements.
→ **Appearance** Dress, hairstyles, body adornment, etc.
→ **Non-verbal aspects of speech** The way in which speech is delivered and the information that is conveyed by this: pitch, intonation, volume, etc.

Body language

Body language has itself been further broken down into eight categories or aspects (Argyle 1988).

→ **Proximity** This refers to the physical distance between people. Hall identified four spatial zones, invisible space bubbles that we try to maintain around us. The smallest is the *intimate zone*, which extends to about 50 cm. Normally, we would expect only someone who was very close to us (e.g. a lover or family member) to come this near. Next is the *personal zone* (0.5–1.5 m), the distance favoured by most Western people when chatting at a party or other social event. The *social zone* (1.5–4 m) is often used for business transactions – e.g. dealing with shop assistants and trades people.

Take note

Experiments suggest that when verbal and non-verbal communication conflict, we tend to believe the NVC.

"People speak with the vocal organs but communicate with the whole body"

G. Abercrombie

Don't forget

Cultural differences are important in NVC. People in some cultures might feel more relaxed about people entering their intimate zone.

Finally, the *public zone* (4 m +) is used when delivering a speech to a sizeable audience.

→ **Orientation**   This refers to the way that we position ourselves in relation to others. If our body is pointing away from someone, this may emphasize our desire for separateness, while bodies pointing towards each other can signal interest and friendliness. Sitting on opposite sides of a desk, facing each other, can be associated with competition and confrontation, while sitting alongside each other (or at right angles) tends to signal harmony and cooperation.

→ **Facial expression**   The face is the most expressive part of the body, and a huge number of different meanings can be conveyed by facial expressions. Some facial expressions are innate (natural) and are the same in every culture. These include expressions registering happiness, anger and fear. Others have to be learned and can differ from one culture to another (e.g. in China sticking out one's tongue can be a sign of surprise). Facial expressions are an important source of *feedback* in conversational interaction.

→ **Eye contact**   is important at the beginning and end of a conversation, and during an interaction shows attention and interest. Frequent eye contact is often an indication of confidence and friendliness, while infrequent eye contact can mean lack of confidence and low self-esteem.

→ **Gestures**   often provide an important accompaniment to speech and can be used for emphasis or clarification (e.g. pointing in a particular direction). Particular gestures convey specific meanings (e.g. rhythmic jabbing of the forefinger during an argument is a sign of aggression).

→ **Posture**   can reflect our emotional state (e.g. sitting on the edge of our seat can show anxiety and tension) or our feelings towards others (e.g. leaning towards another person usually signals interest). *Postural echo* occurs when our posture mirrors that of another person and is usually a sign of empathy and equality.

→ **Head movements**   The slightest inclination of the head can mean a great deal. Nodding of the head shows agreement and understanding and is an important element in conversational feedback. Shaking the head can register disagreement or disbelief, while tossing the head back often accompanies laughter.

→ **Touch**   This is important in social situations, and handshakes, kisses, etc. are used in greetings, farewells, offering congratulations and so on. Who we touch, when and in what way can depend on *gender* (e.g. women kiss more, men shake hands more); *relationship* (e.g. we are more likely to kiss close friends or relatives than strangers); *culture* (e.g. British people are quite reserved about touching).

Watch out!

Context is always important in the interpretation of NVC. The same NVC signals may have different meanings in different contexts.

Checkpoint

Do you know which other facial expressions are thought to be innate?

Watch out!

Be careful not to over-generalize. Body movements do not always mean the same thing – e.g. sitting on the edge of one's seat might signal interest rather than anxiety.

Exam question   answer: page 64

Discuss the contribution of body language to conversational interaction.
Support your answer with examples. (45 min)

Non-verbal communication 2

In this concluding section on non-verbal communication, we focus on appearance and the non-verbal aspects of speech (sometimes known as **prosody**).

> *"It is impossible to wear clothes without sending out social signals"*
>
> M. Argyle

Appearance

Aspects of appearance include clothing, body adornment (such as jewellery), hairstyles and physique (especially relevant when people seek to achieve a particular physique – e.g. body builders). Appearance can combine with spoken language and with other aspects of NVC to convey a variety of messages.

In particular, a person's appearance may reflect occupation (e.g. uniforms, business suits); membership of social groups (e.g. punks and other youth groups are partly identified by their dress); status (e.g. a judge's gown and wig); self-image (e.g. high or low self-esteem); the image that we choose to present to others; and setting or context (e.g. dressing casually for a party).

Checkpoint 1

Try to think of more examples to illustrate these points about the significance of appearance.

Non-verbal aspects of speech

When we say something, a great deal of meaning is conveyed by the *way* that we say it. Non-verbal aspects of speech such as intonation, pitch and volume are sometimes known as **prosodic features**. The expressive power of prosodic effects was demonstrated in an experiment conducted by J. R. and L. J. Davitz (1959). Eight people were asked to recite part of the alphabet ten times, on each occasion attempting to convey a different emotion. They were heard by a group of students, who had to decide which emotion was being expressed on each occasion. The ten emotions were anger, fear, happiness, jealousy, love, nervousness, pride, sadness, satisfaction and sympathy. The experiment showed that for each emotion the rate of correct identification was far higher than could have been achieved by random guessing.

Action point

You might like to duplicate this experiment in class or with a group of friends!

Prosodic features

The main prosodic features are discussed below:

→ **Intonation**   This can significantly alter meaning. 'Well done!' can be made to sound like sarcasm or genuine praise. Variation of tone enlivens our speech, making different shades of meaning or emotion more distinct and helping to retain a listener's attention. Contrastingly, a flat monotone will not engage the listener and will lessen the listener's ability to comprehend fully what is being said.

→ **Pitch** is most noticeable when it is unusually high or low. Researchers who have studied the voices produced by people in different emotional states have found that someone who is depressed usually speaks slowly and with a low and falling pitch. A raised pitch can indicate excitement, enthusiasm or anxiety.

→ **Pace**   Slow, measured speech can convey calmness and reassurance, while interest or enthusiasm are often reflected in more rapid delivery. Fast, muddled speech may be the result of anxiety or panic.

Checkpoint 2

Can you think of other meanings that fast or slow speech might have?

- **Pauses** in a conversation may reflect awkwardness between the participants and can have a menacing effect, but often they are relaxed and free of tension. Hesitation in speech may be an indication of uncertainty, stress or fatigue.
- **Volume** Loudness can reflect attitudes and emotional states. For example, if 'Close the window, please' is said quietly it is likely to be a polite request; shouted loudly it will sound more like an angry demand. Volume level may be linked to status: superiors are more likely to raise their voices to subordinates than the other way round.
- **Stress** Individual words have patterns of stressed and unstressed syllables, and the grammatical structure of an utterance influences the amount of emphasis placed on the different words that make up the utterance. Changes of emphasis draw our attention to particular words and may change the meaning of an utterance.

Prosodic features and personality

As we have seen, prosodic effects can influence the messages conveyed by particular utterances in particular contexts. They can also give a more general impression of personality. Sometimes these impressions are deceptive and misleading, but there does seem to be some relationship between voice quality and personality. Extroverts, for example, tend to speak more loudly and more rapidly than others, and also at a higher pitch and with fewer pauses. Others see this speech style as assertive and often associate it with competence. So-called Type A personalities, who are driven, ambitious and susceptible to early heart attacks, often have a loud, fast, 'explosive' style of speech (Argyle 1993).

Accent

Accent – the pronunciation of words – is an important expression of identity and influences the impressions that others form of a speaker. Researchers have investigated the associations, positive and negative, that particular accents have. The RP accent, for instance, is socially prestigious and is associated with authority and competence, but it is regarded by many as sounding less warm and friendly than most rural accents. People are conscious of their own accents and may seek to modify them in particular contexts (e.g. accents often move closer to RP in more formal situations). Individuals may seek (not always consciously) to modify their accents more permanently, perhaps in order to gain acceptance in a new community or as a means of acquiring social status.

Checkpoint 3

Will someone who has status and authority always speak loudly?

Example

Note how placing the emphasis on a different word each time significantly alters the meaning that is conveyed:
HE gave the money to me.
He GAVE the money to me.
He gave the money to ME.

Links

Accents are discussed more fully on pages 86–9. The discussion of accommodation theory on page 50 is also relevant here.

Examiner's secrets

The aspects of NVC discussed in the previous section (pages 58–9) could also be included in an answer to this question.

Exam question   answer: page 64

'It's not what you say, it's the way that you say it'. Discuss. (45 min)

Answers
Language in use: spoken language

Spoken language: types, functions and influences

Checkpoints

1 Additional examples of monologue include presentations and news reports. Other examples of dialogue include press conferences and radio transmission (e.g. between airline pilots and air traffic controllers).

2 Phatic exchanges between strangers serve as 'ice breakers' and are often a prelude to more serious, purposeful conversation. They establish a social rapport between speakers, an atmosphere of friendly cooperation.

Exam questions

1 Many different answers are possible.
Referential: You will need to answer two questions in the exam.
Expressive: I'm very disappointed you said that.
Transactional: I'd like five kilos of potatoes please.
Interactional: Do you fancy going for a drink tonight?
Phatic: Nice to meet you.

2 Again, many answers are possible.
Audience A teacher explaining something to a class would need to consider such factors as the age range of pupils, their previous knowledge of the subject, etc.
Setting People in a crowded lift often speak less, because being in such close proximity to strangers has an inhibiting effect.
Topic A conversation between two people exchanging opinions of a particular country as a holiday destination contains a large number of place names.
Purpose A conversation between two people negotiating a business deal would have a transactional function. The language used is likely to involve expressions of agreement or disagreement, explanations of points of view, references to relevant facts and figures, etc.

Features of spontaneous speech

Checkpoints

1 Any written texts that aim for an informal, conversational tone might have some of these features. Examples include personal letters, email messages, tabloid newspaper articles, etc.

2 The sentence 'I'll meet you back here in five minutes' contains four examples of deixis: *I'll, you, here, in five minutes.*

Exam question

Here are some relevant features.
LEXIS Colloquial language: 'first off', 'telly', 'next thing', 'cos', 'hanging about'
Contractions: 'didn't', 'he'd', 'it's'

GRAMMAR Disjointed constructions: 'we were just walking across it's only across the road' 'on the screen was this shot just an empty stage'
Non-standard grammar: 'really quick' (instead of 'really quickly')
NON-FLUENCY FEATURES Fillers: 'you know', 'anyway'
Unvoiced pauses: There are a large number of these.
Repetitions: 'waste of time (.) complete waste of time'
False starts: 'server down server busy' 'quarter past twenty past eight'

Structure of conversations 1

Checkpoints

1 Such expressions can be described as phatic – the linguistic term for 'small talk'. See page 42.

2 Body movements that might follow the end of an utterance include shrugging the shoulders and lowering the head. In more formal situations (e.g. a school lesson), a listener may indicate a desire to speak by raising a hand.

Exam question

Most conversations are certainly cooperative in the sense that the participants adhere to a set of unwritten rules and conventions. Conversation will be more competitive if each participant is seeking to dominate the other.

Structure of conversations 2

Checkpoints

1 Other examples of adjacency pairs include: introduction + introduction (Hello. I'm John O'Brien from the planning department – Hello. I'm the site manager); farewell + farewell (See you – 'Bye).

2 People do not enjoy being corrected by others, especially if it happens repeatedly. It damages our confidence and may make us feel that the other person is arrogant, pedantic and insensitive.

3 At a committee meeting, the chairperson may ask if there is any other business before formally concluding the meeting. Business transactions conducted by telephone (e.g. booking train tickets) often end with the salesperson going over the main details of the transaction again and requesting confirmation.

Exam question

Material in the previous section (pages 46–7) is also relevant to this essay. As with all answers, you should aim to have a clear structure. One approach would be to discuss in sequence (after an introductory paragraph) the main stages in a conversation: openings; development of the conversation (this would be the longest part of the answer and would cover such aspects as turn taking, changes of topic and feedback); and ways of closing a conversation.

Conversation theory 1

Checkpoints

1 Received pronunciation is more commonly heard on Radio 3 and Radio 4 than on other BBC stations, reflecting the fact that much of their audience is drawn from the middle and upper classes. RP accents are much less likely to be heard on popular music stations (e.g. Radio 1), where the speech of the presenters may incorporate current teenage slang. Local radio stations often feature presenters with appropriate regional accents.

2 Here are some specimen utterances, with the maxims they show awareness of in parentheses:

'I don't want to bore you with all the details'. (maxim of quantity)

'Can I go back to something you said earlier?' (maxim of relevance)

'I'd better start from the beginning'. (maxim of manner)

'I'm not sure, but I think there's supposed to be a bus every 20 minutes'. (maxim of quality)

Exam question

As indicated, the material on pages 52–3 is also relevant to this question. There are various aspects of conversation theory that might be discussed.

Accommodation theory and audience design theory are relevant in that they suggest that speakers adjust their speech according to their audience. In particular, convergence can be seen as an attempt by speakers to move closer (socially) to their listeners.

Grice's cooperative principle is based on the idea that conversations are successful if the participants work together to achieve their goals and purposes. In this sense, observing Grice's maxims means that we are taking account of the needs of other participants in the conversation.

Goffman's work on face shows how we respect the face needs of others, accepting the image of themselves that they present to us. The various ways of showing politeness also demonstrate sensitivity to others' needs.

Conversation theory 2

Checkpoints

1 This is a matter of opinion, but most people would accept that respect for other people's privacy is a characteristic of British culture (excluding perhaps the British media). British reserve is also evident in non-verbal behaviour, with less physical contact in everyday social encounters than is found in some other parts of the world (e.g. Latin America, the Middle East).

2 Here are some more specimen utterances to illustrate the maxims:

Don't impose 'Could you possibly spare the time to . . .' 'I know you're very busy but . . .'

Give options 'You don't have to' 'Just say no if you'd rather not'

Make your receiver feel good 'It was really good to see you' 'You've hit the nail on the head'

Exam question

Key points of the question here are *appropriate theory* and *relevant examples*. A very generalized discussion of what 'politeness' means would gain low marks. You need to show specific knowledge of the work of theorists such as Goffman, Brown and Levinson, and Lakoff. As with most answers, specific examples of language use are also required.

Gender and conversational behaviour

Checkpoints

1 Some theorists would argue that asking questions reflects lack of confidence. This approach argues that women are less assertive than men and are more likely to seek agreement and reassurance from others. Robin Lakoff is associated with this view of women's conversational behaviour (see page 53).

2 Some readers may feel that differences have become less marked in recent years, especially with regard to topics of conversation. Men have been encouraged to feel less embarrassed about revealing and discussing their feelings (though simultaneously the growth in magazines, television programmes, etc. aimed specifically at young men has reinforced stereotyped notions of traditional male interests). At the same time, interest in some male topics (e.g. football) seems to have increased among women.

Exam question

This is a good example of an essay question containing a ready-made plan. An answer would have two main parts: the evidence that suggests that men and women do behave differently in conversation, and the explanations that have been offered for these differences.

Specimen texts

Exam questions

The advice on answers given here will look at Text A in some detail, then identify a few key features of Texts B and C.

TEXT A

Structure – This is a transactional exchange and as such remains focused on a single topic, the student's essay. The topic is introduced by the teacher's opening words ('so this essay' – an utterance of this kind is known as a *topic marker*). The conversation that follows has a logical structure, determined by the teacher:

- comparison with the student's previous essay
- strengths of the essay
- weaknesses of the essay
- advice on ways of ending essays

Language There are many features that are typical of spoken language:

Informal vocabulary – e.g. 'yeh'; 'a bit more'; 'a bit abrupt'; 'might've'; 'upfront'; 'that bit'; 'the only weak bit'

Deictic expressions – e.g. 'this essay', 'this here', 'this last sentence'

Disjointed constructions – e.g. 'what you say here about prejudice and stereotyping (.) you explain it really well'

Non-standard grammar – e.g. 'there's good good examples'

Non-fluency features – e.g. unvoiced pauses; fillers ('you know'); repetitions ('good good examples'); false starts ('I think it was (.) it gave you the chance to write about the local accent')

Interaction – the teacher dominates and controls the conversation. This is evident in various ways:

- he says more than the student
- he controls what is talked about, moving the conversation along as various aspects of the student's essay are discussed
- he twice interrupts the student
- he uses an imperative ('read it now')

The teacher does try to involve the student by asking questions (though he tends to interrupt the answers) and by frequent use of the second person pronoun 'you', often in an encouraging way ('you explain it really well'; 'you had some good'). The student does express his views, though he sometimes sounds tentative ('I thought that bit might've sounded a bit biased'). Both teacher and student offer each other positive feedback ('yeh the analysis one').

TEXT B

This text is interesting as an example of a mixed-sex interaction. The female (Wendy) initiates the topic and clearly wishes to describe her experiences of the previous night. The male (Stephen) is more interested in Becky's car and whether or not she has passed her driving test. He ignores much of what Wendy says, most notably when she asks him 'where'd you go?'

When Wendy apparently succeeds in moving the conversation along by getting Stephen to tell her where he went the previous night, there is a topic loop as Stephen again returns to Becky and her driving test ('Becky told me she failed on her 3-point turn').

TEXT C

Like Text A, this is a transactional exchange. Kate leads the discussion and begins with a topic marker ('the next item on the agenda . . .') before inviting Carla to speak. Several of Kate's subsequent contributions are questions, seeking clarification of Carla's views. Sarah, who clearly disagrees with Carla, also asks questions, using these as a way of

framing her objections. Clara's expression of her views is very emphatic: 'everyone seems to think', 'there must be somewhere', 'there always seems to be'. Although the conversation begins quite formally, the exchange that follows has many of the features of informal conversation, with several interruptions and examples of overlapping speech. As the participants have contrasting views, the conversation tends to be competitive rather than cooperative, and there is little evidence of supportive feedback.

Non-verbal communication 1

Checkpoint

Examples include standing up as a mark of politeness when someone enters the room; clapping at the end of a speech; maintaining a minute's silence at times of remembrance. Other innate facial expressions might include those for sadness, disgust and surprise.

Exam question

The pitfall to avoid here is to write down everything you know about body language. Make sure you focus throughout on the part that body language plays in *conversational interaction*.

Non-verbal communication 2

Checkpoints

1 Additional examples include football supporters wearing their team's strip (membership of social group); different uniforms worn by people of different status in an organization – e.g. the different uniforms seen in a hospital (occupation and status); bold, unconventional clothing reflecting self-confidence (self-image).

2 Slow speech might accompany careful explanation of something important or difficult. Fast speech can sometimes reflect annoyance or anger.

3 Not necessarily. They may speak relatively quietly because they know that others will listen to them – they feel no need to raise their voices.

Exam question

This is a broad question, which offers the opportunity to discuss many different aspects of NVC.

Language in use: written language

The analysis of written texts is a feature of all AS syllabuses and is usually required at A level as well. Two other sections of this book are of particular relevance to these kinds of questions. The first section ('Language basics') explains much of the terminology you will be expected to use in your answers, and the resource section at the end of the book has four pages of advice on answering analysis questions (pages 178–81). In this section the particular features of certain types of text are identified. It focuses on the types of text that are often set in examinations: newspapers, advertisements, literary works, and instruction and information texts. In addition, there are several specimen texts for you to analyse. You should remember that written texts come in many forms, and other types of text can always be set. However, as is explained in the resource section, there are fundamental principles of analysis that can be applied to the study of all texts. Your aim should be to apply these principles to whatever texts are presented to you in a rigorous, detailed way.

Exam themes

→ Newspapers.

→ Advertisements.

→ Instruction texts.

→ Information texts.

→ Literary texts.

Topic checklist

O AS ● A2	AQA/A	AQA/B	EDEXCEL	OCR	WJE
Newspapers 1	O●	O	O●	O●	O●
Newspapers 2	O●	O	O●	O●	O●
Newspapers 3	O●	O	O●	O●	O●
Advertisements 1	O●	O	O●	O●	O●
Advertisements 2	O●	O	O●	O●	O●
Instruction and information texts	O●	O	O●	O●	O●
Literary texts	O●	O	O●	O●	O●
New technology	O●	O	O●	O●	O●

Newspapers 1

This section outlines the differences between **broadsheet** and **tabloid** newspapers and identifies some graphological features commonly employed in the presentation of news stories. Newspaper headlines are also considered.

Types of newspaper

Newspapers are categorized as broadsheet or tabloid. These terms refer to page size, which is the most obvious difference between the two types of newspaper: broadsheets have larger pages.

Other differences include the following:

→ The tabloids have larger circulations and so are often known as 'popular' newspapers or, collectively, 'the popular press'.

→ The tabloids (excluding the *Daily Mail*, *Daily Express* and their Sunday equivalents) tend to have a mainly working-class readership. Readers of the broadsheets are more likely to be middle- or upper-class. The *Daily Mail*, *Daily Express*, *Mail on Sunday* and *Sunday Express* also have a large proportion of middle-class readers and are sometimes referred to as 'upmarket tabloids' or 'middle-market newspapers'.

→ The content of tabloids tends to be more lightweight: there is more coverage of sport, television and other forms of entertainment, and more stories about celebrities. In the broadsheets, more space is devoted to serious news stories and coverage of the arts and 'highbrow' culture. The middle-market newspapers tend to fall between these two extremes. Because of their content, broadsheets are sometimes called 'quality' newspapers.

→ Presentation also differs. In the tabloids, articles are generally shorter and easier to read, and there is greater use of photographs. Broadsheets make more demands upon the reader and tend to assume a more educated readership. Again, the upmarket tabloids occupy the middle ground in these respects.

Graphology

Some common **graphological features** of newspapers are as follows

→ **Banner headline**   At top of the page, extends across the whole width.

→ **Strapline** (or **overline**)   Additional headline above the main headline.

→ **Sub-headline** (or **sub-deck**)   Subsidiary headline below the main one.

→ **Crosshead**   Sub-heading that appears in the middle of a story, breaking up the text.

→ **Byline**   Text that credits the writer; occasionally accompanied by a photograph.

→ **Standfirst**   Introductory material separated from the main article.

→ **Reverse out**   When white print is used against a black background.

→ **Drop letter**   Letter that is dropped down so that it extends over two, three, or more lines, usually the first letter of an article.

→ **Caption**   Wording beneath a photograph or illustration.

Checkpoint 1

Name some newspapers that are (a) broadsheets and (b) tabloids.

Watch out!

Don't expect a tabloid or broadsheet article to be typical in every respect.

Links

See pages 68–9 for a fuller account of these differences.

The jargon

Graphology refers to the visual aspects of a text.

Action point

Look in a newspaper for examples of these devices.

Examiner's secrets

Other devices include varied type sizes and fonts (including bold print and italics), upper and lower case letters, underlining, photographs and illustrations.

Headlines ●●●

Headlines can serve a number of purposes and also have several distinct linguistic features.

Purposes

→ *Conveying information*   Often a headline simply summarizes the facts of the story (e.g. INFLATION FALLS AGAIN).

→ *Creating drama, excitement and sensation*   Tabloid headlines in particular often seek to arouse the interest of readers in this way. *Hyperbole* (exaggeration) may be present. Sometimes headlines aim to shock or surprise.

→ *Persuasion*   Headlines may be intended to influence the reader's point of view.

→ *Humour*   Some headlines aim to amuse. A story about a train delay due to a flea bothering a passenger was headlined FLEABLE EXCUSE.

Linguistic features

→ *Compression*   Most headlines have a 'telegraphic style' in that complete sentences are generally avoided. Instead, words and grammatical elements (such as verbs and determiners) are omitted and word order changed to make the headline as brief as possible. Short words are favoured over longer ones and abbreviations (e.g. EURO for EUROPEAN) are used.

→ *Informal language*   Tabloid headlines in particular often use informal language (e.g. ADAMS OKAYS PEACE DEAL instead of ADAMS AGREES TO PEACE DEAL).

→ *Journalese*   Certain words are especially associated with newspapers and constitute a kind of newspaper language. They are found not only in headlines but often in the rest of the story as well. Again, tabloids tend to use these words more often than broadsheets.

→ *Familiar phrases*   Headlines sometimes make use of familiar phrases and sayings, often giving them a new twist. The headline for a story describing how medical research had indicated that moderate amounts of alcohol were good for a person's health changed the expression 'hale and hearty' to ALE AND HEARTY.

→ *Playing on words*   Often headlines play with words, using *puns* and exploiting such things as ambiguity and similar-sounding words. A story about big business organizations attempting to take over leading Premier League football clubs was headlined BATTLE TO BUY CRÈME DE LA PREM (a play upon *crème de la crème*, meaning 'the cream of the cream' or 'the very best').

→ *Phonology*   Headlines may seek to have an effect by using the sounds that words make, e.g. *onomatopoeia, alliteration, rhyme*.

→ *Present tense*   Even though they usually refer to past events, headlines often use the present tense to create a sense of immediacy.

Exam question   answer: page 82

Comment as fully as you can on the headlines shown on page 70 (Text A). (45 min)

> *"The headline is the axis around which everything in a newspaper revolves"*
>
> Tony Loynes, Editor, *UK Press Gazette*

Checkpoint 2

Compare the headlines BLAIR'S EURO TRIUMPH and BLAIR NEGOTIATES NEW EU DEAL.

The jargon

Ellipsis is where part of the usual grammatical structure of a sentence is omitted.

Example

These words are all journalese: SLAM, BLAST, STORM, ROW, FURY, SHOCK, SLUMP, SPIRAL, SOAR, PROBE.

Action point

Try to find more examples of these features by looking at the headlines in a newspaper.

Links

You can find more about these devices using sounds on pages 20–1.

Newspapers 2

In this section, we focus on newspaper style and look more closely at the differences between tabloid and broadsheet newspapers, considering the following elements: graphology; headlines; vocabulary; grammar; and tone and bias. The style of middle-market newspapers such as the *Daily Mail* and the *Daily Express* tends to fall midway between the two sets of contrasting characteristics.

> *"Tabloid prose at its best – excitable, exuberant, always vigorous, sometimes vitriolic – is a lively and valuable asset to the language"*
>
> Keith Waterhouse

Graphology

tabloids	broadsheets
→ extensive use of graphological features to make text eye-catching and accessible → headlines often big and bold → dense text avoided – stories usually short and paragraphs very brief. Text broken up by crossheads → typographical variation – different type sizes and styles, bold print, italics, etc. → photographs often large and prominent	→ use of graphology more restrained → headlines usually occupy less space but often contain more words → more dense text – stories and paragraphs both longer. Limited use of crossheads → less typographical variation → photographs less prominent. Illustrations (e.g. maps, tables) may be used to present quite complex information

The jargon

Polysyllabic words contain more than one syllable (usually three or more).

Headlines

tabloids	broadsheets
→ often dramatic, emotive, sensational → use of journalese (*horror, hell, row,* etc.) → simple vocabulary → language often informal – use of slang, everyday expressions, abbreviations → often humorous and inventive. Frequent use of puns and alliteration → bias may be obvious	→ more factual, informative → less reliance on journalese → more use of complex, polysyllabic vocabulary → language more formal. Less use of compression/ellipsis → humour sometimes present but often ironic, sophisticated → bias may be present but is likely to be less obvious

Checkpoint 1

List some additional examples of **modifiers** favoured by tabloid newspapers.

Vocabulary

tabloids	broadsheets
→ simple, direct. Avoidance of complex, polysyllabic words → often dramatic, sensational, forceful (*huge, massive, stamp out, crack down* etc.). Use of hyperbole → use of journalese (e.g. *rap, snub, dash, clash, boost, bid*) → modifiers often have an emotional impact (e.g. *tragic, brave, proud*) → use of collocations (e.g. *bubbly blonde, love rat, Hollywood hunk*) → informal (e.g. *kids, cops, docs*) → bias may be very apparent through the use of words with obviously positive/negative connotations → individuals who feature in stories may be referred to familiarly (e.g. use of first names)	→ more complex, sophisticated. Use of polysyllabic words → more formal, factual and informative → modifiers used to provide information rather than for emotional impact → bias may be evident through choice of lexis but is usually less blatant → individuals who feature in stories may be referred to more formally

Checkpoint 2

List some additional examples of **collocations** commonly used by the tabloid press.

Grammar

tabloids	broadsheets
→ short sentences, often simple or compound	→ longer sentences that make more demands on the reader. More frequent use of complex sentences. More subordinate clauses. Sentence structure more varied
→ compound sentences often broken up to form two simple sentences. Sentences frequently begin with 'And' or 'But'	→ grammar more formally 'correct'
→ constructions may resemble speech – e.g. grammatically incomplete sentences, use of contractions	→ punctuation more formal and more complex
→ subordinate clauses often enclosed within dashes rather than commas or parentheses	→ wider range of cohesive devices employed
→ frequent use of pre-modification, often for emotional effect (see **vocabulary** above)	
→ use of simple connectives (especially *and*, *but*, *now*) to achieve cohesion	

Links

Simple, **compound** and **complex sentences** are explained on pages 12–13. **Cohesion** is explained on pages 22–3.

Tone and bias

tabloids	broadsheets
→ tone often forceful, emphatic	→ tone usually more moderate, restrained
→ lighthearted, playful approach also common	→ approach to news stories less lighthearted; when humour is present usually dry, ironic
→ address to the reader may be informal, familiar, conversational	→ address to reader depends on type of story/article. Occasionally informal but often formal, impersonal
→ bias may be quite blatant and evident in headlines, lexical choice, and the organization and selection of material	→ bias usually less obvious. More attempt to be factual and balanced by presenting information and reporting the views of both sides in an argument
→ views with which the writer agrees are likely to be given more prominence (e.g. described first and at greater length)	→ headlines, lexical choice, etc. may still show bias, but more subtly
→ views with which the writer disagrees may be given less prominence and described in ways that show the writer's disapproval	→ as with tabloids, bias may reflect the political stance of the newspaper
→ bias may reflect the political stance of the newspaper	

Examiner's secrets

When students compare tabloid and broadsheet articles, they sometimes overstate the differences, or refer to differences that do not actually exist. Always study the texts carefully and only make points you are able to support with evidence.

Discourse structure

tabloids	broadsheets
→ opening paragraph usually summarizes key facts	→ opening paragraph also usually a summary, but may give more information
→ short paragraphs – often only one sentence long	→ paragraphs usually longer
→ closing paragraph may contain the 'latest' news	→ articles usually longer, more detailed
	→ closing paragraph may give background information

Examiner's secrets

Your knowledge of the differences between tabloid and broadsheet newspapers should help you with this question, but remember not to assume that tabloid or broadsheet articles are always typical in all respects.

Exam question   answer: pages 82–3

On 24 October 1999, southern England suffered severe storms. Texts B and C on page 71 show how the storms were reported the next day in the *Sun* (Text B) and the *Guardian* (Text C). Compare the two articles, commenting on overall structure, tone, vocabulary, grammar and any other linguistic features you consider relevant. (45 min)

Newspapers 3

Here are some specimen texts, which were referred to in 'Newspapers 1 and 2'.

Text A

1 After a collision a car careered off a road bridge and landed in the back garden of a house. No one was hurt.

CAR, BLIMEY

2 Art students staged a protest by attacking a modern art exhibit which consisted of an unmade bed.

FAN HITS SHEET

3 Archaeologists said they might have discovered the tomb of King Alfred.

KING ALFRED TOMB FOUND

4 A new crackdown on incompetent doctors was announced.

BAD DOCS FACING BLITZ

5 Four British people were sentenced to imprisonment in the Far East.

SLAVE HELL FOUR JAILED

6 Scientists revealed that wearing tinted spectacles may help people with reading difficulties.

TINT HINT ON READING

7 The policies of Foreign Secretary Robin Cook were denounced as hypocritical.

COOK's ETHICAL POLICY EXPOSED AS SHAM

Chaos as storms sweep the South

STORMS lashed the south of England yesterday, flooding villages, felling trees and wrecking an historic pier.

Sussex and Kent were hit by 60mph winds and torrential rain, forcing hundreds of people living near the sea to evacuate their homes.

Sixty feet of the end of Bognor Regis's 19th century pier was washed away.

Several areas of Kent lost power as electricity lines were brought down and roads were blocked by fallen trees. A man was knocked out by a falling branch in Crawley, Sussex. And seafront promises were flooded in Brighton.

A fireman needed hospital treatment after being knocked down by a freak wave at Eastbourne. And police had to abandon a car near Folkestone, Kent, after getting caught in a flood.

Last night homes and caravan sites from Sussex to Cornwall were evacuated as high tide brought new floods.

Source: The Sun 25/10/1999

Examiner's secrets

You may choose to analyse each article in turn, but must remember to *compare* the two texts. You can do this by referring back to Text B as you are analysing Text C, pointing out similarities and differences.

END OF THE PIER SHOW: FLOODS AND GALES LASH THE SOUTH

The end of the pier at Bognor Regis (above) was washed away, homes were flooded, and holidaymakers evacuated as heavy rain and strong winds lashed the south of England yesterday.

Severe gale warnings were in place on the coast after force eight southwesterly winds, an environment agency spokeswoman said. A Sussex police spokesman said about 60ft of the pier had been washed away. Nobody had been injured.

Police evacuated a snooker hall and amusement arcade on the pier. A caravan park at Selsey, also in West Sussex, was also evacuated. The agency spokeswoman said that the floods had been caused by a combination of gale-force winds, low pressure and an equinox tide.

Agency workers were trying to shore up sea defences at Medmerry before the high tide last night. A red flood warning had been issued for Selsey. An amber warning was in place at Medmerry, and an amber warning was also issued from Lymington in the New Forest to Chichester harbour in West Sussex.

The Dorset coastline was placed on the lesser yellow alert and yellow warnings were in place on several rivers. Kent police reported trees down throughout the county blocking roads.

A royal navy fisheries protection vessel, HMS Shetland, went to the aid of a yacht taking on water off Ramsgate in Kent. A lifeboat took off the yacht's eight crew. The floods came nearly a year to the day since the last severe flooding. The agency spokeswoman said that it had warned that climate changes could lead to more flooding in Britain, and had this week launched a £2m warning campaign.

The agency is funding a 24-hour emergency advice line on 0845 988 1188.

Source: The Guardian 25/10/1999

71

Advertisements 1

There are many types of advertisement. As well as commercial advertising aimed at the consumer, there are classified ads, personal ads, government health awareness campaigns and information announcements, advertisements for charities and so on. The link between them is that they usually aim to persuade or to inform (or both).

Useful terms

Target audience   The specific social group that is addressed.
Copy   The written text of an advertisement.
Hook   The initial piece of attention-seeking language used to draw the reader in. Often this takes the form of a question.
Signature line   The bottom-line summary that often appears at the end of an advertisement.

Analysis of advertisements

First you should establish clearly in your mind the following:

→ Who is the advertiser?
→ Who is their target audience?
→ What is their message?

Then you can go on to examine the advertisement in more detail. Listed below are some common features you might look at.

Visual elements/graphology

→ *Layout* – e.g. how much written text is there and how is it presented?
→ *Typographical variations* – e.g. use of different typefaces, bold face, italics, upper and lower case letters, etc.
→ Use of *logos*, *illustrations* and *colour*.

Form and structure

→ Does the advertisement adopt the *form* of a particular style of writing? E.g. junk mail advertising often adopts the form of a personal letter.
→ Has the advertising copywriter created a 'voice' for the advertisement – a *narrator*? For example, we may be asked to believe that an ordinary housewife, a famous celebrity or a cartoon character is speaking to us.
→ Consider the *order* in which items in a text are presented. For example, advertisements often begin with a hook (see above).

Attitudes to reader/audience

→ Often the *tone* is informal, but occasionally it may be deliberately formal. Try to define the tone – is it respectful, familiar, ironic, etc.?
→ Does the advertisement flatter the audience?
→ Use of *direct address* ('you', 'your') – this is usually intended to involve the readers, making them feel they are being personally addressed.

Checkpoint 1

Two possible components that might help to define a target audience are age and gender. Can you think of any others?

Watch out!

Always consider the *effects* of these visual elements.

The jargon

A *logo* is a sign or symbol used to identify and represent a product or company.

Examiner's secrets

Don't discuss the features listed here in isolation. Consider how they work *together* to create the overall impact of the advertisement.

→ Use of *interactive* features – e.g. some advertisements include questionnaires, forms to complete, etc.

Vocabulary

→ *Brand names* (and their associations) are often important.
→ *Slogans* and *catchphrases* (e.g. 'Have a break, have a Kit-Kat').
→ Use of *positive lexis* (e.g. 'special', 'extra'), *comparatives* (e.g. 'brighter', 'cleaner'), *superlatives* (e.g. 'brightest', 'cleanest').
→ Words that suggest the *uniqueness* of the product (e.g. 'only', 'exclusive').
→ *conversational* language, *everyday* expressions, *familiar* sayings.
→ *puns, wordplay.*
→ *technical* or *scientific* language.
→ *non-standard spellings* (e.g. 'Beanz meanz Heinz').

Grammar

→ Use of *short sentences*, sometimes *grammatically incomplete*; e.g. 'The new Hoover 5 000 is expertly designed. And surprisingly inexpensive.' Short sentences make the copy easier to read and may be part of an attempt to imitate spoken language. They also enable the advertiser to give extra emphasis to particular points by putting them in separate sentences.
→ Constructions that make the copy resemble *everyday speech*.
→ Use of first, second or third person – what is the effect? The first person plural ('we') is sometimes used to make a company seem less impersonal ('Telephone the number below and we'll be happy to discuss your mortgage needs with you'). Using the second person (as this example also does) speaks directly to the reader.
→ Use of *imperatives* (commands).
→ *Punctuation* may also be important (e.g. use of exclamation marks).

Phonology

→ Use of sound-related effects such as *rhythm, alliteration, rhyme*, etc.

Content

→ Use of *stereotyping* – e.g. gender stereotypes (beautiful women, strong men); age stereotypes (angelic children); national stereotypes (Australians in Castlemaine XXXX ads, the English in Ikea ads).
→ Use of *humour.*
→ *Intertextuality* This occurs when a text includes a reference to another text. For example, an RSPCA advertisement stating 'A dog is for life, not just for Christmas' included the intertextual reference 'Toys Aren't Us'.

Checkpoint 2

Why might an advertisement use technical or scientific language? Can you think of any advertisements that use this kind of language?

The jargon

When sentences are compressed, and part of the grammatical structure is omitted, this is known as *ellipsis.*

Watch out!

You may also have studied advertisements in GCSE English or in Media Studies. This can be helpful, but remember that in AS or A2 English Language your approach must be different – you need to focus very closely on the *language* that the advertiser uses.

Examiner's secrets

Remember that it is helpful to begin by clearly identifying the advertiser, their target audience and the advertiser's message.

Exam question   answer: page 83

Discuss how the advertisements on pages 74–5 use language to fulfil their purposes. You do not have to compare the advertisements. (60 min)

Advertisements 2

Here are some specimen texts, which were referred to in 'Advertisements 1'.

Text A ●●●

GRADUATE RETAIL CAREERS

HMV

WHERE WILL YOU BE IN A FEW YEARS' TIME?

Contrary to popular belief, there aren't many overnight successes in the music and entertainment business.

Pulp gigged in pubs up and down West Street in Sheffield for years before they hit the headlines. Kate Winslet was plying her trade in Casualty as far back as 1989. And if there's a job Republica's Saffron hasn't done, we'd like to hear about it.

Management at HMV is no different. If you want to be running your own store in two years, you'd better be prepared to work extremely hard.

At some point we'll probably ask you to move to another area of the country to take advantage of an opportunity that doesn't exist locally. The work is tough. The pressure is intense. And the competition is fierce.

But if you're up to it, we don't believe you'll find a more rewarding and exciting challenge in retail.

Of course, you'll go through one of the best management development programmes in retail. But you'll already have many of the qualities we need - like an entrepreneurial streak a mile wide, a flair for business, and the ability to recognise exceptional customer service.

Impress us by sending in one side of A4 that explains why you're right for HMV. Send it, quoting ref: GR/NME, to: Graduate Recruitment, H.R. Department, HMV UK Ltd., Film House, 142 Wardour Street, London W1V 4LN.

*This is a genuine HMV graduate recruit and, er, a genuine lookalike. If you'd like to find out more about what it's like to be an HMV management trainee, write to the address above and we'll send you a brochure.

Just before she started her career, **MADONNA** was sacked from a donut bar in Manhattan for squirting jam at a customer. Just before she started her career, **YEMMI BRYAN** was a law graduate, wondering if she'd be jammy enough to get out of what threatened to be the dullest career imaginable.

Reproduced courtesy of HMV UK Ltd.

Eveleigh Grange, Cheshire
Beautifully appointed homes in an idyllic setting

Regent Homes, *one of the north west's fastest growing property development companies, has just announced a unique opportunity for discerning homebuyers to acquire luxury living accommodation in one of Cheshire's prime locations.*

Our latest development of superb four- and five-bedroomed detached homes at Eveleigh Grange is in the heart of the Cheshire countryside. The delightful village of Eveleigh has quiet, peaceful surroundings and magnificent views across the Cheshire plain.

Yet the city of Chester is just a few miles away, and with quick access to the region's motorway network Liverpool and Manchester are within easy reach.

The excellent location of this prestigious development means it is ideal for busy professionals looking for a rural retreat that offers the very best in country living.

Local amenities are available in the village and the area's primary and secondary schools are among the best in the region.

Eveleigh Grange is a select development of just ten properties, each individually designed to provide purchasers with a home of character and a sound investment for the future. At Regent Homes we have a reputation for building exclusive homes with meticulous attention to design, layout and specification.

All Eveleigh Grange houses include as standard:

▸ Spacious bedrooms and entertaining rooms
▸ Fitted luxury kitchen, complete with hob, oven, microwave, fridge-freezer, dishwasher, cooker hood and washer-dryer
▸ Luxury fully tiled bathrooms and shower rooms
▸ uPVC double-glazed windows
▸ Gas central heating system
▸ Lawned gardens
▸ NHBC 10-year guarantee

For further details please contact our sales office: **01796 823555**

Regent Homes
The lifestyle you deserve

Instruction and information texts

Instruction texts and information texts are closely linked. In some cases, individual texts cannot be rigidly defined as one or the other. Here are some key features of such texts.

Instruction texts

The style and content of an instruction text will be influenced by the intended *audience*. For example, if the audience is assumed to have specialist knowledge of the subject, the language is likely to be more complex than it would be in a text aimed at the general reader.

Listed below are some distinctive features of the language commonly found in instruction texts.

Overall structure

Material is likely to be presented in a logical order, often with a sequence of actions for the reader to perform. Paragraphs will usually be brief and may be numbered. To aid cohesion, there is often a high degree of repetition and anaphoric reference.

Graphology

Diagrams and illustrations may be present to help understanding. Paragraphs are likely to be short and may be spaced out.

Tone

Often formal and impersonal, but second-person pronouns (*you*, *your*) may be used in some texts to create a more friendly tone.

Vocabulary

Often simple – complexity increases as the subject and/or the audience become more specialist.

Vocabulary needs to be precise and unambiguous. Words have literal, denotative meanings rather than connotative meanings.

Where there is a narrow focus on a particular subject, field-specific lexis will often be present.

Abbreviations may be used.

Grammar

Sentences will often be simple and compound rather than complex, usually with a conventional word order. There may be repetitive patterns in the sentence structuring. Imperative verb forms (commands) are common, as are passive verb forms.

Information texts

There is not always a rigid distinction between information texts and instruction texts – e.g. a health information leaflet might contain instructions on how to clean your teeth properly – and many of the features of instruction texts referred to above can also be found in information texts.

Examples

Such texts can include recipes, technical manuals, instructions accompanying self-assembly furniture and so on.

Links

Cohesion and **anaphoric reference**: see pages 22–3.

The jargon

Graphology refers to visual aspects of the text.

Checkpoint 1

Explain the difference between **denotation** and **connotation**.

Checkpoint 2

Explain what is meant by **field-specific lexis**.

Examples

Imperative: '*pull* the lever'
Passive: 'Make sure the chain *has been firmly secured*'.

Consideration of *audience* is again important. Educational texts are often aimed at young children, and this will mean that an attempt is made to simplify vocabulary and grammar. On the other hand, texts aimed at an older, more educated or more specialized audience will use more complex language. In presenting complex information, a high degree of **modification** is likely to be present.

The primary purpose of information texts is to inform, though there may also be an intention to *persuade* (e.g. health information leaflets). As a result, features and techniques associated with advertisements are sometimes found in such texts.

Exam question   answer: pages 83–4

The extract below is from the introductory section of a government information booklet, 'What everyone should know about the Millennium Bug'. The booklet was distributed free to every household in the United Kingdom in 1999. The original text was accompanied by illustrations, but for the purposes of this text you will be focusing on the written language used.

Comment on the use of language in the text, considering such matters as overall structure, tone and address to reader, vocabulary, and grammar. (45 min)

ABOUT THE BUG

Every time you read a paper or watch a video, even when you're choosing what to buy for dinner, somewhere along the line a computer or electronic system will have been involved. Because we rely so heavily on these systems, the government and business have taken the Millennium Bug very seriously.

What is the Millennium Bug?

It's not a virus and you certainly can't catch it. In a nutshell, the Millennium Bug is what happens if a computer or electronic system doesn't recognise the year 2000.

The root of the problem lies in the early days of computing when memory capacity was limited. Programmers saved memory space by representing dates with two digits rather than four (e.g. 99 rather than 1999).

So when the date changes to 2000, unlike you and I, these systems might not recognise the two digit 00 date. They might think it's 1900 or even some other date and potentially create problems in systems that use a year date to function.

Also, since 1900 was not a leap year and 2000 is, some systems might not recognise the 29th February 2000 and may move straight from the 28th February to the 1st March. This could result in problems because computer calendars would then be running a day ahead of real time.

What happens when computers get the date wrong?

Computer systems that are affected may shut down, not start or produce incorrect or erroneous information.

For example, in 1992 Hilda celebrated her 104th birthday, so she was rather puzzled when her local nursery school invited her to enrol for a class. Because the nursery school database logged Hilda's birthday as being in '88, it mistook these two digits for 1988, rather than 1888. Because it stored dates in just two digits, the database thought she was 4 years old.

The jargon

Modifiers are words that describe nouns. Pre-modifers come before a noun, post-modifiers after.

Watch out!

Texts can often have more than one purpose. Always be on the lookout for less obvious, 'hidden' purposes.

Examiner's secrets

Before you begin a detailed analysis, you will find it helpful to consider the *purpose* of the text and its intended audience.

Literary texts

The main difference between literary texts and non-literary texts is that writers of literature are usually involved in creating an imaginary world. Doing this successfully entails a heightened use of language: the best writers of literature stretch the resources of language to their limits, manipulating vocabulary, grammar, phonology and so on in original and unexpected ways.

Examples

Literary texts include novels, stories, plays and poems.

The jargon

The linguistic analysis of literature is known as *stylistics*.

Checkpoint 1

Can you think of a book (or part of a book) you have read recently that tries to do any of these things?

Purposes of literary texts

These can include:

→ to entertain, amuse or excite;
→ to arouse an emotional response (e.g. sympathy, fear, disgust);
→ to influence the way we view some aspect of the world;
→ to explore the personality of an imaginary character;
→ to evoke the atmosphere of a place.

Aspects of literary texts – what to look for

Author's attitude
What is the author's attitude towards the people and places he or she has created, and what attitude does the author intend the reader to have?

Narrative voice
What kind of narrative voice is employed? Often there is a first person narrator, telling us directly of his or her own experiences. How does the writer use language to give the character a distinctive voice?

Narrators (especially in modern texts) often use informal, conversational language, encouraging a more intimate relationship between narrator and reader.

Alternatively, an omniscient third person narrator may be used, who may influence the reader's response by commenting directly on characters and events. Or the writer may guide us more subtly, using hints and suggestions.

The jargon

Omniscient means all-knowing.

Characters
How is language used to create the characters? For example, characters may 'come alive' for us through their speech, their actions or the author's descriptions of their appearance.

Examiner's secrets

Rhetorical techniques might include metaphors, similes, personification, repetition, antithesis, onomatopoeia and alliteration

Rhetorical techniques
These are especially common in literary texts: ask yourself, what techniques are present and what are their effects?

Vocabulary
The connotations of words are especially important in literary texts. How does the writer's choice of words help the writer to develop a consistent viewpoint?

Grammar
Look for ways in which word order and sentence construction are manipulated to achieve particular purposes. In the following example (from

Hard Times by Charles Dickens), the repetitive structures and vocabulary of the sentence, together with its length, convey the grey uniformity of an industrial town and the monotonous lives of its inhabitants.

> It contained several large streets all very like one another, and many small streets still more like one another, inhabited by people equally like one another, who all went in and out at the same hours, with the same sound upon the same pavements, to do the same work, and to whom every day was the same as yesterday and tomorrow, and every year the counterpart of the last and the next.

In contrast, short sentences can seem forceful and direct.

Dialogue

Dialogue is a means of creating character and is especially important in plays. Different characters may be given different ways of speaking, and spoken exchanges help to reveal relationships. Writers often succeed in giving the illusion of natural, everyday speech, but there are usually considerable differences between created dialogue and real conversations. Dialogue in literary texts is more organized, and there is usually an absence of non-fluency features and fewer interruptions and repetitions.

Checkpoint 2

Try to analyse this sentence in more detail: in what ways is its structure repetitive?

Exam question   answer: page 84

The extract below is the opening of a novel, *The Catcher in the Rye*, by J. D. Salinger, published in 1951. The narrator is Holden Caulfield, an American teenager. How does the writer use language to create the character of the narrator and to address the reader? (45 min)

> If you really want to hear about it, the first thing you'll probably want to know is where I was born, and what my lousy childhood was like, and how my parents were occupied and all before they had me, and all that David Copperfield kind of crap, but I don't feel like going into it. In the first place, that stuff bores me, and in the second place, my parents would have about two haemorrhages apiece if I told anything pretty personal about them. They're quite touchy about anything like that, especially my father. They're *nice* and all – I'm not saying that – but they're also touchy as hell. Besides, I'm not going to tell you my whole goddam autobiography or anything. I'll just tell you about this madman stuff that happened to me around last Christmas before I got pretty run-down and had to come out here and take it easy. I mean that's all I told D. B. about, and he's my *brother* and all. He's in Hollywood. That isn't too far from this crumby place, and he comes over and visits me practically every week-end. He's going to drive me home when I go home next month maybe. He just got a Jaguar. One of those little English jobs that can do around two hundred miles an hour. It cost him damn near four thousand bucks. He's got a lot of dough now. He didn't *use* to. He used to be just a regular writer, when he was home. He wrote this terrific book of short stories, *The Secret Goldfish*, in case you never heard of him. The best one in it was 'The Secret Goldfish'. It was about this little kid that wouldn't let anybody look at his goldfish because he'd bought it with his own money. It killed me. Now he's out in Hollywood, D. B., being a prostitute. If there's one thing I hate, it's the movies. Don't even mention them to me.

Examiner's secrets

An additional point to bear in mind here is that this passage uses an international variety of English – 'American English'.

New technology

New technology has revolutionized the ways in which we communicate with each other. Its impact on the language that we use has already been far-reaching and may become still greater in the future. Here we briefly consider some of the ways in which language has been affected by new technology and identify some of the distinctive linguistic features of electronic texts.

Email

Email has been described as occupying a space somewhere between the telephone and the letter, combining elements of written communication and spoken conversation. It is used for one-to-one communication but can also function as a broadcast medium, enabling companies and other organizations to send the same message to thousands of people at very little cost. It is both personal and impersonal. Internet users are often portrayed as sitting in front of their computer screens in lonely isolation for hour after hour but, paradoxically, their very anonymity encourages many users to be frank, open and intimate when exchanging online messages.

Email style

Much of the terminology associated with email derives from letter writing: *email*, *mailbox*, *email address*. However, the style of email messages is notably more *informal* than that of letters. Formal greetings and farewells are often dispensed with, the writer letting the on-screen display of information regarding sender, date, time and subject serve as an introduction. Grammatical constructions and lexical choice are often casual and spontaneous, and punctuation is similarly relaxed (dashes instead of commas). Spelling mistakes are frequently left uncorrected.

The informality of email messages means that there are strong resemblances to everyday conversation, but there are also differences. The formal conventions of letter writing may be overlooked, but often the phatic communication associated with speech is also omitted in the interests of speed and directness. Although much of the vocabulary used is drawn from everyday speech, emails have also generated their own specialized lexicon (see below).

The spontaneity of email messages is seen by many as a positive characteristic. The language that results is vigorous, alive and immediate. Some also believe that emails have revived the art of letter writing, which had steadily declined during the 20th century because of the use of the telephone. Others, however, see the casual approach to language use as yet another sign of falling standards and argue that the disappearance of the different levels of formality associated with letter writing makes the email a blunter and less sophisticated tool.

Checkpoint 1

What is mean by *phatic communication*?

"E-mail colours digital diction. It seems to elicit succinct sentences packed with colloquialisms and punchy Anglo-Saxon words"

Constance Hale, *Wired* Magazine

Email vocabulary

Computer technology has created a huge number of new words: *motherboard*, *modem*, *online*, *offline*, *homepage*, *download* and so on. Most of these terms originate in the United States, and this has had an influence on our spelling. When the context is computers, *programme* is spelled *program* and *disc* is spelled *disk*.

There is also an enormous amount of computer slang. Examples include *newbie* (a new user of the internet), *facetime* (offline, face-to-face communication) and *techie*, *gearhead* and *propellerhead* (all alternatives for 'nerd').

Abbreviations are another common feature of computer language. Some are quite technical and formal – as in DOS (disk operating system) and DAT (digital audiotape) – but many are informal and are used in emails and internet chatrooms. Some of these are listed below.

The list also contains a selection of 'emoticons'. These are graphical symbols (also known as 'smileys') used to represent facial expressions and body language.

Emoticons		Abbreviations	
:-)	smile	BRB	be right back
:-(	anger, displeasure	FWIW	for what it's worth
>:P	sticking out tougue	BTW	by the way
{ }	a hug	WB	welcome back
:-{	sadness	AFK	away from keyboard
<:/&	stomach in knots	IMHO	in my humble opinion
;-)	a wink	IMNSHO	in my not so humble opinion
:-0	shock	TMOT	trust me on this
(:/)	sarcasm	IRL	in real life
:09	hungry	IOW	in other words

Text messages

Some of the abbreviations and emoticons listed above are also used in mobile phone text messages. Here there are several reasons for keeping messages as short and concise as possible. Shorter messages cost less, take less time to compose and reach the person they're intended for more quickly. The small screen size (which usually accommodates about 160 characters) and the small keypad also encourage compression. In addition to abbreviations, linguistic techniques used in text messages include **phonetic spelling** (e.g. *LUV*), **letter homophones** (e.g. *C* for 'see', *U* for 'you') and **number homophones** (e.g. *2* for 'to', *4* for 'for'). Texting is especially popular among young people (a survey by a mobile phone company in 2002 found that 80% of customers over 45 had never sent a text message). As well as being quick and inexpensive, text messages have the advantage of privacy, which is part of their appeal to teenagers: messages cannot be overheard by others.

Links

These words illustrate some of the processes of word formation outlined on pages 152–3.

Checkpoint 2

If you use the internet regularly, you might be able to add to these lists.

Exam question　　　　　　　　　answer: page 84

Consider the strengths and weaknesses of electronic texts compared with traditional forms of written text. (45 min)

Answers
Language in use: written language

Newspapers 1

Checkpoints

1 Broadsheets include *The Times*, *Daily Telegraph*, *Guardian*, *Independent*, *Sunday Times*, *Sunday Telegraph*, *Independent on Sunday* and *Observer*. Tabloids include the *Sun*, *Mirror*, *Daily Star*, *Daily Mail*, *Daily Express*, *News of the World*, *Sunday Mirror*, *Mail on Sunday* and *Sunday Express*.

2 BLAIR'S EURO TRIUMPH encourages readers to admire what Tony Blair has achieved. BLAIR NEGOTIATATES NEW EC DEAL is a more neutral statement of the facts and is therefore less biased.

Exam question

In answering this question, you should comment both on the purpose of the headlines (e.g. to amuse, inform, persuade) and on the linguistic techniques employed.

Headline 1 (CAR, BLIMEY) and 2 (FAN HITS SHEET) are clearly intended to be humorous. All of the other headlines are at least partly intended to inform, most obviously the bald statement of headline 3 (KING ALFRED TOMB FOUND). Headline 7 (COOK'S ETHICAL POLICY EXPOSED AS SHAM) is am example of a political headline that seeks to influence the viewpoint of the reader.

Each of the humorous headlines involves a play on words, and each also uses a familiar phase usually associated with informal speech. CAR, BLIMEY is a play on 'cor blimey', while FAN HITS SHEET is an inventive inversion of a well-known obscenity.

Another example of informal lexis is DOCS (headline 4). This is also journalese, as are BLITZ (from the same headline), HELL, JAILED (both headline 5) and SHAM (headline 7). BLITZ and HELL involve the use of hyperbole. A phonological effect is achieved by the use of rhyme in headline 6 (TINT HINT).

Grammatical compression is evident in many of the headlines, such as the omission of auxiliary verbs and determiners in BAD DOCS (are) FACING (a) BLITZ and COOK'S ETHICAL POLICY (has been) EXPOSED AS (a) SHAM. Compression is achieved in headline 5 by using the nouns SLAVE and HELL as adjectives: SLAVE HELL FOUR JAILED.

Newspapers 2

Checkpoints

1 Additional examples include 'lonely', 'distraught', 'grieving'.

2 Additional examples include 'rising star', 'trouble-torn' and 'passionate fling'.

Exam question

The plan suggested by the question can be followed, looking in turn at overall structure, tone, vocabulary and grammar. A separate paragraph could be devoted to each of these topics, with an additional paragraph if necessary on 'any other linguistic feature you consider relevant'. In each paragraph, the two texts could be compared. An alternative approach would be to discuss each text separately. This approach can be effective, but you need to be careful not to spend too long on the first text you write about, and you also need to make sure you really do *compare* the texts and not simply discuss them as separate entities. Listed below are some features of the articles that might be noted:

Overall structure – the *Sun* article begins with a paragraph that offers a general summary and overview. The second paragraph has a more specific focus on Sussex and Kent. The third, fourth and fifth paragraphs are more specific still, describing specific incidents that occurred during the storms. The final paragraph moves the story forward in time and reports the latest news, referring to events that occurred last night.

The *Guardian* article also begins with a general overview, referring like the *Sun* to the south of England. However, there is also a focus on the pier at Bognor Regis, providing a link with the headline. The second and third paragraphs contain more information about the pier. The main body of the article is based on information obtained from the Environmental Agency, which is mentioned several times. The *Sun* makes no reference to the agency, and the specific incidents referred to in the two articles are generally different, though the damage to the pier is prominent in both. The *Guardian* article concludes with a more general discussion of climate changes in Britain, again based on statements from the Environment Agency. The final sentence gives the agency's helpline number.

Tone – the *Sun* article has a dramatic tone, emphasizing the ferocity of the storms and the chaos they have caused. The opening sentence has several powerful verbs, which the grammatical structure emphasizes: 'lashed', 'flooding', 'felling', 'wrecking'. The heightened tone continues in the next two paragraphs with 'hit', 'torrential', 'forcing' and 'washed away'. The tone then moderates; verbs continue to be emphasized, but they are a little less forceful: 'brought down', 'blocked', 'abandon', 'getting caught'.

The *Guardian* strikes a more humorous, ironic note in the first half of its headline, playing on the double meaning of 'End of the pier show'. The second half of the headline is closer to the *Sun*, however: 'Floods and gales lash the south'. The opening sentence, like that in the *Sun*, emphasizes the impact of the storms by using a series of verbs, though their cumulative effect is less dramatic (partly because they are passive rather than active): 'washed away', 'flooded', 'evacuated', 'lashed'. In the rest of the article, the general impression is of a more restrained presentation of the facts: 'Nobody had been injured', 'An amber warning was in place at Mermerry', 'A royal navy fisheries protection vessel, HMS Shetland, went to the aid of a yacht'.

Vocabulary – in the *Sun*, journalese is evident in words such as 'Chaos', 'sweep', 'lashed' and 'felling'. The use of forceful verbs (see above) creates a sense of drama and excitement. Vocabulary is occasionally quite informal:

'knocked out', 'knocked down', 'getting caught'. The *Guardian* employs some of the same vocabulary as the *Sun*: 'lashed', 'flooded', 'evacuated'. However, some more complex and more formal vocabulary is also present. This includes vocabulary that is often technical and precise: 'severe gale warnings'; 'force eight south-westerly winds'; 'the lesser yellow alert'; 'a combination of gale-force winds, low pressure and an equinox tide'.

Grammar – both headlines use the present tense ('lash' and 'sweep') – this is common in headlines and creates a sense of immediacy. The *Sun* headline uses grammatical compression, as does the first half of the *Guardian* headline, though the second half is a complete sentence ('Floods and gales lash the south'). In the *Sun* article, two sentences begin with 'And', creating shorter sentences by dividing what could be one longer sentence into two. The effect is also of a cumulative listing of the damage caused by the storm. The *Guardian* does not break up sentences in this way, though, as in the *Sun*, sentences are often short: 'Nobody had been injured'. Passive verbs are generally used in the *Sun* to describe this damage, presenting the people and places described as victims of the severe weather: 'Sussex and Kent were hit', 'A man was knocked out', 'seafront premises were flooded'. The *Guardian* is more varied in its use of passive and active verbs.

Advertisements 1

Checkpoints

1 Other possible components include social class and occupation/income.
2 Technical or scientific language is usually designed to impress the reader. Often the language used is not intended to be understood. The aim is rather to create a vague impression of scientifically proven effectiveness or technological power and sophistication.

Exam question

Some features of the advertisements that might have been commented on are outlined below.

The HMV advertisement is aimed at university graduates. It seeks to persuade them that the company's management training programme offers a career with prospects. It initially engages the reader's attention by means of an unusual and intriguing visual image: a Madonna lookalike is shown squirting jam at another woman. The point of the photograph becomes clear only when the caption beneath is read. Madonna worked in a donut bar before becoming famous; the other woman was a law graduate before joining HMV. The implication is that both women have gone on to greater things. The excitement of a career at HMV is contrasted with the dull stuffiness of a legal career. The captions use humour in the play on 'jam'/'jammy' and in the contradictory reference to the Madonna figure as a 'genuine lookalike'. The advertisement also features a hook, which asks a direct question of the reader: 'Where will you be in a few years' time?' The idea that HMV is offering a job with a future has been clearly established.

The main text of the advertisement begins by making the point that the music and entertainment business doesn't feature many overnight successes. The example of Madonna is added to with details of the early careers of Pulp, Kate Winslet and Saffron of Republica. The advertisement uses film and music stars likely to appeal to its intended audience. It also implies that HMV, as a music retailer, is part of the same entertainment industry, making a career with the company seem exciting and glamorous.

The advertisement addresses the reader directly and in a subtly flattering way. Emphasizing the demands of the job ('you'd better be prepared to work extremely hard'; 'if you're up to it') challenges readers to respond that they do indeed have the qualities needed to cope with those demands. The company uses the first person plural to refer to itself ('we'd like to hear about it'), giving a very large business organization a more personal identity. Informal, conversational language is used ('a mile wide', 'Of course', 'er'), strengthening the impression that HMV is not a dull, conventional company.

The Regent Homes advertisement targets a wealthy, upmarket audience – specifically, the 'busy professionals' referred to in the fourth paragraph. The audience are flatteringly referred to as 'discerning homebuyers', and there is throughout an emphasis on exclusivity, with the use of such adjectives as 'prestigious', 'exclusive' and 'select'. The development has 'just' ten properties, implying that only a fortunate few will be able to live there and encouraging readers to take advantage of this 'unique opportunity' while they can. The kind of positive lexis often found in advertising is very much in evidence, with frequent use of such premodifiers as 'unique', 'luxury', 'delightful', 'magnificent', 'excellent' and 'meticulous'. Superlatives ('the very best in country living', 'among the best in the region') underline the effusive tone. Much of the advertisement seeks to persuade the reader that the development combines the beauty and tranquillity traditionally associated with the countryside with easy access to the amenities and employment of urban centres. The attractiveness of the rural environment is evoked in such phrases as 'idyllic setting', 'quiet, peaceful surroundings' 'magnificent views' and 'rural retreat'.

Instruction and information texts

Checkpoints

1 *Denotation* refers to the straightforward, literal meanings of words. *Connotation* refers to the associations that words have.
2 *Field-specific lexis* is vocabulary associated with a particular topic (or 'field').

Exam question

The question explains that the leaflet from which this extract is taken was distributed to every household in the United Kingdom. Its audience might be described as adult members of the general public. In addition, the point might be made that although the subject matter is related to new technology, the leaflet aims to be understood by people with little knowledge of computer systems. The purpose is to inform readers about the millennium bug and its attendant dangers. An additional purpose is perhaps reassurance, in that the reader is told the government and business 'have taken the Millennium Bug very seriously'.

The extract has a clear structure, which is made explicit by the use of sub-headings. After an introductory paragraph about our dependence on computer systems (establishing why we need to take the bug seriously), the extract goes on to answer the question 'What is the Millennium Bug?' The extract concludes by looking at the possible consequences of the bug, focusing on a particular example (the case of Hilda).

The leaflet addresses the reader in a direct, friendly way ('Every time you read a paper'). The reader is encouraged to think of the writer of the leaflet as someone with whom they can identify ('unlike you and I', 'we rely so heavily on these systems'). The tone and vocabulary are often quite informal, with extensive use of contractions ('you're', 'It's', 'can't') and expressions such as 'In a nutshell' and 'somewhere along the line'. This kind of language is in keeping with the leaflet's attempt to simplify the subject matter for the general reader. There is some field-specific lexis ('memory space', 'programmes', 'database'), but the leaflet generally avoids technical vocabulary. The simplification process is also evident in the personification of computer systems ('They might think it's 1900') and in the use of short paragraphs, linked by clear and simple connectives ('So', 'Also', 'For example').

Literary texts

Checkpoint

The sentence contains a large number of clauses, several of which are connected by the simple, coordinating conjunction 'and'. Certain pre-modifiers ('the same', 'every') are repeated, as is 'like one another'. There is also a repetitive pattern of contrasting pairs: 'large streets . . . small streets', 'in and out', 'yesterday and tomorrow', 'the last and the next'.

Exam question

This extract creates the impression of an opinionated, outspoken American teenager speaking directly and candidly to the reader. An analysis might focus on such features as the use of informal vocabulary (including American slang), the presence of non-standard grammar (e.g. 'He just got a Jaguar') and the manipulation of sentence structure in order to mirror the rhythms of everyday speech (sentences are generally short and direct, but the opening sentence has a looser structure).

New technology

Checkpoint

Phatic communication (or *communion*) is the linguistic term for 'small talk' – pleasantries that have little meaningful content but are an important part of informal social interaction. See page 42.

Exam question

Reference could be made here to the debate about falling standards of literacy (allegedly exacerbated by new technology). The discussion of speech and writing on pages 30–1 is also relevant. Electronic texts share some of the characteristics (and therefore some of the strengths and weaknesses) of both speech and conventional written texts.

Much of this chapter is concerned with **sociolects**, the different varieties of language used by different social groups. Variation in language use may be based upon differences in regional origin, social class, gender or occupation. The use of slang is one way that membership of a particular social group might be expressed, though slang serves other purposes as well. The idea that language reflects power relationships in society is considered next, followed by a consideration of how language may encourage us to view minority groups in particular ways (the section 'Representation'). This latter theme is continued in the sections 'Sexism' and 'Political correctness'. 'Taboo Language' (language that society considers offensive or unacceptable) is the subject of the next section, and the chapter concludes by outlining some of the issues and debates relating to 'Language and education'.

Exam themes

→ Language variation.
→ Language and power.
→ Representation.

Topic checklist

O AS ● A2	AQA/A	AQA/B	EDEXCEL	OCR	WJE
Accents and dialects 1	●	○	●	○	○
Accents and dialects 2	●	○	●	○	○
Pidgins and creoles; British Black English	●	○	●	○	○
Language and social class	●	○	●	●	●
Male and female language use	○	○	●	●	●
Occupational dialects	●	○	●	●	●
Jargon	●	○	●	●	●
Slang	●	○	●	○	●
Language and power	●	○	●	●	●
Representation	○	○	●	●	●
Sexism	○	○	●	●	●
Political correctness	○	○	●	●	●
Taboo language	○	○	●	○	●
Language and education	●	○	●	●	●

Accents and dialects 1

Links

Received Pronunciation and **Standard English** are discussed more fully on pages 34–5.

Watch out!

Remember: Standard English is *not* an accent.

Action point

Think about your own attitudes towards particular accents. Are they similar to the attitudes found by researchers? How do you feel about your own accent?

Take note

The southern Irish accent is frequently found to be the most popular, while the Birmingham accent is frequently the least liked.

In studying accents and dialects, we are mainly concerned with **regional variation** in language use, though Received Pronunciation and Standard English are, respectively, an accent and a dialect that are no longer regionally based. **Social variation** is also relevant, as the speech of people higher up the social and occupational ladder tends to have fewer regional features than that of people lower down.

Key terms

Accent   This refers to the *pronunciation* of words. A **regional accent** is an accent spoken in a particular geographical region.

Dialect   This refers to *vocabulary* and *grammar*. It is a broad term and sometimes includes accent as well. A **regional dialect** is the dialect of a particular geographical region.

Received Pronunciation (**RP**)   This is the accent associated with upper-class speakers of the language. It is sometimes known as 'BBC English' or 'public school English'. Unlike other accents, it does not indicate a speaker's regional origin.

Standard English (**SE**)   The dialect (vocabulary and grammar) associated with educated users of the language. It is the form of English considered to be formally 'correct' and is used in most written texts. Like RP, use of Standard English does not indicate regional origin – SE can be spoken with a regional accent.

Attitudes to accents

The evidence

People tend to make assumptions about others based on the way that they speak. Research findings concerning common attitudes towards accents include the following.

→ RP is the most socially prestigious accent, associated with wealth and social status.

→ RP is an accent associated with competence and authority. In surveys it tends to receive high ratings for such qualities as intelligence, self-confidence and determination. However, RP speakers emerge less favourably than speakers with a regional accent in terms of their personal attractiveness. They score less well for qualities such as sincerity, good-naturedness and sense of humour.

→ Rural accents (e.g. the Somerset accent) are viewed more positively than urban accents (e.g. Cockney).

The Howard Giles Capital Punishment Experiment

This experiment suggested that people find regional accents *more persuasive* than the RP accent. Giles presented five groups of students with an identical set of arguments against capital punishment. One group read a printed text; the other four groups heard an oral presentation. The four oral presentations were given by speakers with different accents. One group heard an RP speaker, another a Somerset speaker, another a South Welsh speaker and the last group a Birmingham speaker. The students were first asked about how *impressive* they found the presentations. Those who had read the printed text and those who had heard the RP speaker were the most impressed. Least impressed were those who had heard the Birmingham speaker. Giles then assessed the *persuasiveness* of the accents by comparing the students' views on capital punishment before and after the presentations. Those hearing regional speakers were more likely to have changed their minds than those hearing the RP speaker or reading the printed texts.

The causes

Possible reasons for these attitudes include:

→ RP is seen as the accent of the 'upper' or 'ruling' class (e.g. the royal family are RP speakers) – hence people associate it with authority and status. However, most people do not belong to this class themselves and may feel socially distanced from it. Therefore, they do not associate the RP accent with personal warmth and attractiveness.
→ People make connections between accents and the regions from which they derive. Most people have a positive view of the countryside (associating it with beautiful landscapes, tranquillity, etc.), so they respond favourably to rural accents.
→ The stereotypes associated with accents are often reinforced and perpetuated by the mass media.
→ People find the sounds of some accents more attractive than others.

The effects

These attitudes mean that people may encounter positive or negative discrimination because of their accent:

→ In the field of employment, call centres are often located in certain parts of the country because companies feel that their businesses will benefit from having telephonists with particular accents.
→ Research suggests that the legal system may be biased against particular accents, and that people with these accents are more likely to be suspected of crime.
→ Individual cases of discrimination are often reported in the press, with some individuals changing their accents because of allegedly hostile attitudes. *Convergence* may occur. People may move their accent closer to RP as they acquire (or attempt to acquire) increased social status. Conversely, RP speakers may add regional features to their accents so that it is easier for them to mix socially.

Checkpoint 1

What does this experiment suggest about people's attitudes towards RP?

Checkpoint 2

What connections would you expect people to make with an urban accent?

Links

See 'Accents and the media' in the next section (page 88).

Example

Many would describe the southern Irish accent as 'soft' and 'melodic'. Urban accents are harsher.

Example

Popular locations for call centres include Wales, Tyneside and Scotland.

Links

Convergence and **divergence** are explained on page 50.

Examiner's secrets

Be careful to avoid over-generalization – make specific points about specific accents.

Exam question   answer: page 114

How much truth is there in the claim that people are judged by their accents? (45 min)

Accents and dialects 2

In this second section on accents and dialects, we consider accents and the mass media and the rise of Estuary English. We then focus on regional dialects, looking at dialect vocabulary and dialect grammar.

Accents and the media

Common attitudes towards accents and the stereotyped images associated with particular accents are often reinforced by the media:

→ In the early years of broadcasting, television and radio presenters and announcers almost always spoke with an RP accent (hence the expression 'BBC English'). This was partly because RP was an accent that could be understood by everybody but also because it carried an air of authority.

→ Today, a much wider range of accents is heard, though national news bulletins are still likely to be read by RP speakers.

→ Regional accents are more likely to be heard on local television and radio. The presence of local accents makes it easier for viewers and listeners to identify with the programmes.

→ Comedy and drama programmes often feature regional stereotypes – e.g. the stereotype of the Cockney wide boy is reinforced by *Only Fools and Horses*.

→ The accents of sports commentators often reflect the social standing of individual sports. Darts commentators, for example, often have strong regional accents, reinforcing the sport's working-class image. In contrast, sports such as show jumping, tennis and cricket frequently have commentators with RP accents.

→ Television and radio advertisements for expensive, upmarket products (e.g. cars, computers) often feature an RP accent. Food and drink advertisements, especially those emphasizing the 'naturalness' of the product, make use of rural accents.

→ The spread of Estuary English has been attributed partly to the mass media (see below).

Estuary English

The term 'Estuary English' was first used in the early 1980s. It describes an accent that originated in London and the south-east (the estuary referred to is the Thames Estuary) and that has spread outwards to several other parts of the country. Researchers claim to have identified elements of Estuary English pronunciation several hundred miles from London (e.g. in Liverpool and in Scotland).

Estuary English is a kind of modified Cockney. Features include the glottal stop (omitting the *t* sound in words such as 'Gatwick' – which becomes 'Ga'wick') and pronouncing *l* as *w* (so that 'milk' becomes 'miuwk' and 'tall' becomes 'tauw').

One reason for the spread of Estuary English is the movement of Londoners away from the capital. Another is that some Cockneys have modified their speech and moved it closer to RP, either because they have moved to another area or because they have acquired higher social status. At the same time as this **upward convergence** there has

---

Example

In 1999, a newsreader with a Welsh accent (Huw Edwards) became the regular presenter of the BBC's *Six O'clock News*. There were complaints from some viewers, who felt that a Welsh accent was unsuitable for reading the national news.

Action point

Gather specific examples of the use of accents in television advertising.

Check the net

There is a wealth of interesting material about Estuary English on the Estuary English website:
www.phon.ucl.ac.uk/home/estuary/home.htm

Examples

The politician Ken Livingstone, the comedians Paul Merton and Ben Elton and the television presenter Jonathan Ross are all Estuary English speakers.

been **downward convergence**, with some RP speakers losing elements of their original accent in an effort to integrate with the rest of society.

Estuary English is also considered fashionable, and as a classless accent appeals to many young people.

Dialect vocabulary

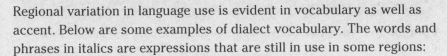

Regional variation in language use is evident in vocabulary as well as accent. Below are some examples of dialect vocabulary. The words and phrases in italics are expressions that are still in use in some regions:

hungry – *clammed, hungered, leer, leery, thirl*
cross-eyed – *boss-eyed, cock-eyed, squint-eyed, glee-eyed, skent*
afraid – *frit, flayit, afeared*

Researchers who record dialect vocabulary have found that it is diminishing – there are now fewer words that are used only in certain regions. The vocabulary that we use has become more standardized. Reasons for this include the following:

→ Communities are less isolated. People travel around the country much more, and communities often include people who have lived elsewhere. Increased contact between the speakers of different regional dialects causes the differences between them to lessen. Some dialect vocabulary ceases to be regional because it spreads to other parts of the country. For example, 'parky' (originally a Midlands dialect word for 'cold') and 'toe rag' (originally a Cockney insult) are both in common use across the country.
→ Universal compulsory education means that everyone is encouraged to use Standard English.
→ The existence of the mass media means that we regularly hear dialects other than our own. In particular, we are used to hearing (and reading) Standard English.

Dialect grammar

Regional dialects continue to employ grammatical constructions that are different from those found in Standard English. Some constructions are especially common and are found in several parts of the country. In many instances, they are usages that have survived from Old or Middle English. They include the following:

→ Multiple negatives, as in 'I don't know nothing about it'.
→ Non-standard past tense forms, as in 'I seen him yesterday', 'We was late', 'She done it'.
→ Use of 'them' for the demonstrative pronoun 'those', as in 'Where did I put them scissors'.

Checkpoint 1

What is the opposite of convergence?

Take note

Estuary English is prevalent in the mass media (it has been called 'the language of the disc jockey'), and this has also encouraged it to spread.

Checkpoint 2

Does this mean that the total number of English words is declining?

Check the net

There are many websites related to specific English dialects – e.g. the Yorkshire Dialect Society can be found at: www.clanvis.com/loc/dialect/home.htm

Take note

Other constructions are more strongly associated with particular regions: e.g. use of 'thou' and 'thee' (northern England).

Exam question   answer: page 114

It has been said that Estuary English may eventually replace RP as our most influential and prestigious accent. How far do you agree with this view? (45 min)

Examiner's secrets

Don't assume that 'influential' and 'prestigious' mean exactly the same thing.

Pidgins and creoles; British Black English

In this section, we discuss further varieties of English, although not all pidgin and creole languages are derived from English. We also look at British Black English, a term for creole-based varieties of English spoken in the UK.

What is a pidgin?

A **pidgin** combines two or more languages, enabling the members of different speech communities to communicate with each other. Pidgins develop when circumstances (such as trade or colonization) force different languages together, creating the need for some means of communication between groups of people who have no language in common. What usually happens is that the dominant language (likely to belong to the group with the greatest social or economic power) becomes adapted and simplified. Use of the pidgin is usually confined to a limited range of situations. Pidgin is used only to communicate with outsiders: members of the same speech community do not use pidgin to communicate with each other, so a pidgin has *no native speakers*.

Characteristics of pidgins and creoles

Pidgins   Because pidgins are restricted in their use, they are usually characterized by limited vocabulary and reduced grammatical structures, with simple clauses and few prepositions.

One of the most studied examples of pidgin is *Tok Pisin* (the name is derived from English, 'Talk Pidgin'). It is spoken in Papua New Guinea and developed from varieties of English spoken in the Pacific region in the 19th century. It was a means of communication between English-speaking Europeans and Pacific islanders. The English derivation of much Tok Pisin vocabulary is very apparent (see examples below). Tok Pisin has grown in importance and is now being acquired by children as their first language. This means it is undergoing **creolization** (see next paragraph).

Tok Pisin vocabulary

Mi	I, me	*antap*	on top	*dok*	dog
Yu	you	*maus*	mouth	*het*	head
Askim	to ask	*stret*	straight away	*kol*	cold

Creoles   Over time, a pidgin may begin to be used more extensively and may become the first language of new generations of speakers. When this happens, the language becomes a creole.

Acrolects, basilects and mesolects

These terms are used by linguists when different varieties exist within a single creole. The **acrolect** is the most socially prestigious variety, and is closest to the language (e.g. English) from which the creole derives. The **basilect** is at the opposite end of the spectrum, and is the variety which has least in common with the 'parent' language. The varieties in between are known as **mesolects**.

Who speaks pidgins and creoles?

Many of the world's pidgins and creoles are a legacy of old colonial power and derive from English, French, Portuguese or Dutch. More recent examples include the pidgins spoken in Germany among migrant workers from countries such as Turkey. Around a quarter of the known pidgins and creoles are English-based. Most creole languages are spoken by the descendants of African slaves. These include the Caribbean creoles derived from English, such as those spoken in Antigua, Barbados, Grenada, Jamaica and Guyana.

A language such as **Jamaican creole** has many grammatical features that distinguish it from Standard English. Examples include:

➜ no –s ending on plural nouns;
➜ multiple negatives;
➜ no verb endings to indicate past tense; instead, the base form of the verb is used ('he go last week');
➜ omission of auxiliary verbs ('me not' = 'I am not');
➜ *fi* used instead of 'to' with infinitives ('I really doan know how fi tell y'u dis' = 'I really don't know how to tell you this').

Attitudes to pidgins and creoles

It was once common for pidgins and creoles to be regarded as corrupt, imperfect varieties of other languages. Linked to this attitude was the view that the speakers of these languages were similarly deficient: socially, culturally and intellectually inferior to speakers of the original (usually European) languages. It is now recognized that these languages are efficient, functional systems of communication, with their own, internally consistent rules and structures. There is also interest among linguists in their importance as an expression of personal and national identity. The attention paid in recent years to **British Black English** is an example of this.

British Black English

'British Black English' is a term used for several different varieties of creole English spoken in Britain. Older Afro-Caribbean immigrants may continue to speak their native creoles, but their children and grandchildren develop, through their contact with local British English varieties, different, modified creoles. These creoles, rather like regional accents and dialects, are an important symbol of group identity and solidarity. They are closely associated with black youth culture and have produced a large body of creole literature, including poems, novels and reggae lyrics.

> *"A Creole is a pidgin which has expanded in structure and vocabulary to express the range of meanings and serve the range of functions required of a first language"*
>
> Janet Holmes

Checkpoint 2

Can you see a parallel here with attitudes towards regional dialects? (see page 113).

The jargon

Another term for British Black English is *patois*.

Exam question   answer: page 114

Janet Holmes, in her book *An Introduction to Sociolinguistics*, reports that some teachers have described the language of their West Indian pupils as 'careless and slovenly'. Explain what might cause attitudes such as this to exist. What arguments could be put forward to persuade these teachers to change their views? (45 min)

Language and social class

Topic link

The rise of Estuary English suggests that class differences in language use might be diminishing. See pages 88–9.

Take note

When the speech of people from different social classes is compared, those from higher social classes have accents that are closer to Received Pronunciation, and the grammatical features of their speech are closer to Standard English.

Checkpoint 1

Why do you think respondents are asked to perform these kinds of tasks?

The jargon

Labov used the term **hypercorrection** to refer to the tendency for some speakers to increase their use of prestige forms in situations where they are conscious of their own speech.

In the sections on accents and dialects (pages 86–9) we looked at **regional** variation in language – how people's use of language has been influenced by their regional origin. In this section, we consider how the language that people use may be influenced by their **social class** – an aspect of social variation. Broadly speaking, researchers have found that as one moves higher up the social scale, regional differences become fewer.

How do we define social class?

This is a controversial question, and one of the problems encountered when comparing research findings is that researchers may have used different systems for identifying the social classes of the people they have studied. The three most common criteria are occupation, education and income.

Labov's New York study (see below) used these criteria and divided people into nine social classes: classes 1–5 were working-class, 6–8 were lower middle-class and 9 was upper middle-class.

Trudgill's Norwich research (also discussed below) used six factors: occupation, education, income, type of housing, locality (area of residence) and father's occupation. He divided his subjects into five social classes: middle middle-class, lower middle-class, upper working-class, middle working-class and lower working-class.

The usual method of researchers is to analyse the language of a sample of speakers drawn from different social classes. Respondents (the people being studied) are often asked to read aloud passages and word lists and to tell a story about an interesting experience. Depending on the research, *phonological* features (pronunciation) and *grammatical* features (e.g. the use of double negatives) may both be considered.

Labov

One of the first studies to establish a link between language use and social class was Labov's New York city research (1966).

He studied the use of the *postvocalic r*, the pronunciation of 'r' in words such as 'farm', 'floor' and 'car'. In New York, the postvocalic 'r' is considered socially prestigious (rather like pronouncing 'h' at the beginnings of words in Britain), so Labov believed that the higher the social class of the speaker, the more likely they would be to pronounce it.

He found that in casual speech upper middle-class speakers used the postvocalic 'r' more than lower middle-class speakers. This confirmed his expectations. However, an interesting finding was that in more formal situations (e.g. reading word lists) the reverse was the case. This suggested that the lower middle-class speakers were more conscious of their own speech and more anxious to make a good impression through the way that they spoke.

Trudgill

Trudgill's Norwich research (1983) examined the relationship between social class and a number of different linguistic variables.

One such variable was the pronunciation of *–ing* at the end of words such as 'fishing' and 'singing'. He found, as he expected, that respondents lower down the social scale were more likely to drop the 'g' in their pronunciation ('fishin', 'singin'). He also found that among all classes pronunciation of the *–ing* ending increased according to the formality of the situation. This confirmed that people are conscious of their speech, adopting more socially prestigious features in more formal contexts.

A grammatical feature he considered was the use of verbs without an 's' ending – e.g. saying 'she go' and 'he run' rather than 'she goes' and 'he runs'. Again, he found that this non-standard feature was much more frequent among working-class speakers. Trudgill also found that the language speakers used was influenced by their *gender*.

Petyt

Petyt (1980) studied speakers in Bradford, Yorkshire. He examined the dropping of the 'h' sound at the beginning of words such as 'house'. He found that there was a close relationship between 'h' dropping and social class. Lower working-class speakers on average dropped 93% of 'h' sounds, upper working-class speakers 67%, lower middle-class speakers 28% and upper middle-class speakers only 12%.

Social networks (Milroy)

An alternative approach to the examination of social variation in language use is the study of **social networks**. Lesley Milroy pioneered this approach when she studied social networks in Belfast (1980).

A social network is a group of people who regularly interact with each other. Any one individual may belong to several networks, interacting with different groups of people at home and at work, for example.

Studies such as those of Labov, Trudgill and Petyt focus on **social stratification** – that is, they tend to assume that society can be divided into separate layers or classes. In practice, people's lives are not so compartmentalized, and someone who is working-class might well have middle-class friends or work colleagues. Looking at social networks shows that the relationships people have can be an important influence on the language that they use.

Exam question   answer: page 114

In what ways might the social class that we belong to influence the language that we use? (45 min)

Links

Bernstein's theory of restricted and elaborated codes, outlined on page 112, offers another perspective on the relationship between language and social class.

Links

Trudgill's findings in relation to gender differences are also discussed in the next section (pages 94–5).

Checkpoint 2

Can you think of any other linguistic variables that might reflect the social class of a speaker?

Examiner's secrets

Try to identify several different specific 'ways', and remember to support your points with reference to relevant research.

Male and female language use

Another factor that may cause variation in language use is **gender**. This section outlines some of the differences in the language used by men and women, and some of the theories that have been developed to explain this behaviour.

Male and female differences ●●●

The main differences in the way men and women use language relates to standard speech forms. Researchers have consistently found that women use more standard speech forms than men. This pattern appears to exist across all social classes and also across different languages: research in many Western countries has produced similar findings. In Britain, this means that women tend to use Standard English more than men do. Important research includes that of Peter Trudgill in Norwich (1983) and Jenny Cheshire in Reading (1982). Cheshire investigated the speech of adolescents at an adventure playground and found similar patterns to those that exist among adults. This suggests that differences in male and female language use are already evident during childhood.

Examples of the speech differences which researchers have found include the following:

→ Men are more likely to drop the 'h' sound at the beginnings of words such as 'house' and 'hat'.
→ Men are more likely to drop the final 'g' sound in words such as 'going' and 'swimming'.
→ There is more use of 'ain't' among men than among women.
→ Correspondingly, there is more use of 'isn't' among women than among men.
→ Men are more likely to use 'seen' and 'done' as past tense forms (e.g. 'I seen him yesterday', 'we done it last week').
→ Men are more likely to use multiple negatives (e.g. 'I don't know nothing about it').

Reasons for differences ●●●

Linguists do not agree on the reasons for these differences. Some of the explanations that have been suggested are outlined here.

Women are more status-conscious

The argument here is that social status is more important to women than men. Speech can be taken by others as an indicator of social class, so women make more effort to conform to standard usage in an effort to demonstrate their status and respectability.

Society's expectations of women

This approach is based on the argument that society expects 'better' behaviour from women than men. This begins in childhood, when boys' misbehaviour is tolerated more than girls'. As adults, it is argued, women are often expected to behave in a 'ladylike' way, and this includes speaking in an appropriate manner. Moreover, society also expects

Links

The characteristics of Standard English were outlined on pages 34–5.

Checkpoint 1

Apart from gender, which other factors might help to explain why speakers use language in this way?

The jargon

Conditioning people as they grow up to perform certain social roles is known as **socialization**.

94

women to play the dominant role in child rearing, and this includes providing children with models of 'correct' speech for them to imitate.

The subordinate role of women

This argument suggests that women's speech patterns are created by their subordinate role within society, which is seen as male-dominated. In the same way that children are expected to speak politely to adults, women must defer in their speech to men, and this results in their greater use of polite, standard forms. This theory is especially associated with the American linguist Robin Lakoff (1975). In addition to the use of standard forms, Lakoff also identified a number of other features that she said were more characteristic of women's speech than men's. She argued that these features reflected women's lack of confidence, in that compared with men their use of language tended to be less direct and less assertive. Examples of such features include the following:

→ hedges and fillers (expressions such as 'sort of', 'you know', etc.);
→ tag questions (questions added to the ends of statements – e.g. 'That's right, isn't it?');
→ indirect request forms (e.g. 'Would you mind closing the window?').

Overt and covert prestige

This approach shifts the focus towards men: why are they more likely in their speech to deviate from Standard English? The explanation usually offered is that men associate non-standard forms with masculinity and toughness. Trudgill, for example, found that when they were asked about their own speech, men tended to claim they used more non-standard forms than they in fact did. This suggests that they were rather proud of using such language and felt that some kind of prestige attached to it. It is said that men tend to desire **covert** prestige, while women seek **overt** prestige:

→ **Covert prestige** is the prestige that derives from behaviour that goes against the norms and conventions of 'respectable' society.
→ **Overt prestige** is the prestige that attaches to respectable, socially desirable behaviour.

In Cheshire's Reading research, for example, the adolescent boy ('Noddy') who used non-standard forms most often also had a reputation for tough, deviant behaviour (e.g. getting into fights and trouble with the police) and was respected for this by his peers. In contrast, another boy ('Kevin'), who used non-standard forms much less frequently, rated low on an index of 'tough' behaviour and was often the victim of other boys' jokes and excluded from group activities.

Checkpoint 2

Some linguists would not agree that these features of women's speech indicate uncertainty and lack of confidence. Can you think of other explanations that might be offered?

Links

Differences in the ways men and women behave in conversation are also relevant to this topic. They are discussed on pages 54–5.

Exam question   answer: page 114

What evidence is there to suggest that men and women use language in different ways? What explanations have been offered to account for these differences? (45 min)

Examiner's secrets

In a question such as this it is important to remember to include the names of relevant researchers.

Occupational dialects

The next two sections concern the language used by occupational groups. **Occupational dialect** is a broad term and includes all the distinctive features (e.g. lexical, grammatical, phonological) associated with the language of a particular occupation. **Jargon**, discussed in the next section, refers more specifically to vocabulary and is a term that sometimes has negative connotations, referring to language that is unnecessarily complex and obscure.

What are occupational dialects?

Every occupation generates its own specialist language. Two examples that we shall shortly be focusing on are teaching and the legal profession, but there are countless others. The list becomes even longer if we include other forms of group activity (e.g. sports, leisure pursuits).

In all of these cases, the existence of a specialist language enables the members of a group to communicate with each other with clarity, economy and precision. Less positively, using occupational dialects can sometimes also be a way of excluding others and of making the user feel more important or more sophisticated.

The most identifiable characteristic of an occupational dialect is usually its *vocabulary*, though in some instances other linguistic features are also involved. Legal language, for example, has certain recurring *grammatical* features (see opposite page). In the case of the Church, the language used in services has distinctive *phonological* features (repetition, call-and-response rhythms, etc.).

Education

If you are studying at a school or college, the terms listed below are likely to be familiar to you:

The language of education

timetable	National Curriculum	homework	GCSE
register	Key stages 1, 2, 3, 4	coursework	pupil
class	record of achievement	assignment	A-level
set	supply teacher	project	reports
form	private study	worksheet	course
year	staff room	mock exam	module

The list of terms (which could have been much longer) is an example of the specialist vocabulary created by a particular occupation or activity. Note that many of the terms are in everyday use, but outside the world of education they have different meanings (e.g. 'class', 'form', 'year'). Education also illustrates how an occupational variety often has *sub-varieties* within it. The terms shown above are likely to be understood by teachers and students alike, but we could compile a second list of terms likely to be used exclusively by teachers: e.g. 'tracking' (monitoring standards in education). Other sub-varieties might include different dialects used in schools, sixth-form colleges and universities.

The jargon

Occupational dialects are also sometimes known as **occupational registers** or **occupational varieties**.

Checkpoint 1

Choose a sport and try to list ten specialist terms associated with it.

Links

The purposes of occupational dialects are discussed more fully in the next section (pages 98–9).

The jargon

A **sub-variety** is a variety that is used by only certain members of a group.

Watch out!

In addition, each individual institution would probably have its own small collection of unique terms.

Legal language ●●●

The language used by lawyers is a highly developed occupational variety, with numerous distinctive features. Most of these features are a result of the following factors:

→ Legal language needs to be as precise and unambiguous as possible.
→ The legal system is rooted in history and tradition.

Some of the main characteristics of legal language are outlined below.

Vocabulary

→ Use of archaic words (e.g. 'hereby', 'thereto', 'hereinafter').
→ Use of French (e.g. *lieu*), and Latin (e.g. *habeas corpus*) vocabulary.
→ Use of *formal* words and phrases (e.g. 'without let or hindrance').

Grammar

Sentences are often lengthy and complex, with many subordinate clauses. This arises from the need to ensure that there is no room for misinterpretation and that all eventualities are covered.

There is a tendency towards repetition and long lists of items. Again this is explained by the desire to eliminate any possibility of uncertainty.

Certain classes of word are especially common, such as modal verbs, (e.g. 'shall', 'may'), hypernyms (e.g. 'vehicle') and hyponyms (e.g. 'moped', 'motor car', 'agricultural tractor').

Critics of legal language argue that it is excessively difficult and obscure. It is said that in a democracy the legal system should be open and accessible rather than the preserve of experts, who are able to charge high fees for acting as translators or interpreters.

Take note

Another feature of legal language is the limited use of punctuation. Lengthy sentences will often have few if any commas. This is because punctuation can subtly alter the sense of a sentence and may cause ambiguity.

Checkpoint 2

What is the difference between a **hyponym** and a **hypernym**?

Links

Recent attempts to simplify legal vocabulary are discussed in the next section (pages 98–9).

Exam question   answer: page 115

The extract below is from a legal agreement between the Department of Transport and the Motor Insurance Bureau (an organization that represents car insurance companies). In what ways is the language used typical of legal documents? Why might such use of language be criticized, and how might it be defended?

If judgement in respect of any relevant liability is obtained against any persons or person in any Court in Great Britain whether or not such a person or persons be in fact covered by a contract of insurance and any such judgement is not satisfied in full within seven days from the date upon which the person or persons in whose favour the judgement was given became entitled to enforce it then MIB will, subject to the provisions of paragraph (2), (3) and (4) below and to Clauses 4, 5 and 6 hereof, pay or satisfy or cause to be paid thereunder in respect of the relevant liability including any sum awarded by the Court in respect of interest on that sum and any taxed costs or any costs awarded by the Court without taxation (or such proportion thereof as is attributable to the relevant liability) whatever may be the cause of the failure of the judgement debtor to satisfy the judgement.

Jargon

The term **jargon** refers to the specialist vocabulary associated with a particular occupation or activity. The marginal notes in this book headed 'The jargon', for example, always refer to terminology associated with the study of the English language. Used in this way, 'jargon' is a neutral term. However, the word is sometimes used more negatively (or pejoratively) to refer to language that is excessively technical and hard to understand.

The jargon

Pejorative is used to describe a word, phrase or tone that devalues or denigrates (it is similar in meaning to **derogatory**).

Positive use of jargon ●●●

Jargon has been described as 'verbal shorthand'. It enables the members of an occupational or other specialist group to communicate with each other clearly, quickly and precisely. This kind of jargon is undoubtedly necessary and helps the group concerned to function more effectively. A person suffering from back pain, for example, might say in casual conversation that she has been prescribed a course of injections. The doctors and nurses administering the treatment, however, would obviously need to be more precise: for them the treatment might involve 'facet joint injections', 'sclerosant injections' or 'epidural injections'.

Negative use of jargon ●●●

Checkpoint 1

What is the linguistic term for a language variety used exclusively by the members of a particular social group?

Jargon is appropriate when it is used for communication between the members of a specialist group. It becomes inappropriate when it is used to address a wider, non-specialist, audience. Medicine again provides an example of this. A doctor advising a patient that his lifestyle is increasing the risk of 'acute myocardial infarction' is unlikely to be understood. Explaining that he has a high risk of a 'heart attack' would be more effective.

Using jargon in this unhelpful way may not be intentional, but the speaker (or writer) can still be criticized for showing a lack of sensitivity to the needs of his or her audience. Occasionally, however, there is a more deliberate desire to confuse. When this occurs, jargon is often a means of expressing membership of an exclusive group. The user feels more important and believes he is demonstrating his superiority over those who do not share his knowledge of specialist terminology. There may also be a desire to keep clients, patients or other outsiders 'in the dark' so that it becomes more difficult for them to question and criticize (doctors and lawyers are often accused of using language in this way).

Checkpoint 2

Can you think of any other occupations that sometimes receive similar criticism?

Features of unhelpful jargon ●●●

Common linguistic features of the kind of unhelpful jargon referred to above include the following:

→ Vocabulary that is unnecessarily complex, scientific or technical and that is unlikely to be understood by the audience. Words are likely to be long and difficult, when shorter, simpler words would be more effective (see medical example above).

→ Vocabulary that is currently fashionable (using 'buzz words'). Often the meaning is vague and imprecise. Examples: 'interface', 'parameters', 'firm up'.

→ Abstract vocabulary, which again makes the meaning of the text hard to pin down.

→ Euphemisms may be used to disguise the reality of what is being described; e.g. a company that is dismissing some of its employees may refer to this as 'downsizing' or 'rationalization'.

→ Unnecessarily elaborate constructions; e.g. nouns become noun phrases: in some schools and colleges libraries have become 'learning resource centres'.

→ Use of the passive voice (e.g. 'It is anticipated that').

Plain English Campaign ●●●

In Britain and the United States, pressure groups have campaigned for greater clarity of expression in government publications and in legal and commercial texts (such as forms and leaflets). In the UK, the Plain English Campaign, established in Liverpool in 1974, has succeeded in raising awareness of the dangers of jargon. It promotes the cause of plain English and also offers advice to businesses and government departments. Organizations can apply for permission to use the Crystal Mark on their documents, a symbol that confirms that the document has been read and approved by the Plain English Campaign. Its annual awards, given for the notable use (or misuse) of language, always receive media attention.

Changes in legal language ●●●

The legal system is an example of an institution where some attempt has been made to make the language used more accessible to non-specialists. In 1999, the language officially used in civil courts was reformed. Many Latin phrases (such as *in camera*) were dropped, together with other expressions that were considered obscure and difficult. Some of the changes are shown below:

Legal terminology – the old and the new

old	new	old	new
writ	claim form	*subpoena*	witness summons
affidavit	statement of truth	plaintiff	claimant
pleading	statement of case	minor/infant	child
in camera	in private	leave of the court	permission of the court
ex parte	without notice	*inter partes*	with notice

Links

Euphemisms are discussed more fully on page 110.

Action point

If you have not heard of the Plain English Campaign, watch for references to it in the media and look out for the Crystal Mark logo on leaflets, etc.

Links

Legal language was also discussed in the previous section (pages 96–7).

Exam questions   answers: page 115

1 Choose an occupational group and discuss the distinctive features and purposes of the group's use of language. (45 min)

2 'Jargon' is an Old French word and originally referred to the meaningless twittering of birds. Explain, with examples, what you understand by the term 'jargon' today. (45 min)

Slang

Slang is a fascinating topic to study and is a popular choice for coursework investigations. In this section, some of the main characteristics of slang are identified, and we also consider the origins and uses of slang. Examples of slang expressions are given, but you will find it useful to add additional examples of your own.

Characteristics: what is slang?

Slang is notoriously hard to define, but these are some distinguishing characteristics:

→ It is *informal*, to the point of often being racy, rebellious and subversive.

→ It is generally found in *speech* rather than writing and refers to *vocabulary* rather than grammar.

→ It is often *short-lived*. New slang expressions are entering the language all the time. Many disappear quite quickly, though others are remarkably enduring. Some slang expressions cease to be slang because they come to be regarded as normal, standard usage.

Examples

Gob was used to mean 'mouth' as long ago as 1550, and the first recorded use of *booze* for 'alcohol' was in 1325.

Examples

Pub, *bike* and *phone* are no longer thought of as slang.

Origins: where does slang come from?

Occasionally, slang creates *completely new words* – e.g. 'barf' (American slang for 'vomit').

More commonly, slang gives *old words new meanings*, as when 'hot' is used to mean 'sexy' or 'popular' and 'bread' is used to refer to money. Sometimes, there is an *inversion of meaning*: used as slang, 'bad' and 'wicked' both mean 'good'. Old words may be put together to form new compounds: 'rip-off', 'hang-up'.

Some slang words are *clippings*, as in 'ciggie' for 'cigarette'.

Slang also *borrows from other languages*: 'dekko', meaning 'look', is taken from Hindi.

Much slang involves the use of *metaphor*. New comparisons are invented, as with the numerous slang expressions meaning 'eccentric' or 'lacking intelligence': 'not playing with a full deck', 'the lift doesn't reach the top floor', 'a few sandwiches short of a picnic' and so on.

Checkpoint 1

What are **clippings**? Can you think of any more examples of slang words that are clippings?

Purpose: what is slang for?

Slang is often *subversive*, reflecting a desire to rebel against respectability and society's conventional norms and values.

Much slang is *humorous* (e.g. the metaphors referred to above).

Slang often expresses *membership of a social group*. It can be a kind of secret language that strengthens the feeling of solidarity among the members of the group while excluding others. The first slang dictionary was a collection of words used by criminals, compiled by a judge in 1565. Today, the criminal underworld continues to have its own slang, with drug dealing creating hundreds of new expressions.

Teenagers are another social group strongly associated with the use of slang. It emphasizes their separation from the world of adults. Each new generation likes to assert its own identity, so teenage slang is constantly changing. The slang terms shown below come from a BBC survey of teenagers in 1998.

boys	lads, chaps, geezers, blokes
girls	birds, babes, chicks
boyfriend	babe, beany, beef
girlfriend	bird, chick, bit of stuff, beany
good	brill, ace, snazzy, wicked, rough
bad	cack, shabby, skankin', fuddy, lame
cool	mental, gnarly, mega, smooth, hard
uncool	feeble, freak, gone, lean, shameful

Occupational groups also have their own slang, but it is often difficult to distinguish between this kind of slang and jargon, though jargon usually refers to more formal, specialized vocabulary (often technical), while slang is informal.

Many *activities* and *subcultures* generate their own slang. Skateboarding, surfing and the dance music scene are examples.

Some slang is *regional*, encouraging a sense of regional solidarity and identity. Here the dividing line between slang and regional dialect is often blurred, though again slang is likely to be more informal and subversive. Cockney rhyming slang (see below) is an example of regionally based slang.

Slang may arise from *the desire to be new, fashionable and up-to-date*. This helps to explain its appeal to young people, and also accounts for the ceaseless flow of new expressions. Long-established Cockney rhyming slang such as 'apples and pears' (stairs) seems very dated, but more recent examples sound less tired: 'syrup' (wig, from 'syrup of figs'), 'Claire Rayners' (trainers).

Some *subjects* have traditionally been fertile sources of slang, such as sex, money and alcohol.

Slang is also often used to express *abuse*: the 1998 *Oxford Dictionary of Slang* listed 138 synonyms for 'fool'.

Attitudes to slang ●●●

Slang is sometimes disapproved of because it is considered 'vulgar' or 'improper'. In recent years, some slang (e.g. relating to sex or to people's nationalities) has been frowned upon as politically incorrect, but slang's rebellious, nonconformist edge is the source of its vitality. It uses language in colourful and inventive ways and is the enemy of the stale and the predictable.

Exam question   answer: page 115

What are the main characteristics of slang. How and why is it used? (45 min)

Checkpoint 2

How many of these terms are familiar to you? Do any of them seem dated? How many alternative expressions can you think of?

Examples

Some examples from the American film industry:
Going shopping – trying to sign up a star
Making a marriage – selling a script
Doing a Dino – going out of business, after a producer who went bankrupt, Dino de Laurentis.

Check the net

There are hundreds of slang-related websites, including an Online Slang Dictionary at.
www.umr.edu/wrader/slang.htm/

Example

The lexicographer Jonathan Green, who has studied the history of slang, estimates that there have been around 2 500 expressions for 'drunk'.

Examiner's secrets

Essays on slang should always include plenty of examples.

Language and power

Language and power is a broad topic that has links with other topic areas. Individuals or social groups might exercise power within society because of their occupation, social class, race or gender. At the same time, the mass media exercise power as they can influence attitudes and opinions. Here we focus on some of the ways in which the *language* used by an individual or group might reflect their status or power.

Forms of address ●●●

In English, the ways in which people address each other are a good indicator of relative status and power. The most common forms of address available to speakers include first name ('Susan'), title ('Doctor'), and title followed by last name ('Doctor Jones', 'Mr Lewis').

Asymmetrical or **non-reciprocal** address forms usually reflect a difference in status. These occur when people address each other in different ways. A teenager who has a Saturday job in a department store might call the manager 'Mrs Roberts', while she addresses him as 'Gary'.

A stage might be reached in a relationship when address forms change and become more symmetrical (people begin to address each other in similar ways). Here it is usually the person of higher status who initiates the change.

More examples

Students are likely to use respectful forms in addressing their teachers: the formal title 'Sir' or 'Miss', or title followed by last name ('Mr Hall'). *Teachers* will address students by their first name or, in more traditional schools, by their last name only. Students who leave school and go on to college where they are invited to address their teachers by their first names often feel uncomfortable at first about doing so.

Race   In the southern United States, social inequalities between blacks and whites used to be reflected in asymmetrical address forms. Whites would address blacks by their first names in situations where they would have used titles and last name if the other person had been white. The derogatory address term 'boy' was also in use. Blacks would normally be expected to address whites by title and surname.

Family   Address forms between family members are also of interest. Younger family members will often use titles when addressing older relatives ('Mum', 'Dad', 'Gran', 'Uncle John'). The reverse almost never occurs, though 'Son' is sometimes used as a form of address.

Other influences on address forms

Context can influence the forms of address that are used. Titles, especially those of an elaborate nature, are more likely to be used in formal situations (e.g. 'Our guest of honour tonight is the Right Honourable Sir Peter Birkdale').

Research suggests that people feel most confident about identifying the appropriate form of address to use if the other person is a *close subordinate* or a *distant superior*. In other situations, they are often more

---

Watch out!

Symmetrical address forms may be encouraged from the very beginning, but it will be the superior in the relationship who takes the decision (e.g. a manager telling a new member of staff 'Call me Chris').

Checkpoint 1

Why do you think this pattern of family address forms exists?

uncertain: if you meet a stranger (a *distant equal*), for example, should you address him as 'David' or 'Mr Barrett'? Often, our reaction to such situations is to avoid using address forms altogether.

Conventions relating to the use of address forms reflect social attitudes. In Britain in recent years there has been a movement towards more symmetrical address forms (students addressing teachers by their first names is an example of this).

Making requests ●●●

This can be another indicator of status. Where clear differences of status exist, **imperatives** (commands) may be used by superiors to subordinates (e.g. a judge to a witness: 'Answer the question'). Where there is equality of status, or a subordinate is addressing a superior, requests tend to be less direct (e.g. 'Would you mind opening the window?').

Research suggests that men use more imperatives than women, whose requests tend to be expressed more indirectly.

Status and power in conversations ●●●

There are a number of ways in which the position of dominance in a conversation might be apparent: initiating, changing and closing topics of conversation; saying more than the other person; ignoring what the other person says; asking questions. The sections on conversation (pages 46–57) are relevant here.

Language and power – other links ●●●

Using language that the other person is unfamiliar with can be a way of asserting status. A specialist might try to emphasize his superior knowledge by using jargon or technical vocabulary. Language of this kind excludes others. Accents can have a similar effect – e.g. some people feel intimidated by an RP accent.

Non-verbal communication is also important. Dominance can be expressed through appearance (e.g. uniforms), body language, and by the prosodic features of speech, such as volume, tone and emphasis.

Checkpoint 2

Why do you think this movement towards more symmetrical address forms has occurred?

Watch out!

Imperatives are also used with close friends or family members ('Answer the phone!') and do not always reflect differences in status.

Example

An analysis of medical interviews in the USA (West 1983) found that doctors asked 91% of questions, patients only 9%. Research also indicates that men do all of these things (apart from asking questions) more than women.

Watch out!

Power often depends on *context*. A police officer arresting a doctor for a driving offence is in a position of power, but if he were a patient in a hospital the roles would be reversed.

Exam question   answer: page 115

The conversation below between a white policeman and a black doctor took place in the USA. Analyse the conversation in the light of your knowledge of the relationship between language and power. (45 min)

'What's your name boy?'
'Dr. Pouissant. I'm a physician.'
'What's your first name, boy?'
'Alvin.'

(SOURCE: John Pride and Janet Holmes (eds)
Sociolinguistics, Penguin, 1980)

Representation

This section is concerned with how language is used to portray (or *represent*) reality. The relationship between language and thought is considered, together with the ways that language both reflects and moulds our social values.

Language and thought

Many theories have been developed regarding the relationship between language and thought. These can be roughly put into three categories:

1. Some theories argue that language *controls* the way we think, because the language we learn to use teaches us to perceive the world in certain ways. This approach is known as **linguistic determinism** and is most strongly associated with the *Sapir–Whorf hypothesis* (see below).
2. An opposite view is that language *reflects* the way we think. The beliefs, attitudes and values of a society are expressed in (but not influenced by) the language that the people of that society use.
3. Many linguists favour a position between these extremes, seeing language and thought as *interdependent*, each influencing the other.

The Sapir–Whorf hypothesis

This theory was developed by two linguists, Edward Sapir and his pupil Benjamin Lee Whorf. The theory argues that the language we learn determines the way we view the world, and that people who use different languages perceive the world in different ways.

Kay and Kempton (1984) studied the Mexican language Tarahumara, which has a single word for the colours blue and green. In an experiment they found that English speakers were better at differentiating between shades of blue and green, suggesting that their knowledge of colour terms influenced their perception of colour.

Grammatical differences between languages are important to the theory as well as differences of vocabulary. Whorf studied Hopi Indians in North America and claimed that whereas English verbs can signify past, present or future, the Hopi language does not divide time in this rigid way. He argued that as a result their whole conception of the nature of time is different. Later researchers, however, have argued that Whorf's analysis of the Hopi language is seriously flawed.

Criticisms of the Sapir–Whorf hypothesis

Language is more flexible than the theory suggests and can be used to describe unfamiliar concepts.

Moreover not having the language does not necessarily mean we do not understand the concepts. Some Australian Aboriginal languages do not have a developed system of words for numbers (instead they rely on words meaning 'many', 'some' and so on), but they are still able to count and calculate.

"We see and hear and otherwise experience very largely as we do because the language habits of our community predispose certain choices of interpretation"

Edward Sapir

Watch out!

A famous language 'myth' evolved after a passing reference in an article by Benjamin Whorf to Eskimo words for snow. Whorf implied that Eskimos had more words for snow than existed in other languages and that as a result they perceived snow differently, distinguishing between different types of snow more efficiently than (for example) English speakers. Following the article's publication in 1940 other linguists and anthropologists repeated and developed Whorf's argument. Eventually, however, it became clear that the argument was based on a fundamental misunderstanding of Eskimo language and had no real substance.

If language controlled our thoughts, language change would not occur because we would never have any new ideas or concepts. In fact language is continually changing in response to developments in society (new attitudes, new inventions, new ideas).

Few linguists today would support an extreme version of the Sapir–Whorf hypothesis. They would not accept that language totally determines the way we think. However, many would agree that there is some truth in the idea that language *influences* our perception of the world, for example through its influence on our social values.

Language and social values

In recent years, much attention has been paid to the way that language is used to refer to minority groups. For example, there is more awareness now that some language is *sexist*. It is said that to an extent the existence of such language is simply a reflection of the way society is: some people have sexist attitudes, and that is why there is sexist language.

However, it is also argued that the existence of sexist language helps to perpetuate sexist attitudes. If a boy grows up learning that the male should always come first in expressions such as 'men and women', 'male and female', 'Dear Sir or Madam' and so on, he may unconsciously assume that this means men are more important. It follows that reducing the use of sexist words and expressions will help to change society's perception of women. This is what many feminists are trying to achieve.

Similar arguments apply to the language used to describe race and people with disabilities:

→ At its most obvious, racist language includes such derogatory terms as 'nigger', 'Frog', 'Paki' and so on. More subtle racism has been perceived in the contrasting associations that the words 'black' and 'white' have in English. 'White' usually has positive connotations: synonyms include 'pure', 'spotless' and 'unblemished'. 'Black' is used in such negative expressions as 'blackmail', 'black look' and 'black sheep'.
→ The vocabulary used to describe people with disabilities includes words that are now rarely used because of their negative connotations, such as 'cripple' and 'spastic'. Again, however, the negative representation can take a more subtle form, as in the expressions 'lame duck', 'blind stupidity' and 'deaf to reason'.

The term **linguistic engineering** is used for deliberate attempts to alter the language that people use. Racist language, for example, is discouraged by laws against its use and by guidelines concerning acceptable language within media organizations such as the BBC.

Links

Attempts have been made to make the language that refers to minority groups more positive. See the section 'Political correctness' (pages 108–9).

Checkpoint 1

Give examples of present-day language usage that seeks to avoid sexism.

Checkpoint 2

Often the derivation of these expressions is not racist, but it is claimed that their effect is to reinforce negative attitudes towards black people. Can you think of any other words or expressions that use 'black' in a negative way?

Exam question   answer: page 115

'The limits of my language are the limits of my world'. Discuss the implications of this statement and consider how far you agree with it. (45 min)

Sexism

'Sexism' means discrimination against others on the basis of their gender. Feminist writers have highlighted the presence of sexism in English vocabulary and grammar. They argue that the language we use not only reflects the fact that we live in a patriarchal (male-dominated) society but also helps to strengthen and perpetuate sexist attitudes, ensuring that they are passed on from generation to generation.

Vocabulary

Lexical asymmetry   Male words and their female equivalents are often unequal (asymmetrical) in their associations and connotations. Examples are 'spinster/bachelor', 'mistress/master', 'madam/sir'. 'Bachelor' denotes an unmarried male and 'spinster' an unmarried female, but the connotations of the words are very different. 'Bachelor', in collocations such as 'eligible bachelor' and 'bachelor pad', suggests someone who is youthful and has an enjoyable lifestyle. 'Spinster' suggests a sadder figure: someone who is older, and whose life is dull and unexciting.

Marked and unmarked terms   Terms for females are often marked by the addition of a suffix to the male term, which is unmarked: 'actor/actress', 'sculptor/sculptress', 'usher/usherette'. It is argued that this suggests male roles are more important because the standard, unmarked term is used to refer to them. A sign of changing attitudes is that marked terms are now less common (e.g. 'authoress' is almost unknown), though some (e.g. 'actress') remain in everyday use. A related issue is the existence of expressions such as 'lady doctor' or 'female lawyer', which seem to assume that such high-status positions are usually held by men.

Insulting usages   There are many negative words for females, often with no equivalents for males. Often these words compare women to animals ('cow', 'bitch', 'dog') and many have sexual associations: 'slut', 'slag', 'whore'. Words denoting sexual promiscuity in males tend to be more positive – 'stud', 'Casanova', 'Don Juan' – reflecting differing attitudes to the sexual behaviour of men and women.

Patronizing usages   Patronizing terms for women include 'babe', 'sweetheart', 'dear' and 'love', though these can also be applied to men. There are several words comparing women to food, suggesting perhaps an underlying attitude that one of the purposes of women is to provide men with pleasure: 'crumpet', 'tart', 'sweetie', 'honey'. Also relevant here is the *feminine inanimate.* This is the use of female pronouns (she, her) to refer to inanimate objects such as cars and ships. Such references are often affectionate but can also imply male ownership.

'Man'/'Mankind'   'Man' is sometimes used to refer specifically to males but on other occasions is used *generically* to refer to the whole human race (as in 'Man is a primate'). 'Mankind' is always a generic term. The use of 'man' and 'mankind' has been criticized because it implies that men are more important. 'Humankind' is an alternative that is increasingly used, but it has not yet replaced 'mankind'.

Example

Important feminist writers include Dale Spender (author of the influential study *Man Made Language*) and Deborah Cameron.

Checkpoint 1

Analyse the associations of *mistress/ master* and *madam/sir* in the same way.

Take note

The suffix *–ette* is additionally demeaning because it usually indicates a smaller, lesser version of something (e.g. 'kitchenette').

Example

Even expressions involving males can have this effect: 'male nurse' reinforces the idea that nurses are usually female.

Grammar

Generic 'he'   The masculine pronoun 'he' is used generically (i.e. to refer to both males and females), as in the sentence 'Anyone can choose not to vote in a general election if he wishes'. Use of the neutral plural pronoun 'they' in such constructions ('if they wish') was once common in English, but the grammarians of the 18th and 19th centuries condemned this as incorrect (on the grounds that 'anyone' is singular so must be followed by a singular pronoun). As with 'man' and 'mankind', it is argued that this use of 'he' reinforces ideas of male superiority. Alternatives include using 'he or she' (though placing the male first is also controversial – see below) or using a plural construction ('People can choose . . .').

Order of precedence   Placing the male word first in phrases suggests an assumption that men are of higher status: 'he or she', 'his and hers', 'sir or madam', 'male and female' and so on. Again, this convention was strengthened by the grammarians of previous centuries, who decreed that putting the male first was 'natural' and 'proper'.

Non-sexist usage

Increased awareness of sexism in society has resulted in determined attempts to avoid sexism in language. A few specific examples of this have been referred to above. Additional examples are discussed below:

Inclusive usages   Gender-specific words such as 'policeman', 'fireman' and 'headmaster/headmistress' have been replaced by neutral terms: 'police officer', 'firefighter', 'headteacher'. Guidelines are now issued to media journalists stipulating the use of such inclusive terms. 'Person' has replaced man in many compounds ('chairperson', 'spokesperson', etc.), though its use is sometimes ridiculed. Other alternatives to the generic use of 'man' include 'humankind' instead of 'mankind', 'manufactured' or 'synthetic' instead of 'man-made' and 'workforce' or 'staff' instead of 'manpower' (signs on the tollbooths at the entrance to the Mersey Tunnel once said 'Manned' but now say 'Staffed').

Use of Ms   This came into use because male and female titles are asymmetrical. 'Mrs' and 'Miss' reveal a woman's marital status, whereas 'Mr' does not. 'Mrs' is also followed by the husband's surname, suggesting that the male is the dominant partner in the marriage. 'Ms' is now in common use, but it has been argued that in practice it is not as neutral as 'Mr' because it leads many people to assume that the person is unmarried, divorced or a feminist.

Radical changes   Radical changes that have not been generally accepted include 'womyn/wimmin' (instead of 'woman/women'), 'herstory' (replacing 'history') and 'mistress copy' (for 'master copy').

The jargon

A **generic** term is a term that applies to all the members of a group.

Take note

Despite the strictures of the grammarians, 'they' – which in any case sounds quite natural to most people – is becoming increasingly acceptable.

Checkpoint 2

Apparent exceptions may, on closer inspection, provide further evidence of sexual inequality – e.g. 'mother and father' suggests that bringing up children is primarily the responsibility of the female parent. Can you think of other exceptions?

"The language and its use have to be changed; there is no alternative if one seeks to throw off one's oppression"

Dale Spender, *Man Made Language*

Examiner's secrets

Avoid simply giving a lengthy expression of your opinion. Include plenty of hard evidence – specific examples of language use – to support your case.

Exam question   answer: page 116

'The English language systematically degrades and devalues women'. Do you agree with this statement? (60 min)

Political correctness

'Political correctness' is a broad term used to describe the opinions and attitudes of those who are actively opposed to prejudice on such grounds as race, gender, sexual orientation and physical appearance. In terms of language, they also oppose vocabulary that reflects such prejudices. However, many people who hold these attitudes would not describe themselves as politically correct. This is because the term has acquired negative connotations (as explained below) and is now often associated with extremism, aggression and intolerance.

What is political correctness?

The earliest known use of the term 'political correctness' in print was in the United States in 1970.

The linguist Deborah Cameron, who has researched the history of the term, found that initially it was used ironically by left-wing activists and intellectuals to mock their own attitudes.

During the 1980s, left-wing radicals (especially in the United States) became increasingly concerned with the rights of minority groups and conducted campaigns against discrimination on such grounds as race, age, gender and sexual orientation. Right-wing opponents of these campaigns grouped them together under the disparaging label 'political correctness', and the term came to be associated with extreme, over-zealous attitudes.

It is now often said that it is only the opponents of political correctness who actually use the term. Those who hold 'politically correct' attitudes prefer not to use it because of its negative connotations.

Examples of political correctness

Although supporters of political correctness distance themselves from the term, it is undoubtedly the case that the radical campaigns and movements of the last 20 years have had a real impact on the language that we use. Words and phrases have been identified as sexist, racist, ageist, ableist (discriminating against those with disabilities) and heightist (discriminating on the basis of height, especially against those who are short). Alternatives have been proposed and in many cases are now in general (if not universal) use. Some examples of politically correct and incorrect usage are shown below.

Incorrect	Eskimo	'Eskimo' is considered offensive because
Correct	Inuit	it is possibly derived from an Indian word meaning 'eaters of raw flesh'.
Incorrect	Spastics Society	The Spastics Society changed its
Correct	SCOPE	name in 1994.
Incorrect	Unemployed	'Unwaged' is sometimes preferred
Correct	Unwaged	because not being in paid employment does not necessarily mean that time is not usefully employed.
Incorrect	Christian name	'Christian name' is considered offensive
Correct	First name	to non-Christians.

Links

The section 'Sexism' (pages 106–7) is also relevant to this topic.

The jargon

As well as 'political correctness', other terms in common use are 'politically incorrect' and the abbreviations 'PC' and 'non-PC'.

"The phrase 'political correctness' encapsulates all the dogmatic, puritanical and narrow-minded arrogance that has made people distrust revolutionary politics from Robespierre onwards"

David Lodge

Checkpoint 1

Why do you think the Spastics Society changed its name to SCOPE?

Action point

Find examples of your own to add to this list.

Arguments in favour of political correctness ●●●

Supporters of political correctness argue that much of the language they oppose is offensive and demeaning. In contrast, referring to minority groups in more positive terms encourages them to feel respected and accepted by the rest of society.

Another argument relates to the theory that the language we learn to use influences the way we perceive the world. If the vocabulary we acquire as children encourages us to think of certain minority groups as inferior, we are more likely to view them in this way. It follows that changing the language that people use should change their perceptions: using more positive vocabulary to describe minorities will mean people start to view them more positively.

Criticisms of political correctness ●●●

Opponents of political correctness argue that seeking to control the language we use comes dangerously close to trying to control the way that we think. They regard those who campaign against politically incorrect language as dictatorial and intolerant.

Others who are sympathetic to the causes of political correctness argue that focusing on language is a distraction from the real struggle, which should be directed towards more practical goals, such as tougher laws against discrimination and increased investment to help the disadvantaged. They argue that language reflects social attitudes, and that if attitudes do not change in society the new 'positive' vocabulary will soon acquire the same negative connotations as the old.

Political correctness is often ridiculed through the use of humour. Bizarre, outlandish expressions are invented to satirize the new vocabulary of political correctness: 'boring' becomes 'differently interesting'; 'bald' becomes 'hair disadvantaged'; 'false teeth' become 'alternative dentition'. Stories deriding the excesses of political correctness regularly appear in the press. In the 1980s, it was reported that the left-wing leadership of the Greater London Council had banned references to 'black coffee' in the council cafeteria because 'black' was a racist word; 'coffee without milk' was to be used instead (in fact the story was completely untrue).

Checkpoint 2

Do you know the name given to the theory which suggests that the language we use determines how we think?

"Words make a difference but what is more important is the work ahead to end discrimination"

Ann Robinson, Chief Executive SCOPE (formerly the Spastics Society)

Exam question   answer: page 116

Explain the motives of those who have sought to make language more 'politically correct' and consider the extent to which they have been successful. (45 min)

Examiner's secrets

Remember to include plenty of examples, and try to draw them from a range of areas (e.g. race, gender, disability).

Taboo language

'Taboo language' refers to words that are avoided because they are considered offensive, embarrassing, obscene or unpleasant. Here we look at the nature of taboo language and at the ways language can be manipulated to avoid the use of taboo expressions (e.g. by the use of **euphemisms**).

What is taboo language?

Taboo derives from a Tongan word referring to behaviour that is forbidden; originally the word had religious connotations. We use 'taboo language' to refer to words that we avoid using, either because we find them offensive or because we do not wish to offend others. Certain vocabulary relating to sex, sexual organs and bodily functions is especially strongly condemned: it is described as *swearing* and involves the use of bad language, foul language or four-letter words.

Occasionally, the use of taboo language is prevented by laws and regulations (e.g. every national newspaper will have a policy regarding words it is prepared to print and words it is not). Generally, however, it is a matter of *social custom*: attitudes within society (or within particular social groups) will determine which words are considered unacceptable.

Taboo language is strongly associated with certain subjects, such as sex, religion, bodily functions, illness and death. Because these are socially sensitive subjects, and discussion of them can sometimes cause embarrassment or offence, it is not surprising that there is also sensitivity regarding the language used to refer to them.

Often the *situation* influences whether a word is taboo or not. The word 'died' is in everyday use, but if we were referring to the recent death of someone close to us we might prefer to use 'passed away'.

Avoidance of taboo language

Various linguistic strategies are used to avoid taboo language:

→ Part of the word may be omitted and replaced by dashes or asterisks (as in 'f**k'). The Jewish religion forbids the use of 'God' in writing or print; it is replaced by 'G–d'.
→ A taboo word may be referred to by its initial letter only, as in 'the f-word'. Use of this device has broadened, and it is now often used humorously to refer to words that the speaker is reluctant to mention.
→ The form of the taboo word may be changed, so that it becomes inoffensive. Usually, the initial sound of the word is retained: 'Shit!' becomes 'Sugar!'
→ Most importantly, euphemisms are used.

Euphemisms

A **euphemism** is a mild or indirect expression used instead of one that is considered in some way offensive, painful or unpleasant. An example

Checkpoint 1

Can you think of any other laws or regulations that prohibit the use of certain language?

Take note

Many people will happily swear when with close friends but will avoid such language in the presence of strangers.

Example

There is a longstanding superstition in the acting profession that forbids reference to Shakespeare's *Macbeth* by the play's title. Instead, it is known as 'the Scottish play'.

Example

Some of these amended expressions are so much part of the language that their derivation has been forgotten: 'Crikey!' and 'Cripes!' are inoffensive versions of 'Christ!'

referred to earlier is 'passed away' for 'died'. Others with the same meaning include 'passed on', 'passed over', 'left us' and 'no longer with us'. Some euphemisms take the form of **slang** expressions, as in 'point Percy at the porcelain' for 'urinate'. Others are much more formal, as when 'perspire' is used instead of 'sweat'.

Businesses, governments and local authorities have made increasing use of euphemisms in recent years: the local rubbish tip is now a 'waste reception centre', late trains are caused by 'operating difficulties'. Often this entails the use of **jargon**. This kind of 'official' euphemism has been much criticized on the grounds that it can be used to disguise the reality of what is being described. The language of modern warfare is often cited as an example: 'precision bombs' are used to make 'surgical strikes' (implying clean, clinical efficiency), and the enemy is 'neutralized' or 'terminated' rather than 'killed'.

Links

For more on slang, see pages 100–1.

Links

Jargon is discussed on pages 98–9.

Reasons for using taboo language ●●●

So far, we have focused on the reasons for avoiding taboo language, and the ways of achieving this. In practice, taboo expressions are in regular use – if they were not, they would disappear from the language. Some reasons for using taboo language are outlined below:

→ Using taboo language challenges society's norms and conventions. It may be an expression of defiance or rebellion (e.g. a teenager swearing at an authority figure), or an attempt to change society's attitudes (in the past, writers have deliberately included obscenities in their work to challenge censorship laws).
→ Swear words provide an emotional outlet and are often used to give vent to strong feelings of rage or frustration.
→ Covert prestige may be acquired through swearing. If other members of a social group swear, using language in a similar way expresses solidarity with them.

Checkpoint 2

What is meant by 'covert prestige'?

Attitudes to taboo language ●●●

Taboo language is a reflection of society's attitudes and values. As these change over time, so too do our ideas about acceptable and unacceptable language. In some respects, attitudes towards taboo vocabulary are now more relaxed. Four-letter words appear more frequently in print and are heard more often on television. At the same time, 'official' euphemisms (see above) have increased in number. The rise of political correctness has also created a new taboo vocabulary: words that were once in common use are now avoided because they are thought to discriminate against minorities (e.g. they may be considered racist or sexist).

Links

Political correctness is discussed on pages 108–9.

Exam question   answer: page 116

Taboo words occur in most languages. Why do you think this is? Illustrate your answer with examples of English taboo language. (45 min)

111

Language and education

Standards of literacy among pupils and school leavers are the subject of intense public debate, with continual complaints in the media about poor spelling and ignorance of grammar. Educationalists point to improving examination results as evidence that standards are in fact rising. Recent governments have paid close attention to the teaching of English, and the past 15 years have seen the introduction of the National Curriculum, the Literacy Hour in primary schools and regular National Tests in English. Here we look at some of the controversies surrounding **language and education**.

Language, education and social class ●●●

Working-class children achieve less success in education than children from middle-class families. At school their examination results tend to be poorer, and fewer of them go on to higher education. Research has shown that our language is affected by the social class we belong to, so attempts have been made to discover if there is a link between language, class and educational achievement. Does the language that working-class children use reduce their chances of success, and does the language of middle-class children work to their advantage?

In addressing this question, **deprivation theories** argue that working-class children are disadvantaged by their language; they learn to use language in ways that make educational achievement difficult. **Difference theories** tend to place the blame on the educational system, which is seen as unsympathetic to working-class culture and negative in its attitude towards the language of working-class pupils.

Bernstein's restricted and elaborated codes ●●●

Bernstein's influential theory identifies two types of language, the restricted code and the elaborated code. He argues that our environment (specifically, the social groups to which we belong) determines which kind of language we use.

→ Characteristics of the **restricted code** include short, simple and sometimes incomplete sentences; repetition of a limited range of conjunctions; limited use of adjectives and adverbs; frequent use of idioms; reliance on implicit meaning (meanings are implied or understood rather than openly expressed or explained).
→ Characteristics of the **elaborated code** include more complex, grammatically complete sentences; a wider range of conjunctions, adjectives and adverbs; more explicit meanings.

Bernstein says that all of us are able to use the restricted code. We use it in informal situations and when communicating with close family members and friends. However, the elaborated code, according to Bernstein, is not generally used by lower working-class adults and their children, so that working-class children are at a disadvantage when they attend school, as education makes extensive use of the elaborated code.

Links

The relationship between language and social class is discussed on pages 92–3.

Checkpoint 1

Is Bernstein's theory a deprivation theory or a difference theory?

Checkpoint 2

What are idioms?

Example

Bernstein's theory suggests that working-class pupils have more difficulty working with abstract ideas and concepts.

Criticisms of Bernstein

Bernstein's ideas are controversial and are rejected by some linguists. In particular, his research methods have been questioned. Although he has conducted experiments, it is said that there is only limited evidence to support his ideas. Another criticism is that while the linguistic differences between working-class and middle-class children that he identifies may be a real and valuable discovery, the effects that these differences have on educational performance are harder to assess.

The Standard English debate

A related controversy concerns Standard English and its place in the school curriculum.

An argument associated with John Honey and others is that for many years teachers have neglected the teaching of Standard English. Honey argues that the reason for this is that within educational circles there is the mistaken belief that all dialects are equal and that Standard English should therefore not be given preference over the regional dialects that children hear and learn outside school.

Honey maintains that working-class children (who are less likely to use Standard English than the children of middle-class families) should be taught that Standard English *is* a superior dialect in many situations. He says that encouraging them to continue using their own local dialects will disadvantage them in later life.

Honey's opponents mostly accept that Standard English is appropriate in more formal situations and in many types of written English. However, they reject the notion that Standard English should be regarded as superior to other dialects and are much keener than Honey for regional dialects to be respected and maintained.

English in the National Curriculum

The National Curriculum for England and Wales was introduced in 1987. It identifies English as one of the three core subjects (the others are maths and science) and gives clear guidelines as to how the subject should be taught. Standard English is identified as 'the language of public communication', and its importance is stressed. However, the 'richness' and 'integrity' of non-standard dialects are also acknowledged. Nevertheless, some critics argue that the National Curriculum places too much emphasis on Standard English, and that this emphasis implicitly devalues regional accents and dialects.

> *"nothing more effectively condemns an individual to his class or ethnic ghetto than an inability to communicate clearly and logically in English"*
>
> John Honey

> *"Linguists are agreed that no variety of a language is inherently better than any other"*
>
> Ronald Wardhaugh

Take note

Subsequent documents and reports (e.g. the National Literacy Strategy in 1998) have added to these guidelines.

Examiner's secrets

In a question such as this, you should show an awareness of both sides of the argument. Try to identify strengths and weaknesses in each of the opposing viewpoints.

Exam question　　　　　　　　answer: page 116

Should schools promote Standard English, their pupils' native dialects or both? (45 min)

Answers
Social aspects of language

Accents and dialects 1

Checkpoints

1 The experiment confirms that people tend to regard RP speakers as having authority and intelligence. However, compared with speakers with certain other accents, they are not seen as being as persuasive or trustworthy.
2 Urban environments have a less positive image and may be associated with crime, pollution, industry, etc. This helps to explain why urban accents tend to be regarded less favourably.

Exam question

Research has certainly suggested that the accents that speakers have cause others to make assumptions about them. An answer should explain what these assumptions are, referring to particular accents and the specific characteristics that are associated with them. The argument should be supported with references to research findings and to other relevant evidence, such as the use made of particular accents by commercial organizations (e.g. call centres) and the mass media.

Accents and dialects 2

Checkpoints

1 The opposite of convergence is *divergence*. See page 50.
2 No, because new words are entering the language all the time. The decline is in *regional differences* in the language that we use.

Exam question

This is an interesting question, and a variety of opinions could be expressed in answering it. What you must be careful to avoid is a loose, generalized discussion. It would be logical to begin with clear, precise definitions of estuary English and RP. Each accent could then be examined in turn, focusing on present-day attitudes and possible future trends. It might plausibly be argued that Estuary English is likely to become the country's most influential accent in that it will be the accent spoken by the largest number of people in positions of public prominence. However, as a socially prestigious accent associated with upper-class speakers, it is at present a long way from overtaking RP.

Pidgins and creoles; British black English

Checkpoint

1 Because creoles serve the same range of functions as other fully fledged languages, they are more developed than pidgins. As a pidgin undergoes creolization, grammatical forms become more complex and vocabulary increases.
2 There is a strong parallel. In the past, there has been a tendency to regard regional accents and dialects as inferior to Received Pronunciation and Standard English, though this view is much less prevalent today. See pages 112–13.

Exam question

Creole English has several features that distinguish it from Standard English (an answer should give examples). The traditional regard for Standard English as a prestigious variety can cause other varieties to be regarded as inferior (as mentioned above, there is a parallel here with regional dialects). However, creoles have their own rules and structures and, viewed linguistically, are not inferior to other varieties. They also have an important role as an expression of personal and national identity.

Language and social class

Checkpoints

1 The tasks correspond to different levels of formality. Reading aloud is quite a formal task, and speakers might be expected to be more conscious of their own speech. Telling stories about themselves is a less formal task, and researchers hope that speakers will be more natural and unselfconscious. Giving respondents a variety of tasks helps researchers to gauge the effect that setting and context has on speech.
2 Grammatical features that might reflect the social class of the speaker include the use of double negatives and of non-standard past tense forms (e.g. 'I seen that film last week'). A phonological feature is the pronunciation of *th* sounds as *f* ('fink' instead of 'think').

Exam question

In answering this question, you need to show a knowledge of specific research findings. Some of the ways that phonological and grammatical aspects of language use might be influenced by social class can be explained with reference to Trudgill, Labov and other researchers.

Male and female language use

Checkpoints

1 The main additional factor likely to be an influence here is social class (see previous section). Certain features may also reflect regional differences or age variation.
2 The main alternative explanation is that women are more sympathetic and more supportive than men in conversational interaction. See pages 54–5.

Exam question

The two parts of the question offer a ready-made plan for an answer. In tackling the first part, you should identify relevant researchers and should also be specific about the linguistic differences between men and women that have been found to exist. The use of language in conversational interaction (see pages 54–5) can be included. In answering the second part, you should show an awareness that alternative explanations of male and female differences have been offered.

Occupational dialects

Checkpoints

1 Football is an obvious example: 'goal', 'penalty', 'free kick', 'corner', 'pass', 'defender', 'attacker', 'midfield', 'cross', 'foul', 'tackle', 'offside', 'touch line'.
2 A *hypernym* is a general word, while *hyponyms* are more specific. A single hypernym will usually have several hyponyms. The word 'vehicle' is a hypernym because it is a general word referring to many different forms of transport. Words that refer to specific types of vehicle are hyponyms: 'moped', 'motor car', 'agricultural tractor'.

Exam question

Several of the features commonly associated with legal language are present in this extract, including archaisms ('hereof', 'thereunder'); formal vocabulary ('in respect of', 'attributable'); long, complex sentences (in fact the extract is one continuous sentence); repetition ('person or persons', 'the relevant liability', 'costs', 'judgement').

Jargon

Checkpoints

1 The term is *sociolect*. See page 32.
2 Additional examples include car mechanics, builders, computer retailers, etc.

Exam questions

1 There may be an occupational group of which you have close personal knowledge. Alternatively, you may study the language of one or two specific occupations as part of your A-level course (the way language is used by a particular occupational group is a good topic for a coursework language investigation). Remember to discuss *purposes* as well as language features. The points made on page 98 about positive and negative uses of jargon may be of some help here. The previous section on occupational dialects (pages 96–7) is also relevant to this question.
2 The negative connotations of the word 'jargon' can be traced back to its French origins. An answer should recognize that the term is now not only used negatively and should include specific examples to support the points made.

Slang

Checkpoint

Clippings occur when words are shortened. Examples include 'doc' (for 'doctor') and 'deffo' (for 'definitely').

Exam question

Slang is a difficult word to define, and you should be careful not to begin an answer with a vague, imprecise or incomplete definition. Instead, it would be better to acknowledge the difficulty, then try (as the question suggests) to identify slang's main characteristics. *How* slang is used and *why* it is used are difficult to separate, and you might well discuss them together: explaining the purposes of slang inevitably entails examining how people use it. Your points should be regularly supported with examples of slang words and expressions.

Language and power

Checkpoints

1 The use of titles for older relatives recognizes their seniority within the family.
2 This movement has occurred because in many areas of life there is now greater informality and social equality.

Exam question

The power that the police officer clearly believes he has over Dr Pouissant comes from two sources. First, he is a police officer (power deriving from occupational status), and second, he is white and Dr Pouissant is black (power deriving from the dominance of one racial group over another). Dr Pouissant also has occupational status and tries to assert this when he says 'I'm a physician'. However, the conversation does not take place in a medical context, and his occupational status is not recognized by the police officer. The conversation is controlled by the police officer, who asks questions in an abrupt, intimidating manner. He uses the derogatory term 'boy' – in the past, this was commonly used by whites towards blacks in the American south – and demands to know Dr Pouissant's name. The reply 'Dr Pouissant' is given, but the police officer refuses to accept this form of address and repeats the question in a modified form, asking for Dr Pouissant's 'first name'. The more powerful person in a relationship will often address a subordinate by his first name, when the reverse would not be true. In the southern United States, this pattern of address forms was once common between whites and blacks. Dr Pouissant capitulates and replies 'Alvin'.

Representation

Checkpoints

1 Attempts to avoid sexism in language are discussed in the next section (pages 106–7). Examples include the use of gender-neutral terms such as 'firefighter' (for 'fireman') and 'police officer' (for 'policeman').
2 Other examples include 'black spot', 'blacklist', 'black mark'.

Exam question

This question expresses the view, associated with the Sapir–Whorf hypothesis, that our perception of the world is controlled and limited by the language that we use. An appropriate response would be to explain the Sapir–Whorf hypothesis and then consider its strengths and weaknesses.

Sexism

Checkpoints

1 'Mistress' has sexual connotations and usually means a married man's illicit girlfriend. 'Master' usually has connotations of dominance and superiority. 'Sir' and 'madam' can both be used respectfully, but 'madam' again sometimes has sexual connotations and can refer to a woman who runs a brothel. It can also be used as a derogatory term for a woman who is considered pushy and assertive.

2 'Aunt and uncle' is another exception, along with 'nan and granddad'. This seems to correspond to the pattern of 'mother and father', suggesting that the responsibility for showing affection to younger relatives rests primarily with female family members.

Exam question

An answer to this question might look separately at vocabulary and grammar. The argument that language is now becoming less sexist should also be considered.

Political correctness

Checkpoints

1 'Spastic' had become a term of abuse. SCOPE was chosen as the new name because it was thought to be 'optimistic and engaging'.

2 This theory is known as the Sapir–Whorf hypothesis. See page 104.

Exam question

In answering the second part of the question ('consider the extent to which they have been successful'), it is important to include examples of politically correct usages that have either gained or not gained acceptance. The criticisms made of political correctness (including the ridiculing of some politically correct expressions) could also be discussed here.

Taboo language

Checkpoints

1 The use of abusive or insulting language that is likely to incite racial hatred is against the law.

2 *Covert prestige* is the prestige that derives from acting in ways that defy the norms of conventional, 'respectable' society. See page 95.

Exam question

Reasons for both the avoidance of taboo words and the use of them are relevant to this question.

Language and education

Checkpoints

1 Bernstein's theory is a deprivation theory, as it argues that the language of working-class children places them at a disadvantage when they attend school.

2 Idioms are everyday, colloquial expressions whose meanings cannot be derived from the literal meanings of the words that they contain. See page 18.

Exam question

Most linguists would say 'both', arguing that regional dialects should certainly be respected and kept alive, but that knowledge of Standard English is also essential. An effective answer would express a view but also show an awareness of the range of opinions on this issue.

Children's acquisition of language

Children's acquisition of language is an especially interesting topic and is often chosen by students as the focus for a coursework language investigation. In studying how children's use of language develops, you need to be aware of the main stages that they pass through and also of the different kinds of development that occur. A child has to acquire not only vocabulary (lexical and semantic development) but also a knowledge of *phonology*, *grammar* and *pragmatics* (the way language is used in social situations). As well as having an understanding of how a child's use of language changes during the early years of its life, you need to be aware of the main theories that seek to explain the processes involved in language acquisition. In addition, this chapter considers how children learn to read and write, and the ways that adults speak to children (including the influence that this has on their language development).

Exam themes

→ Stages in language acquisition.

→ Types of language development.

→ Theories of language development.

Topic checklist

O AS ● A2	AQA/A	AQA/B	EDEXCEL	OCR
Beginnings of language development	O	●	●	O
Phonological development	O	●	●	O
Lexical and semantic development	O	●	●	O
Grammatical development 1	O	●	●	O
Grammatical development 2	O	●	●	O
Pragmatic development	O	●	●	O
Theories of language acquisition 1	O	●	●	O
Theories of language acquisition 2	O	●	●	O
How adults speak to children	O	●	●	O
Learning to read and write	O	●	●	O
Specimen texts	O	●	●	O

* WJEC does not include this topic area.

Beginnings of language development

In this section, we look at the earliest stages of language development – from birth to a child uttering its first word, which usually happens when the child is about a year old.

Stages of development ●●●

Children all around the world seem to acquire language by passing through a similar set of *stages*. The time taken to move from one stage to the next can vary from child to child, but the stages themselves and the order in which they are negotiated appear to be universal: the same pattern of development applies regardless of the language being acquired.

Before birth

It is possible that even before birth a baby has started to become acclimatized to the sounds of its native language. Research by Mehler and others (1988) found that French babies as young as four days old were able to distinguish French from other languages. When they were exposed to French, they sucked on dummies more strongly – a sign of increased interest – than when they listened to English or Italian. The research suggests that while in the womb babies become used to the rhythms and intonation of the language being spoken around them.

Crying

During the first few weeks of life, the child expresses itself vocally through crying. Different kinds of cry can be identified – signalling hunger, for example, or distress or pleasure – and research has found that English parents can interpret the cries of foreign babies as readily as they can those of English babies. This suggests that the cries are instinctive noises, and as such they cannot really be considered a 'language'.

Cooing

Cooing (also known as gurgling or mewing) is another universal development and generally occurs when babies are around six to eight weeks old. They make sounds such as 'coo', 'goo' and 'ga-ga'. It is thought that during this phase the child is developing increased control over its vocal cords.

Babbling

Babbling is the most important stage during the first year of a child's life. It usually begins when the child is aged between six and nine months and often continues for some months after the child has started to use actual speech. At the onset of babbling, the baby begins to make sounds that more closely resemble those of adult language.

Combinations of consonants and vowels are produced, such as 'ba', 'ma', 'ga', 'da'. Sometimes these sounds are repeated, producing what is known as **reduplicated monosyllables** (e.g. 'baba', 'mama'). Such sounds still have no meaning, but parents are often eager to believe that their baby is speaking its first words.

Don't forget

Children do not develop at the same pace. Children of six months, nine months or any other age will often differ markedly from each other.

Watch out!

Make sure you always put these stages in the correct sequence.

Example

Such eagerness is reflected in the fact that words resembling 'mama', 'papa' and 'dada' are used the world over to mean mother and father.

The typical baby makes more noises during this period than previously, and evidently enjoys exercising its mouth and tongue. As well as babbling, it is likely to blow bubbles and splutter.

Phonemic expansion and contraction

During the babbling phase, the number of different phonemes produced by the child increases initially. This is known as **phonemic expansion**. Later (usually by the age of about nine or ten months) a reduction in the number of phonemes (**phonemic contraction**) begins to occur. The range of sounds made by the child shrinks, becoming increasingly restricted to those of the child's native tongue. In other words, the baby retains the sounds of its native language but suppresses or discards those sounds that will not be needed.

We know that this happens because the noises made by children of different nationalities begin to sound different from each other. In experiments, adults asked to listen to babies of different nationalities have successfully picked out the babies from their own countries.

Intonation and gesture

Another development during the babbling stage is that the patterns of intonation begin to resemble speech. Often, there is a rising tone at the end of an utterance, as if the child were asking a question. Other variations of emphasis or rhythm may suggest greeting or calling. Researchers have also noted during this phase that children, although they do not have the power of speech, show through their gestures a desire to communicate. They may, for example, point to an object and look at an adult with a facial expression that seems to say, 'What's that?' or 'Look at that'.

Understanding ●●●

Although the child may not yet have begun to speak, this does not mean that he or she does not understand the meaning of certain words. Signs of word recognition are usually very evident by the end of the first year. Words that are likely to be recognized include names of family members, basic responses such as 'No' and words relating to familiar situations or experiences (e.g. 'Bye-bye').

The first word ●●●

A child is usually about a year old when it speaks its first recognizable word. This, and some of the later stages in language acquisition, will be discussed in the next few pages. We shall focus on four specific aspects of linguistic development: *phonology*; *lexis and semantics*; *grammar* and *pragmatics*.

Checkpoint 1

What is a **phoneme**?

Checkpoint 2

What term is used for the kind of development that involves learning to interact with others?

Take note

A feature common to several stages of language acquisition is that children demonstrate an ability to understand language used by others before they begin to use the same language themselves.

Exam question   answer: page 140

'A child spends the first year of its life preparing to speak'. Discuss early language development in children in the light of this comment. (45 min)

Phonological development

In this section, we consider the **phonological** aspects of language acquisition – that is, how children develop the ability to use and understand the *sounds* of language.

The first year

Along with other aspects of early language acquisition, the phonological development that occurs during the first year of a child's life was outlined in the previous section (pages 118–19).

Trends in phonological development

It is impossible to be precise about later **phonological development** because the order in which vowels and consonants are acquired can vary from child to child. When a sound has apparently been mastered, it may be used only in the pronunciation of certain words and may be missing or pronounced incorrectly in others. Moreover, a child will often pronounce the same word in a variety of ways before using the correct pronunciation regularly. However, researchers have identified certain general trends, and some of these are listed below:

→ Command of all the vowels is achieved before command of all the consonants. By the age of two and a half, the average child has mastered all of the vowels and around two-thirds of consonants. At four, the child is likely to be having difficulty with only a few consonants, but it may be six or seven before confidence in the use of all of them has been acquired.
→ Consonants are first used correctly at the beginnings of words; consonants at the ends of words present more difficulty. For example, a child will find the *p* and *b* sounds in 'push' and 'bush' easier to pronounce than those in 'rip' and 'rib'.
→ In general, sounds that occur frequently in a large number of words will be acquired before sounds that occur less frequently.
→ To make words easier to say, children *simplify* their pronunciation in certain ways (see below).

Simplification: deletion

Children will often simplify pronunciation by **deleting** certain sounds:

→ Final consonants may be dropped (e.g. the *t* sound in 'hat' and 'cat').
→ Unstressed syllables are often deleted (e.g. 'banana' becomes 'nana').
→ Consonant clusters are reduced (e.g. 'snake' becomes 'nake', 'sleep' becomes 'seep').

Simplification: substitution

Another form of simplification involves **substituting** easier sounds for harder ones. Common examples include:

r (as in 'rock' or 'story') becomes *w*
th (as in 'there', 'that' or 'thumb') becomes *d*, *n* or *f*
t (as in 'toe') becomes *d*
p (as in 'pig') becomes *b*

Links

See 'Beginnings of language development' on pages 118–19.

Watch out!

Be careful about making sweeping generalizations when writing about language acquisition. Show that you are aware that no two children develop in exactly the same way.

Checkpoint 1

What is a **consonant cluster**?

Reduplication of sounds is another common phenomenon. This occurs when different sounds in a word are pronounced in the same way (e.g. 'dog' becomes 'gog').

Understanding ●●●

Comprehension of phonological patterns and the meanings they represent develops more quickly than the child's ability to reproduce them. Berko and Brown (1960) described how a child referred to his plastic fish as a 'fis'. When the observer responded, 'This is your *fis*?' the child said, 'No – my *fis*.' He continued to reject the adult's mimicry of his speech until he was told, 'This is your *fish*.' He then replied, 'Yes, my *fis*.' In another study, a child whose pronunciation of 'mouse/mouth', 'cart/card' and 'jug/duck' were indistinguishable could nevertheless point to pictures of the objects in a comprehension task.

Links

There is a link here with other aspects of language acquisition: comprehension is often ahead of speech (e.g. see page 119).

Intonation ●●●

As explained in the previous section (page 119), children seem to be consciously altering the tone and rhythm of their voices before they can speak. A range of messages is conveyed in this way (e.g. questions, demands, greetings and feelings of surprise or pleasure).

As the child grows older, a wider range of meanings is expressed through intonation. When the child is producing two-word utterances, emphasis is used to alter meaning: the straightforward statement 'my car' becomes 'MY car' when the child's ownership of the toy seems to be under threat.

Links

Two-word utterances are discussed on page 124.

Although children are able to reproduce the main patterns of intonation from quite an early age, understanding of their meaning is apparently still developing as they enter their teens. In an interesting study (Cruttenden 1974), adults and children listened to a recording of a set of football results (e.g. 'Tottenham Hotspur 3, Arsenal 1'). The intonation used in announcing the first team's score enabled the adults to predict accurately whether the result was a home win, an away win or a draw. However, among children aged 7 to 11, the youngest achieved very little success at all and even the oldest were significantly less successful than the adults had been.

Checkpoint 2

Can you think of any other factors that might help to explain the results of this experiment?

Examiner's secrets

As previous sections have explained, this is an important general principle of language acquisition: there is usually a significant gap between understanding and being able to express this understanding in speech.

Exam question   answer: page 140

'Children's understanding of the sounds of English and their ability to make these sounds in a confident, meaningful way do not always develop at the same rate'. Explain what you understand by this, supporting your argument with appropriate examples. (45 min)

Lexical and semantic development

This section focuses on a child's acquisition of words (**lexical development**) and word meanings (**semantic development**).

How fast do children acquire vocabulary? ●●●

The average child begins speaking at the end of its first year and by the age of 18 months has a vocabulary of about 50 words. By the age of two, a child usually has command of about 200 words.

After this, there is a remarkable explosion in the child's vocabulary. Figures can only be very rough estimates, but it has been said that an average child is using around 2 000 words by the age of five, and twice as many as this at seven.

All of these figures refer to words actively *used* by the child. The number of words that are *understood* is higher at each stage – e.g. it has been estimated that at 18 months a child understands about 250 words, five times as many as it uses.

When a word is added to a child's vocabulary, the child is not aware immediately of the word's full range of meanings. Further time is needed to acquire this additional knowledge.

First words ●●●

Studies have shown that there are predictable patterns in the words and types of words first acquired by children. The table below shows some typical words used by a child of 18 months.

Entities
Names for people: *daddy, mummy*, etc.
Words referring to

Food	*drink, juice, milk, water, toast, apple, cake*		
Humans	*baby*	Animals	*dog, cat, duck, horse*
Clothes	*shoes, hat*	Toys	*ball, doll, blocks*
Vehicles	*car, boat, truck*	Other	*bottle, key, book*

Properties   *hot, allgone, more, dirty, cold, here, there*
Actions   *up, sit, see, eat, go, down*
Personal – social   *hello, bye, no, yes, please, thank-you*

Source: *Contemporary Linguistics* by W. O. Grady *et al.* (1996).

A large proportion of a child's first words refer to people (*mummy, daddy*), familiar objects (*shoes, ball*) and social interaction (*hello, bye*).

Nouns make up the largest class of words, followed by verbs, then adjectives. Nouns are *concrete* rather than *abstract*. It is only later, usually between the ages of five and seven, that a child begins using more general, abstract nouns.

The first verbs that the child uses are action words such as 'go' and 'eat'.

Noticeably absent are words that serve only a grammatical function, even though these are very frequent in adult language (e.g. 'the', 'of', 'to').

Watch out!

Never suggest that the acquisition of vocabulary 'ends' at a certain age. We continue hearing and learning new words throughout our lives.

Checkpoint 1

Explain the difference between **concrete** and **abstract** nouns.

Checkpoint 2

Why do you think function words such as 'the' and 'of' are not acquired until later?

Underextension

Underextension is a common semantic error made by children. It occurs when a word is given a narrower meaning than it has in adult language. An example is using the word 'cat' for the family pet but not applying it to other cats.

Overextension

Overextension, the opposite of underextension, is also a feature of children's early language. This occurs when a word is given a broader, more general meaning than it should have.

Common examples include using the word 'daddy' not just for the child's father but for other men as well, and using 'dog' to refer to other four-legged animals (cows, horses, etc.).

Overextension occurs more frequently than underextension and is the main semantic error made by young children (when a child has a vocabulary of 50 words, it is estimated that about a third of these are likely to be overextended).

As the child's vocabulary grows, the meanings of overextended words narrow and the meanings of underextended words broaden. There is a marked decrease in the number of overextensions after the age of about two and a half, because the child's vocabulary is increasing rapidly and plugging the gaps that overextended words had previously been used to fill (e.g. the child now knows the names given to apples, tomatoes and cherries and doesn't refer to them all as 'apples').

Children's understanding of word meanings is ahead of their ability to produce the corresponding words. For example, a child who overextends the word 'dog' when speaking may identify the correct picture when shown pictures of a variety of four-legged animals and asked to point to the one that shows a dog.

Labelling, packaging and network building

Aitchison (1987) identified three stages or processes that occur during a child's acquisition of vocabulary: labelling, packaging and network building.

1   **Labelling** is the first stage and involves making the link between the sounds of particular words and the objects to which they refer (e.g. understanding that 'mummy' refers to the child's mother).
2   **Packaging** entails understanding a word's range of meaning. Underextension and overextension (see above) occur before this stage is successfully negotiated.
3   **Network building** involves grasping the connections between words: understanding that some words are opposite in meaning, for example, and understanding the relationship between *hypernyms* and *hyponyms*.

Exam question   answer: page 140

Exam question

Explain some of the difficulties that a typical child might encounter in the acquisition of vocabulary, from the time it speaks its first words up to the age of seven. (45 min)

Action point

Do you have a younger brother or sister (or other relative) whose vocabulary includes words that are overextended, or underextended? Any such words will give you more examples to include in answers.

Examiner's secrets

Try to relate your points to approximate ages, and support them with specific examples of the kinds of words that the child might use.

Grammatical development 1

This first section on grammatical development is primarily concerned with **syntax** – that is, the development of a child's ability to create grammatical constructions by arranging words in an appropriate order.

One-word stage

The average child is about a year old when it speaks its first words.

Roughly between the ages of a year and 18 months, the child speaks in single-word utterances ('milk', 'mummy', 'cup' and so on). In the development of language, this is known as the **one-word stage**. Occasionally more than one word may appear to be involved, but this is usually because a group of words has been learned as a single unit (e.g. 'allgone').

In many situations, the words the child uses simply serve a naming function, as when a parent points to a picture of a ball in a book and the child says 'ball'. Sometimes, however, single words convey more complex messages. Words used in this way are termed **holophrases**.

For example, the word 'juice' may be used to mean 'I want some juice', 'I want more juice' or 'I've spilt some juice'. The situation and the child's use of gestures and intonation enable the parent to understand what the child means. On these occasions, single words are in effect taking the place of more complex grammatical constructions, which the child has not yet mastered.

Although its own utterances are limited, the child's *understanding* of syntax is more advanced. Children show this to be the case because they respond to two-word instructions such as 'kiss daddy' and also understand more unusual requests (e.g. 'tickle book').

Two-word stage

Two-word sentences usually begin to appear when the child is about 18 months old, though single words will continue to be used for some months after this. This is the **two-word stage**.

The two words are usually in a grammatically correct sequence, often subject + verb (e.g. 'Jenny is sleeping' becomes 'Jenny sleep'). Other common constructions include:

Verb + object ('Draw doggie').
Subject + object ('Suzy juice', meaning 'Suzy is drinking juice').
Subject + complement ('Daddy busy').

When a child tries to repeat what an adult says, it may omit some of the words, but those that are retained will again usually be in an appropriate grammatical order:

ADULT – Look, Ben's playing in the garden.
CHILD – Play garden.

The above example also demonstrates how utterances focus on key words. Words that convey less information, or that primarily serve grammatical functions (e.g. 'in', 'the') are omitted.

Links

Intonation was discussed in the section 'Phonological development' (pages 120–1).

Links

The terms **subject**, **verb**, **object**, etc. were explained on pages 10–11.

Meanings of two-word utterances

A child's two-word sentences can express a range of complex meanings. For example, they may indicate possession ('Mummy car' for 'Mummy's car') or somebody performing an action ('Paul eat'), or be used to explain location ('Teddy bed'). Bloom (1973) observed that the same sentence may be used to express different meanings. 'Mummy sock' could mean 'This is Mummy's sock' (said when the child was picking it up) or 'Mummy is putting my sock on me' (said when the child's mother was doing this).

The ambiguity of some two-word utterances arises partly because inflectional affixes are absent. These include, for example, –s at the ends of words to show either possession or that a noun is plural, and –ed verb endings to indicate past tense.

Telegraphic stage

From the age of about two, children begin producing three- and four-word utterances.

Some of these utterances will be grammatically complete:

Subject + verb + object ('Amy likes tea').
Subject + verb + complement ('Teddy looks tired').
Subject + verb + adverbial ('Mummy sleeps upstairs').

Others will have grammatical elements missing: 'Daddy home now', 'Laura broke plate', 'Where Stephen going?' The condensed structure of many of these utterances explains why they are described as **telegraphic** (the term is also sometimes applied to two-word utterances). Like telegrams, they include the key words but omit such words as determiners (e.g. 'a', 'the'), auxiliary verbs (e.g. 'is', 'has') and prepositions (e.g. 'to', 'for').

A child will begin to show command of a wider range of structures – questions and commands will be used, for example, as well as simple statements.

Progress during the telegraphic stage is rapid. By the age of three, items that were previously omitted (such as determiners) are beginning to be used regularly. Soon sentences with more than one clause (e.g. 'want to go to bed') start to appear, and coordinating conjunctions ('and', 'but') begin to be used.

Inflectional affixes (e.g. –ing, –ed and –s endings) are gradually acquired during this period.

By the age of five, many of the most basic grammatical rules have been learned, though some (e.g. the use of the passive voice) have yet to be mastered.

Checkpoint 1

Can you define the term **inflectional affixes**?

Checkpoint 2

How does the *order* of the words in these utterances compare with the order you would find in equivalent adult sentences? What conclusion do you draw from this?

Links

The acquisition of inflectional affixes is discussed more fully in the next section (pages 126–7).

Exam question answer: page 140

'Although their utterances do not meet all the conventional expectations of a sentence, children might be said to speak in "sentences" from a very young age'. Discuss. (45 min)

Grammatical development 2

In this section, we examine some other aspects of grammatical development, beginning with the acquisition of inflections. Next, we look at some of the evidence suggesting that children unconsciously absorb grammatical rules as they acquire the language. Finally, we consider how children develop the ability to ask questions and to use negative constructions accurately.

Acquisition of inflections

Research has identified a predictable pattern in the acquisition of inflectional affixes (e.g. word endings such as *–ed* and *–ing*). Functional words such as determiners ('a', 'the') and auxiliary verbs also seem to be acquired in a regular order.

Brown (1973) studied children's language development between the ages of 20 months and 36 months and found that the sequence shown below occurred regularly (features are listed in the order in which they were acquired):

1 *–ing*
2 plural *–s*
3 possessive *–'s*
4 'the', 'a'
5 past tense *–ed*
6 third person singular verb ending *–s*
7 auxiliary 'be'

Another study by Cruttenden (1979) divided the acquisition of inflections into three stages:

1 Initially, children memorize words on an individual basis and have no regard for general principles or rules. This means, for example, that they may at first produce the correct plural form of 'foot' ('feet') and the correct past tense for 'run' ('ran').
2 During the second stage, they show an awareness of the general principles governing inflections and as a result may apply regular endings to words that require irregular inflections. For example, they observe that plural nouns usually end in *–s*, so they use 'foots' as the plural of 'foot'. In the same way, they observe that past tense forms usually end in *–ed*, so instead of 'ran' they say 'runned'. This kind of error is known as **overgeneralization** or **overregularization** (for further examples see 'Understanding of grammatical rules', below).
3 In the third stage, correct inflections are used, including irregular forms.

Understanding of grammatical rules

Children produce accurate grammatical constructions from a remarkably early age, and researchers have attempted to discover whether they have in fact grasped grammatical rules or are simply imitating what they have heard others say.

One famous experiment was carried out by Berko (1958), who showed children pictures of fictitious creatures he called 'Wugs'. At first

Examiner's secrets

Make sure you remember examples that you can use when explaining these stages.

126

they were shown a picture of one creature and told, 'This is a Wug'. Next they were shown a picture of two creatures and told, 'Now there is another one; there are two of them'. Then the children were asked to complete the sentence, 'There are two . . .'. Children aged three and four replied 'Wugs'. As they could never have heard this word before, they were clearly applying the rule that plurals usually end in –s.

Children between the approximate ages of two and a half and five years often show an awareness of rules in the grammatical errors they make. As explained opposite, they tend to overgeneralize or overregularize the language, trying to make it more consistent than it actually is. Words such as 'sheeps', 'wented' and 'mouses' are the result.

Checkpoint 2

Try to think of some other examples of overgeneralization.

Questions

Asking questions involves quite complex constructions. Research suggests that children acquire this skill in three stages:

1 Initially (during the two-word stage) questions rely on intonation alone – e.g. 'Daddy gone?' said with a rising tone.
2 During their second year, children acquire question words: first 'what' and 'where', then 'why', 'how' and 'who'. This results in constructions such as 'Where daddy gone?' The child has not yet begun to use auxiliary verbs (an adult would say, 'Where *has* daddy gone?').
3 In their third year, children begin to use auxiliary verbs and also learn to form questions by reversing the order of subject and verb – e.g. 'Joe is here' becomes 'Is Joe here?' However, questions involving *wh–* words are not always inverted correctly, producing such constructions as 'Why Joe isn't here?'

Don't forget

Although children apply grammatical rules in this way, they are not conscious that they have acquired them and would not be able to explain them.

Examiner's secrets

Look for evidence of these different stages in the texts that you study.

Negatives

The correct expression of negation again seems to be acquired in three stages:

1 At first, there is a single dependence upon the words 'no' and 'not', used either singly or in front of other expressions: 'No want', 'No go home'.
2 During the third year, 'don't' and 'can't' begin to be used. These words, together with 'no' and 'not', also begin to be placed after the subject of the sentence and before the verb: 'I don't want it', 'Sam can't play'.
3 In the third stage, more negative forms are acquired (e.g. 'didn't', 'isn't'), and negative constructions are generally used more accurately.

Exam question   answer: page 141

'When a three-year-old child says "We wented there", I feel like congratulating him on his knowledge of English grammar'. With reference to this statement, explain some of the ways in which young children demonstrate knowledge of English grammar. (45 min)

Pragmatic development

Pragmatics is the study of the part that language plays in social situations and social relationships. As well as learning the sounds, words and meanings of language, children have to acquire what the linguist Del Hymes calls 'communicative competence'. This means developing all the skills associated with conversation: they must learn when to speak, how to respond to others, which registers are appropriate for which situations, and so on.

The functions of children's language

Children are motivated to acquire language because it serves certain purposes or functions for them. Halliday (1975) identified seven functions that language has for children in their early years.

The first four help the child to satisfy its physical, emotional and social needs. Halliday calls them the instrumental, regulatory, interactional and personal functions:

Instrumental   This is when the child uses language to express its needs (e.g. 'Want drink').
Regulatory   This is where language is used to tell others what to do (e.g. 'Go away').
Interactional   Here language is used to make contact with others and form relationships (e.g. 'Love you, daddy').
Personal   This is the use of language to express feelings, opinions and individual identity (e.g. 'Me good girl').

The next two functions are the heuristic and the imaginative. Both help the child to come to terms with its environment:

Heuristic   This is when language is used to gain knowledge about the environment (e.g. 'What that tractor doing?').
Imaginative   Here language is used to tell stories and jokes, and to create an imaginary environment.

Last, there is the **representational** function: the use of language to convey facts and information.

Early years

Even before they can speak, children are being introduced to the important role that language plays in everyday life. Adults and others speak a great deal to them, and routine events such as feeding and bathing are accompanied by regularly repeated utterances. They are learning about a world in which language accompanies most activities.

Interactions between child and parent (or other adult) prepare the child for later participation in conversations. Bancroft (1996) observes that the traditional game of 'peek-a-boo' has several parallels with a typical conversation:

➔ There is turn taking. Even though the child may not initially understand its part in the game, the adults acts as though it does.
➔ Each participant responds to the contribution made by the other.

→ The participants have a common purpose and understand the sequence they should follow.
→ The activity gives the participants pleasure.

At first, the adult begins the exchanges and the child may take little active part, but as the child grows older it takes more control, and by the age of 9 or 10 months will probably be regularly initiating the game itself. Other spoken interactions similarly follow the structures and conventions of conversations. Adults will ask questions, express agreement and give other approving or disapproving responses, even though the child is not yet speaking.

First conversations ●●●

When a child first starts to speak, its utterances take the form of statements rather than questions, and they are not always directed at anyone else. In conversation, the child will often seem to ignore what the other speaker says. A typical conversation will be initiated by an adult and will be very much dependent on the adult's continued input to keep it going. Nevertheless, the child is beginning to use language for social interactions and to express its needs (e.g. 'Milk!').

Later development ●●●

A child's conversational skills develop considerably between the ages of two and four. It becomes a much more active participant and is able to initiate conversation. It learns some of the conventions of turn taking and begins to respond to questions, greetings and so on in an appropriate manner. It also makes increasing use of politeness forms ('Please', 'Thank you').

Researchers have found some aspects of young children's language use to be remarkably sophisticated. Youssef (1991), for example, studied a group of children on the Caribbean island of Trinidad. She found that they responded to different social contexts by using different varieties of English. Janet, a child aged 3 years and 9 months, produced 100% Standard English past tense verb forms in conversation with her mother (who encouraged her to use Standard English), but decreasing amounts with the family helper (a Trinidadian English speaker), her brother and children of her own age.

Further skills are acquired after children have started school. In particular, they develop increasing sensitivity to the needs of their listeners and a greater understanding of the language appropriate to more formal situations.

Links

The structures associated with adult conversations are described on pages 46–9.

Checkpoint 1

If speech is adjusted so that it moves closer to that of the other participant in a conversation, what is this known as?

Checkpoint 2

What term is used for a form of language appropriate to a particular situation?

Exam question   answer: page 141

In what ways do young children show an awareness that language enables us to interact with others? (45 min)

Theories of language acquisition 1

The next two sections consider some of the main theories that have been developed to explain children's ability to acquire language. We shall look at the theories in a chronological sequence, beginning in this section with the theories of **imitation and reinforcement**, and **innateness**.

Imitation and reinforcement

This approach argues that children acquire language by **imitating** the speech of others. When a child produces words successfully it receives approval and encouragement, and this motivates the child to repeat the behaviour.

This theory is especially associated with Skinner (1957) and regards language as similar to other kinds of human behaviour: if we do something and it has positive, pleasurable consequences, we are more likely to do it again; if it has unpleasant consequences, we are less likely to repeat the action.

In terms of language, when the child speaks words and, later, sentences, it is rewarded in various ways: it may, for example, get something that it has asked for (e.g. if it has requested a drink), or simply see that its parents are excited, happy and approving. This **reinforcement** shapes the child's use of language and ensures that it develops successfully.

Evaluation

It is clear that imitation plays an important part in phonological development. The fact that children develop regional accents indicates that they imitate the sounds they hear around them. However, it is unlikely that imitation and reinforcement account for the acquisition of all aspects of language. Criticisms of the theory include the following:

→ All children seem to pass through the same stages of language development regardless of the type and amount of reinforcement they receive. If the acquisition of language was entirely dependent on parental reinforcement, there would be much more variation between individual children.

→ Children develop an understanding of how grammar works. They show this by trying to apply grammatical rules in a consistent way: a child might say 'wented', applying the rule that past tense verbs usually end in –*ed*, and 'mans' (for 'men'), applying the rule that plural nouns usually end in –*s*. They are clearly not imitating what they have learned here and have not been encouraged to make these mistakes.

→ This understanding of grammar means that they have the capacity to understand an infinite number of sentences, and to produce sentences that are entirely original. In both cases, they are not limited to sentences they have heard spoken by others.

Checkpoint 1

When might this theory suggest that the child would receive a negative response, and what form might this take?

Checkpoint 2

What term is used to refer to this kind of error?

Links

For more on children's understanding of grammar, see the section 'Grammatical development' (pages 124–7).

Innateness ●●●

Criticism of Skinner's approach was led by Chomsky, whose alternative theory of language acquisition was proposed in 1965. Chomsky argued that children have an **innate** (inborn) ability to extract the rules underlying language from the words they hear being spoken around them. He called this ability the 'language acquisition device' (LAD).

According to Chomsky, different languages have difference **surface structures**, but they all share the same **deep structure**. For example, utterances containing a subject, verb and object are common to all languages. Children are said to possess an innate awareness of this deep structure, and this explains why they are able to develop language proficiency so rapidly: from birth their brains are ready to analyse what they hear and to understand how the language system of the society they have been born into works.

Evaluation ●●●

Supporters of Chomsky argue that the existence of an innate LAD would explain:

→ The impressive speed with which children learn to speak.
→ The fact that children from all cultures pass through similar stages of language development.
→ The existence of grammatical features that are common to all languages. (These features are known as **linguistic universals**).

The main criticism of Chomsky is that it underestimates the role of interaction with others in language development.

Chomsky's theory implies that if a child is exposed to language, the acquisition of that language will happen automatically. Critics argue that the child is more dependent on interaction with others than this suggests. Bard and Sachs (1977) studied a child called 'Jim', who was the son of deaf parents. Jim was not deaf himself and, because they wanted him to speak normally, his parents taught him little of the sign language they used to communicate with each other. Jim spent a lot of time watching television and listening to the radio, which meant he heard a lot of spoken language. Despite this, his speech development was seriously retarded until he began attending sessions with a speech therapist, after which his speech improved at a rapid pace. Jim was clearly *ready* to learn to speak, but he needed human contact with the speech therapist to become a competent speaker.

Examiner's secrets

Remember the names of the scholars (e.g. Chomsky) associated with each theory.

Links

Theories that place more emphasis on the importance of interaction are discussed in the next section (pages 132–3).

Exam question   answer: page 141

Discuss the strengths and weaknesses of the argument that children have an innate capacity for language. What other explanations of language acquisition by children have been offered? (45 min)

Examiner's secrets

It would also be relevant to bring into this answer material covered in the next section (pages 132–3).

Theories of language acquisition 2

This section considers **cognition** and **input** theories.

Cognition theories

Intellectual development in children – the development of mental abilities and skills – is known as **cognitive development**. Cognitive theories of language acquisition suggest that cognitive development is the overriding influence on the development of language. The main theorist associated with this approach is Piaget.

Stages in language acquisition are said to be linked to stages in cognitive development:

→ One example is the development of **object permanence**, which is the ability to understand that objects have an independent existence. Before they develop this ability, children appear to believe that if an object moves out of their sight it ceases to exist; if an object is hidden they do not look for it, because they assume it no longer exists. The development of object permanence begins during the first year but is not usually complete until the child is about 18 months old. Soon after this age, there is a sharp increase in children's vocabulary. Cognitive theorists argue that these two events are linked: once children have realized that objects have an independent existence, the next step is to learn the names for those objects.

→ Another example is a child's ability to arrange objects such as sticks in order of increasing or decreasing size. Children who are not yet able to do this usually describe the objects as 'long' or 'short', whereas children who understand the task use comparative terms such as 'longer' and 'shorter'. Again, it is argued that an aspect of linguistic development (the use of comparative adjectives) is a consequence of the development of a cognitive skill.

Evaluation

While there are almost certainly close connections between language development and cognitive development, many argue that the role of cognitive development is overstated by cognitive theorists. Some aspects of linguistic development appear to be separate from cognitive development.

The main evidence suggesting this is that in some children there is not a close match between the two kinds of development. Several studies have been made of children whose mental development has been retarded but who have still been able to speak fluently. In particular, it seems that a child's ability to develop a grasp of grammar and sentence structure is independent of its general cognitive development.

Input theories

Input theories are the most recent of the theories of language acquisition outlined in this and the previous section. They stress the role of **interaction** in the development of language, focusing in particular on the interaction that takes place between children and parents (or other carers). A child's language acquisition is said to depend on the contribution (or **input**) made by parents and others.

Don't forget

Jean Piaget (1896–1980) was a Swiss psychologist whose ideas about intellectual development in children have had a major influence on teaching and education.

Watch out!

Be careful not to be too dismissive of any of the theories. There is probably some validity in all of them.

Links

The Bard and Sachs study of 'Jim' suggested that interaction was important. See page 131.

Much attention has been paid to the language that parents and others use towards children, and to the ways in which this encourages language development. We look more closely at the characteristics of this language in the next section. Here though are some key points that are relevant to input theories of language development:

→ Parents speak more slowly to children than they do to other adults. They use simplified constructions and less complex vocabulary. This makes it easier for a child to imitate its parents, and the task of learning the sounds and structures of language is made less demanding.
→ Parents tend to expand their children's speech. If a child says, 'Sweets allgone', an adult might reply by saying, 'Yes, the sweets are gone – you've eaten them all, haven't you?' Through this kind of interaction, the child's vocabulary and awareness of sentence structure is gradually extended.
→ Parents often introduce new words by using familiar sentence frames. For example, a parent might have a habit of saying, 'What's this? It's a flower. And what's this? It's a tree. And what's this? It's a bush'. The child's attention is drawn to the new word because the rest of the sentence is familiar. In this way, the acquisition of new vocabulary is encouraged.
→ Parental interaction with children introduces them from an early age to the conventions of conversation: turn taking, question-and-answer sequences and so on. This helps pragmatic development.

Evaluation

The precise relationship between parental input and children's linguistic development has proved difficult to measure. When a child advances another stage in its acquisition of language, it is hard to be certain about what has caused this. Moreover, it does not seem essential that adults address children in a particular way, because children reared in cultures where adults do not alter their speech when addressing children still succeed in acquiring language. However, it is probable that interaction does play an important part in language development, and that future research will shed further light on this.

Conclusion ●●●

All of the theories that have been looked at have some validity. It is most likely that all of the factors that have been mentioned contribute to language acquisition and that they all need to be present for a child to become a fully competent user of language. What remains unclear is the relative importance of the various factors, and the exact nature of their relationship to each other.

Exam question   answer: page 141

Compare input and innateness theories of language acquisition. Are the two approaches incompatible? (45 min)

Checkpoint 1

What term is used for the language that adults use towards children?

Checkpoint 2

The major theories are not mutually exclusive and sometimes 'overlap'. What other theory is alluded to here?

Don't forget

Also of relevance here is research (e.g. Clarke-Stewart 1973) suggesting that children whose mothers talk to them more have more extensive vocabularies.

Links

Researchers have studied how the game of 'peek-a-boo' helps to introduce a child to the routines of conversation. See page 128.

Links

For more on children raised in these kinds of cultures, see page 135.

Examiner's secrets

Look for contrasts between the theories. The innateness approach was discussed on pages 130–1.

How adults speak to children

This section considers the distinctive characteristics of the language used by adults when they speak to children. Various terms refer to such language, but one that is in common use is **child-directed speech**. Studies of child-directed speech have attempted to discover the influence that such speech has on children's language development.

Links

The study of child-directed speech is especially relevant to **input** theories of language acquisition (see page 132).

Terminology

At first, researchers were especially concerned with the language that mothers used towards children. The term '**motherese**' was used for this. Studies of the speech of fathers led to the creation of an accompanying term, '**fatherese**'. However, recognition that natural mothers and fathers were not always the main or only significant adults in children's lives resulted in the use of the alternative term '**caregiver**' (or **caretaker**) speech. '**Child-directed speech**' is a broad term now commonly used by linguists. However, it should be noted that although there are similar patterns in the language used by adults of various kinds towards children, there are also differences. For example, research has suggested that fathers tend to be more demanding than mothers, using more direct questions and a wider range of vocabulary.

Features of child-directed speech

Here are some of the most common features of child-directed speech.

Phonology

→ Slower, clearer pronunciation
→ More pauses, especially between phrases and sentences
→ Higher pitch
→ Exaggerated intonation and stress.

Lexis

→ Simpler, more restricted vocabulary
→ Diminutive forms (e.g. 'doggie')
→ Concrete language, referring to objects in the child's immediate environment.

Grammar

→ Simpler constructions
→ Frequent use of imperatives
→ High degree of repetition
→ Frequent questions
→ Use of personal names instead of pronouns (e.g. 'Mummy' not 'I').

Action point

Your own knowledge and experience of adult–child interactions may enable you to add other features to this list.

Effects of child-directed speech

Speaking slowly and using simplified vocabulary and grammatical structures makes language more accessible for a child. The combined task of comprehending the language and developing the ability to use it is therefore made easier. Understanding of word meanings, for example, is clearly facilitated when a parent focuses the child's attention on an object in the immediate environment and slowly repeats the name for it.

The use of a higher pitch and exaggerated intonation, together with similarly exaggerated gestures and facial expressions, may serve to retain a child's attention, so that it listens more intently to what is being said.

Research suggests that the frequent use of questions improves children's understanding of auxiliary verbs (words such as 'did', 'have', 'will', etc.). This is because questions include more auxiliary verbs than statements (e.g. saying 'Did the man fall over?' instead of 'The man fell over').

Asking questions and pausing for a reply (which parents tend to do even before their children have begun speaking) also help to introduce children to the rules and conventions of conversation. Children become used to the idea of turn taking, and the pattern of alternating is associated with conversational interaction.

However, some argue that **baby talk** – the use of such expressions as 'doggie', 'moo-cow', 'gee-gee' and so on – actually interferes with language development because it provides children with an inaccurate and distorted version of normal speech.

The use of child-directed speech by parents and other carers may aid language acquisition, but it does not appear to be essential. There are cultures where adults do not modify their speech when addressing children (e.g. Samoa and parts of Papua New Guinea), and in these societies children appear to acquire their native language at normal rates of development.

Use of child-directed speech in other contexts ●●●

The kind of language that adults use when addressing children is also sometimes found in other situations.

→ Lovers may use baby talk in a humorous, affectionate way when addressing each other.
→ The language used to address pet animals has strong similarities with child-directed speech.
→ Researchers have identified parallels between child-directed speech and the language carers and others tend to use when addressing elderly people. For example, there is a tendency to use simpler sentences, to repeat statements and to talk more slowly and in a higher pitch. This may reflect negative stereotyping of older people and an assumption that old age means reduced mental capacity. Certainly, research (e.g. Coupland 1991) has found that some elderly people consider this style of speech patronizing and demeaning. However, others, especially those suffering from frailty, deafness or short-term memory loss, view it more positively and describe it as encouraging and helpful.

Links

Auxiliary verbs were explained on pages 6–7.

Checkpoint 1

Do you share the view that baby talk is harmful?

Checkpoint 2

Why do you think these different situations are associated with similar kinds of language use?

Exam question   answer: page 142

Explain what is meant by child-directed speech and consider the role that it plays in language development. (45 min)

Learning to read and write

Don't forget

The stages represent an *ideal* pattern of reading development. Individual children develop at different rates and in some cases are unable to reach the later stages.

The jargon

High-frequency words are words that are often used (e.g. 'go', 'come', 'big' etc.).

Take note

For more able students, reading comprehension becomes more effective than listening comprehension of the same material during Stage 4.

Example

The Department of Education's National Literacy Strategy (1998) states that in infant schools there should be 'a strong and systematic emphasis on the teaching of phonics'.

The acquisition of spoken language is a natural process. In all cultures, children pass through the same stages of language development and learn to speak without the help of formal instruction. Learning to *read* and learning to *write* are very different: they are skills that need to be *taught*. In this section, we consider how children acquire the ability to read and write, and the specific kinds of skills that they need to master.

Stages in reading development

Shown below are six stages in the development of reading skills identified by the American researcher Jeanne S. Chall (1983). The ages relate specifically to children educated in the American school system, but we can assume a broad correspondence with the ages of English children.

Stage 0: Pre-reading and pseudo-reading (up to the age of 6)   Children may 'pretend' to read, turning the pages of a book and repeating a story that has previously been read to them. They are increasingly able to name letters and may start to write their own names.

Stage 1: Initial reading and decoding (ages 6–7)   Children begin to learn the relationship between sounds and letters and are able to read simple texts comprising short, high-frequency words. Their understanding of spoken language is far in advance of their understanding of written language. Chall estimated that a child now understands approximately 4 000 spoken words and 600 written words.

Stage 2: Confirmation and fluency (ages 7–8)   This is a period of consolidation, during which children steadily increase their reading skills and their vocabulary. By the end of this stage, Chall estimated, a child understands 9 000 spoken and 3 000 written words.

Stage 3: Reading for learning (ages 9–14)   Reading ceases to be an end in itself and becomes a means of gaining knowledge and pursuing individual interests. The child tackles a wider range of reading material: magazines, newspapers, reference books and so on.

Stage 4: Multiplicity and complexity (ages 14–17)   Reading material is increasingly complex and varied.

Stage 5: Construction and reconstruction (age 18 onwards)   Ideally, young adults are now confident readers, able to read a diverse range of material rapidly and efficiently. They recognize the practical and recreational benefits of reading and read for a variety of personal and occupational purposes.

The teaching of reading

The teaching of reading has been debated for decades, and it continues to be a controversial issue within education. Many different schemes and methods have been proposed, but the main division is between phonic and whole-word approaches:

→ The **phonic** approach focuses on the sounds of language. Children are taught the relationship between letters and sounds and are encouraged to use this knowledge to construct or decode words.

When a child encounters a new word, it attempts to read it by 'sounding out' the letters.

→ The **whole-word** approach (also known as 'look and say') teaches the child to recognize individual words as wholes, rather than as units made up of individual letters or sounds.

Learning to write ●●●

Learning to write involves the acquisition of a variety of skills:

→ Initially, a child must master the physical coordination required to write with a pen or pencil. In the first years of writing, accuracy and neatness steadily improve.

→ The structures and conventions of written language must be learned, e.g. spelling, punctuation, sentence construction, paragraphing, etc.

→ The child needs to become aware of the different purposes that written language can serve, and the different styles of writing that are appropriate to these purposes.

Stages in learning to write ●●●

B. M. Kroll (1981) identifies the following four stages in the development of writing skills (ages are approximate):

Preparatory stage (up to the age of 6)   The child masters the physical skills required to write and learns the basic principles of the spelling system.

Consolidation stage (ages 6–8)   At this stage, children tend to write as they speak. They are likely to use short, declarative sentences, grammatically incomplete sentences or longer sentences linked by simple conjunctions such as 'and', 'then' and 'so'.

Differentiation stage (ages 8–mid-teens)   Children become more aware of the differences between writing and speech. There is increasing confidence in handling the conventions and grammatical structures associated with writing. Sentences become more complex, with more subordinate clauses and the use of more sophisticated connectives. There is also more variety, as the child begins to learn the different writing styles required for different purposes and audiences.

Integration stage (mid-teens upwards)   The writer develops a personal 'voice' and adapts confidently to the requirements of different situations. These skills continue to develop in adulthood.

Don't forget

Many educationalists favour an integrated approach, which combines elements from both methods.

Checkpoint 1

In what ways does the development of *reading* skills assist the development of *writing* skills?

Checkpoint 2

What are **declarative sentences**?

Examiner's secrets

An answer is likely to include some general observations about the differences between reading/writing and speech, but also some more specific contrasts between the kinds of skills and behaviour involved, perhaps with reference to particular ages.

Exam question   answer: page 142

In what ways does the development of reading and writing skills differ from the development of speech? (45 min)

Specimen texts

Here are three specimen texts with questions to test your knowledge of various aspects of children's acquisition of language.

TEXT A

answer: page 142

Listed below are typical utterances spoken by children at different ages. Discuss what the data reveals about the language abilities of children of these ages and consider how their ability develops between these ages. (45 min)

15 months	Bye Mummy
	Isee
	Allgone
20 months	All fall down
	Teddy tired
	Gone, where Mummy gone?
	More juice
28 months	Teddy's hat came off
	Harry's got a big, big green truck
36 months	Little Luke hit me, he did
	I am going to see Harriet another day tomorrow
	I don't like faces, I want to see children's ITV
40 months	Look at my knee. I felled over in the playground.
	Once upon a time there was a little girl and she got beautiful hair and then the monster killed her and then she got dead and then and then the beautiful fairy came and made them better again.

TEXT B

answer: page 142

The conversation below is between Paul, aged 22 months, and his grandmother.
Comment on the *grammatical* features of the child's use of language. (15 min)

GRANDMOTHER: (*lifting Paul on to footstool*) Say 'I'm king of the castle'

PAUL: king of castle

GRANDMOTHER: and you're the dirty rascal

PAUL: I'm dirty rascal

GRANDMOTHER: No, I'm the dirty rascal. You say it. YOU'RE (*pointing to herself*) the dirty rascal

PAUL: (*pointing to himself*) I'm dirty rascal

TEXT C

answer: page 142

The conversation below is between a mother and her daughter Gemma, aged 28 months. Analyse the conversation, considering the following aspects of the child's language abilities at this age: lexical/semantic; grammatical; phonological; pragmatic.

(.) = brief pause

GEMMA: Where man gone?

MOTHER: He's gone back to work.

GEMMA: Gone to work.

MOTHER: Can you help me put these toys away?

GEMMA: Me do it.

MOTHER: I can't find your pencil case.

GEMMA: I know where 'tis.

MOTHER: Good girl. Shall I keep this picture and show it to Daddy?

GEMMA: Yes (.) What's that? What's that Mummy?

MOTHER: That's a screwdriver. The man left it, didn't he?

GEMMA: What's it?

MOTHER: A screwdriver.

GEMMA: Crewdriver.

MOTHER: Screwdriver.

GEMMA: Man's crewdriver. Heavy.

MOTHER: Yes, it's a big one, isn't it? Do you want to do some more drawing?

GEMMA: OK (.) No paper.

MOTHER: Here's some paper. You could draw the man.

GEMMA: Yes (.) I draw him with a long coat, isn't it? (.) He fix the light.

MOTHER: Yes. Are you going to draw his ladder?

GEMMA: Yes. Big big big ladder. And long long coat.

MOTHER: Good.

GEMMA: And funny hat.

MOTHER: Funny hat? He didn't have a hat, did he?

GEMMA: Yes. I want it.

MOTHER: OK.

Answers
Children's acquisition of language

Beginnings of language development

Checkpoints

1 A *phoneme* is the smallest unit of sound in a language. The word 'cat' has three phonemes: *c-a-t*. Note that phonemes are not the same as syllables. See page 20.
2 *Pragmatic development* is the term used for the development of social skills, acquired as the child learns how to interact with others. See page 128.

Exam question

The stages of language development common to all children provide an appropriate structure for an answer to this question. The child can be said to be 'preparing to speak' in that with each stage it moves closer to the utterance of its first word.

Phonological development

Checkpoints

1 A *consonant cluster* occurs when two or more consonants appear next to each other at the beginning or end of a syllable – e.g. the beginning letters of *'spread'* and the closing letters of *'mist'*.
2 Another factor is that adults are more likely to be used to hearing such broadcasts so are more familiar with announcers' intonation patterns.

Exam question

The focus here is on phonological development, though it is worth explaining that comprehension is also ahead of speech in other aspects of language acquisition. Berko and Brown's research (the 'fis/fish' exchange) is clearly relevant to this question. Knowledge of the main trends in phonological development, and of the ages at which they may be evident, should also be shown.

Lexical and semantic development

Checkpoints

1 Concrete nouns refer to things that physically exist. They are the names given to things that can be seen, touched and felt. Dog, ball and bottle are all concrete nouns. Abstract nouns refer to feelings, ideas, qualities. Happiness and friendship are abstract nouns. See page 4.
2 Nouns (especially concrete nouns) are more readily acquired by children because it is easier for a child to identify what the words refer to. Words which have a more abstract meaning, or which do not convey clear information, are acquired more slowly.

Exam question

The focus of this question is on the *difficulties* a child commonly experiences in acquiring vocabulary rather than on the progress that a child makes in learning new words and meanings. Difficulties that might be discussed include:

- not understanding a word's full range of meanings;
- taking longer to acquire abstract nouns than concrete nouns;
- acquiring grammatical function words ('to,' 'for', 'the', etc.) relatively slowly;
- underextension (giving words meanings that are too narrow);
- overextension (giving words meanings that are too broad). Overextension is a more frequent error than underextension.

The ages at which these difficulties are likely to occur, and how and when they are overcome, should also be explained.

Grammatical development 1

Checkpoints

1 *Inflectional affixes* are parts of words that tell us something about their grammatical functions. In English, inflectional affixes are always suffixes (suffixes are single letters or groups of letters commonly found at the ends of words). Examples of inflectional affixes include *–s* added to a noun to make it plural (*toy* + *s*); *–ed* added to a verb to make it past tense (*open* + *ed* = *opened*); *–er* added to an adjective to make it a comparative (*small* + *er* = *smaller*). See page 14.
2 Although grammatical elements are missing from these utterances, those elements that are present are in the correct order: 'Daddy [is] home now', 'Laura broke [the] plate', 'Where [is] Stephen going?' This is significant as it indicates that children have an understanding of grammatical structure.

Exam question

The stages of grammatical development provide a logical structure for an answer. During the one-word stage, single-word utterances are often in effect expressing meaning that would conventionally be expressed in sentences. These utterances are known as *holophrases*, and examples should be included (e.g. 'milk' meaning 'I want some milk'). At the two-word stage, the *order* in which words are placed obviously begins to become significant. Some of the elements found in conversational sentences (e.g. determiners) may be missing, and words themselves may be grammatically incorrect (e.g. they may lack inflectional affixes). However, the words that are present are usually in a grammatically correct sequence. Examples of common structures include subject + verb ('Mummy drink') and subject + complement ('Teddy tired'). At the telegraphic stage, when three- or four-word utterances are produced, some utterances are grammatically complete. Others have elements missing, but those that are present are again generally in the correct grammatical order (see Checkpoint 2 above).

Grammatical development 2

Checkpoints

1 *Auxiliary verbs* are verbs that are placed in front of main verbs. They include words such as 'is' ('he is laughing'), 'have' ('I have eaten my dinner'), 'can' ('I can do it'), etc.

2 Common examples of mistakenly adding *–ed* to verbs to form past tenses include 'goed', 'taked' and breaked. Examples of incorrect plurals include 'mans', 'foots' and 'geeses'.

Exam question

This question invites a discussion, with examples, of overgeneralization. However, the reference in the question to 'some of the ways' indicates that other elements of children's grammatical knowledge can also be mentioned (e.g. ability from a very early age to use words in the correct grammatical sequence).

Pragmatic development

Checkpoints

1 When speech styles move closer to one another, this is known as *convergence*. See page 50.
2 A form of language appropriate to a particular situation is a *register*. See page 36.

Exam question

An explanation and discussion of the seven functions that language has for children (as identified by Halliday) could form the early part of this answer. This would show knowledge of relevant theory and an understanding of what motivates children to use language. All of these functions involve interaction with others, which is the central theme of the essay.

The early interactions between parent and child that precede the child's first use of language (e.g. 'peek-a-boo' games) might be mentioned, but not at length as you need to focus on interaction through language. You should discuss the nature of early conversations, when two-way exchanges are limited but act as an important prelude to the rapid development of conversational skills that occurs between the ages of two and four.

During this later period, the child begins to initiate conversation, responds more to the speech of others, learns some of the conventions of turn taking and makes increasing use of politeness forms.

Theories of language acquisition 1

Checkpoints

1 If a child uses language incorrectly and the parent is unable to understand what is being said, it may not get what it wants. This negative reinforcement, according to the theory, helps to motivate children to use language accurately. Alternatively, if a parent understands the child it might respond by correcting the child's use of language – repeating the word or sentence back to the child, but in its correct form – encouraging the child to *imitate* the parent's speech.
2 This kind of error is known as *overgeneralization* or *overregularization*. See page 126.

Exam question

This question asks for an evaluation of the strengths and weaknesses of the approach to language acquisition that is most strongly associated with Chomsky. Initially, the theory itself should be briefly outlined. Evidence in support of the theory includes the similarities in the nature of language and language development across cultures; the existence of linguistic universals (grammatical features present in all languages); and of common stages of language development in all children. The speed and facility with which children acquire language also lend weight to the theory. The main weakness is that the theory overlooks the role of interaction in language acquisition. Bard and Sachs's study of 'Jim' – which suggests that without human intervention a child will not acquire language – is very relevant here. The second part of the question offers the opportunity for a brief overview of other theories: imitation and reinforcement; cognition; input.

Theories of language acquisition 2

Checkpoints

1 The language used by adults towards children is known as *child-directed speech*. Other terms in use include 'caregiver language', 'caretaker language', 'motherese' and 'baby talk'. See page 134.
2 The role of *imitation* is recognized here. See page 130.

Exam question

The main contrast between the two theories is that the innateness approach argues that a child has a *natural* tendency to acquire language, while the input approach argues that language is acquired through interaction with others. Extreme versions of the two theories, arguing that language acquisition is *solely* dependent on one or other of the factors, are incompatible. However, it is perfectly possible to argue that *both* factors play a role: a child is born with an innate capacity for language, but interaction is needed to *develop* that capacity.

Examiner's secrets

Be careful not to be too dogmatic in examination essays. Recognize the strengths and weaknesses of opposing viewpoints.

How adults speak to children

Checkpoints

1 This is a matter of opinion. Arguments in support of baby talk are that it is playful and that it increases children's confidence by offering them 'words' that they are able to articulate. Others object that it misleads children and does nothing to aid the acquisition of correct, standard vocabulary.

2 The use of baby talk between lovers is playful and affectionate. Used towards pets it can again be an expression of affection, as well as reflecting an assumption that the animal will not be able to understand adult language (though it is unlikely to understand baby talk either). As is explained on page 135, there are contrasting views and interpretations of the use of such language towards elderly people.

Exam question

This is a relatively straightforward question and a good example of a question with a clear structure, which can be duplicated in an answer. Child-directed speech should first be defined and its main features outlined. The part that it plays in language development (see 'Effects of child-directed speech' on page 134) should then be discussed.

Learning to read and write

Checkpoints

1 Reading texts means that children encounter models of correct usage which they can attempt to imitate. It also helps to introduce children to the notion that different styles of writing serve different purposes.

2 *Declarative sentences* are sentences that make statements. See page 13.

Exam question

An answer might begin with the important distinction that while speech is at least partly innate, reading and writing are not natural skills and have to be taught. In comparing the acquisition of reading skills with the acquisition of speech, the main point to emphasize is that spoken language develops far more rapidly than the understanding of written language. This can be supported by reference to Chall's estimates of the numbers of spoken and written words understood by children at specific ages. The development of writing skills is again slower than the development of speech, but there is an important link between the two in that early children's writing tends to mimic speech. Only from the age of about eight onwards does a child become aware of the distinct conventions and grammatical structures of writing.

Specimen texts

TEXT A

These utterances illustrate some of the typical language features of children at key stages in their development. At 15 months, the child is usually at the one-word stage. Sometimes pairs of words may be spoken, but usually as a single unit ('Isee', 'Allgone'). By 20 months, the child is normally at the two-word stage. Grammatical elements are often missing from utterances, but words are in a correct grammatical sequence: 'Teddy tired' for 'Teddy is tired', 'More juice' for 'I want more juice'. At 28 months, children are beginning to produce grammatically complete – though short – utterances: 'Teddy's hat came off'. The limits of a child's vocabulary may be reflected in the repetition of certain words ('Harry's got a big, big green truck'). Both these utterances also illustrate that children's vocabulary continues to be primarily concrete. At 36 months, utterances are more complex, including for example auxiliary verbs ('am', 'don't'). Time is a concept that still causes difficulty ('another day', 'tomorrow'). The reference to 'faces' indicates that there is also difficulty expressing certain other ideas (the child was actually referring here to a news programme). By 40 months, longer utterances are produced. The use of 'felled' is an example of overgeneralization, with the mistaken application of the rule that past tense verbs end in –*ed*. There is command of a limited range of conjunctions, with repeated use of 'and' and 'then'.

TEXT B

Of particular interest here is the fact that Paul is not simply willing to imitate his grandmother. The grandmother's use of 'you're' is interpreted as a reference to the child himself – showing an understanding of how pronouns are usually used.

TEXT C

The mother attempts to extend Gemma's vocabulary by introducing her to the word 'screwdriver', though Gemma has difficulty with the pronunciation of the word. Several of Gemma's utterances omit grammatical elements ('Where man gone?'), and there is a misuse of the first person pronoun ('Me do it'), though constructions follow a correct grammatical sequence. Gemma interacts effectively with her mother, asking questions and responding relevantly to what her mother says. Occasionally, though, her utterances are limited to a repetition of her mother's words.

The first few sections of this chapter offer a historical overview of the development of English. Linguists usually divide the history of English into four main periods (dates are approximate): **Old English** (400–1150); **Middle English** (1150–1450); **Early Modern English** (1450–1700); **Late Modern English** (1700 to the present). The history of English is obviously an immense topic, and for the examination you are expected to have only an outline knowledge of how the language has developed. However, you do need to be able to recognize the characteristic features of texts from the Early Modern English period onwards. The chapter goes on to look at the main types of language change: changes to vocabulary (lexical and semantic change), pronunciation (phonological change) and grammar (grammatical change). The underlying causes of change, and the attitudes that people have towards changes in their language, are also considered. Finally, the greatly contrasting predictions that people have made about the future of English are discussed.

Language change

Exam themes

→ Types of language change.

→ How and why language changes.

→ Debates and controversies regarding language change.

→ Analysis of texts from different times.

Topic checklist

○ AS ● A2	AQA/A	AQA/B	EDEXCEL	OCR	WJE
Origins of English; Old English	●	●	●	○	○●
Middle English; Early Modern English	●	●	●	○	○●
Specimen texts	●	●	●	○	○●
Late Modern English	●	●	●	○	○●
Lexical change	●	●	●	○	○●
Semantic change	●	●	●	○	○●
Phonological change	●	●	●	○	○●
Grammatical change	●	●	●	○	○●
Causes of language change	●	●	●	○	○●
Attitudes to language change	●	●	●	○	○●
The future of English	●	●	●	○	○●

Origins of English;
Old English

Watch out!

Don't fall into the trap of calling all English from the past 'Old English'. Remember these different periods of English, and the names they are given.

Checkpoint 1

Name six languages other than English which belong to the Indo-European family.

Example

Other **Germanic languages** include Dutch, Danish, Swedish and German.

This historical overview of the development of English is divided into three parts. In the first part, we look at the origins of English and at **Old English**, which was in use roughly between 400 and 1150. In the second part (pages 146–7), we focus on Middle English (1150–1450) and Early Modern English (1450–1700). Late Modern English (from 1700 to the present) is considered on pages 148–9.

Origins of English

The many different languages of the world are grouped into **families**. The languages within each family have similarities, which suggests that they have evolved from a common origin.

English belongs to the **Indo-European** family, the most widely spoken group of languages in the world.

The exact source of these languages is not known for certain, but some theories suggest that Indo-European may have originated in Anatolia (now eastern Turkey) around 6000 BC.

The Indo-European family is sub-divided into nine branches (see map below). English is a **Germanic** language and developed from the speech of the Angles, Saxons and Jutes – Germanic tribes who invaded England from northern Germany and southern Denmark in the 5th century.

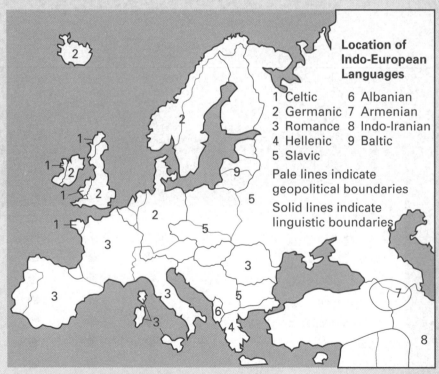

Location of Indo-European Languages

1 Celtic	6 Albanian
2 Germanic	7 Armenian
3 Romance	8 Indo-Iranian
4 Hellenic	9 Baltic
5 Slavic	

Pale lines indicate geopolitical boundaries

Solid lines indicate linguistic boundaries

Source: O'Grady *et al.: Contemporary Linguistics* (Longman)

Old English

The Old English period begins with the invasions of the Angles, Saxons and Jutes and ends around 1150.

At the time of these invasions, England was occupied by Celtic tribes, who were driven out towards the edges of Britain. Welsh, Irish Gaelic and Scots Gaelic are all **Celtic** languages. In England, the Celtic language was almost completely overtaken by Anglo-Saxon, and only a handful of Celtic words survive in modern English. The Celtic influence is however evident in some place names. *Aber* (meaning river estuary) gave rise to Aberdeen, *llan* (meaning church) to Llandudno and Llangollen. The Celtic name for the river Thames was *Tamesa*.

Vikings from Scandinavia began invading England towards the end of the 8th century. Their **Old Norse** language resembled that of the Anglo-Saxon invaders, and much of its vocabulary was absorbed into Old English.

Old English texts look strange to the modern reader. However, many of the words that we use today are of Anglo-Saxon origin. Some are listed here:

Words derived from Old English
    Pronouns: I, you, he, she, it, we, this, that, these, those
    Nouns: friend, husband, anger, window, bull, cake, dirt, sun
    Adjectives: happy, cold, black, bloody, tight, low, ill
    Verbs: can, shall, get, give, want, call
    Conjunctions: and, as, but, so, then
    Prepositions: up, down, in, on, to, by
    Adverbs: while, when, where

Old English words have a muscular quality about them: they are usually short, direct and forceful. Many of the most memorable phrases in English are made up of Old English words, including 'ashes to ashes', 'dust to dust' and 'with this ring I thee wed'.

Although we speak of Old English as a single language, it contained several different **dialects**, and the vocabulary that was used in different parts of the country varied much more than it does now. There was also no single, agreed system of **spelling**.

In terms of grammar, Old English used **inflections** much more than modern English does. Inflections are parts of words (usually word endings) that indicate grammatical functions. In modern English, for example, adding *–s* to the ends of most nouns changes them from singular to plural. Old English was very reliant on inflections, using them for example to indicate whether a noun was the subject or object in a sentence. Compared with contemporary English, meaning was consequently less dependent on word order, so the construction of Old English sentences was also looser and more flexible.

The jargon

Old English is sometimes known as **Anglo-Saxon**.

"The history of English is one of repeated invasions, with newcomers to the islands bringing their own language with them"

David Crystal, 1988

Links

See the specimen text using Old English on page 148.

Checkpoint 2

Can you define the term **dialect**?

Exam question

In the exam, you will not be directly tested on your knowledge of Old English, so a practice question has not been included here. Note though that it can impress the examiner if you occasionally show your knowledge of the roots of English – provided that it is relevant to the question.

Middle English; Early Modern English

The **Middle English** period followed another invasion, by the Norman French in 1066. Their influence on the language was not felt immediately, and the beginning of the Middle English period is usually said to be around 1150. **Early Modern English** (1450–1700) is marked by increasing standardization of the language, a development encouraged by the introduction of printing in 1476.

Middle English

The Norman Conquest of 1066 was followed by a long period of French rule. French became the language of the royal court and of government and the law. There was a great deal of intermarrying between the French and English aristocracies.

English survived as a language but was enormously influenced by French. The mixture of Old English and French produced the language that is known as Middle English.

A huge number of French words (perhaps as many as 10 000) entered the language. Words of French origin tend to be more elegant and refined than their Old English equivalents. Compare, for example, 'premier' (French) and 'first' (Old English). Some more examples of French loan words are shown below:

Words of French origin
> **Government**: government, court, state, city, citizen
> **Relationships**: aunt, uncle, cousin, sir, madam
> **Food**: dinner, supper, sauce, beef, sugar
> **Fashion**: coat, dress, button, bracelet, cotton
> **Recreation**: dance, tennis, amusement, entertain, audience

Phonology was also affected. Speech rhythms became more varied because whereas Old English usually stressed the first syllable of each word, French often stressed all syllables equally. The French influence also brought softer sounds to the language.

The main change to grammar in the Middle English period was the loss of a large number of **inflections**.

There was still no agreed system of **spelling**, and the range of spellings found in manuscripts is even greater than in the Old English period.

Early Modern English

The impact of printing
Printing, introduced to England in 1476 by William Caxton, was a crucial factor in the emergence of an accepted 'standard' English. During the Middle English period there were five main dialects. Caxton chose to use the **East Midland dialect** for the texts that he printed. The East Midland area included London, Oxford and Cambridge – the political and commercial hub of the country and the foremost centres of learning. The East Midland dialect was rapidly confirmed as the most prestigious and 'correct' form of English.

Checkpoint 1

Loan words are words that are taken from other languages. Do you know another term for such words?

Checkpoint 2

With the help of a good dictionary, investigate the origins of the following words: 'great', 'small', 'remember', 'romance', 'good', 'roof', 'purchase', 'renaissance'.

Links

You can find out more about inflections and how they changed on page 158.

With the arrival of printing, *spelling* and *punctuation* slowly became more standardized. Inconsistencies of spelling remained but gradually began to disappear. Most modern punctuation marks entered English after the invention of printing, though it wasn't until the end of the Early Modern English period that something resembling the modern punctuation system began to emerge.

The influence of Latin

The Romans first came to Britain around 55 BC, and they went on to occupy the country for 400 years. During this period they built roads and established settlements, but had surprisingly little linguistic impact. The native population continued to speak Celtic during this period, and it is not until the 16th and 17th centuries that Latin can be considered a strong influence on English. The revival of Latin was partly because during the Renaissance there was an intense interest among scholars in classical texts and authors. A measure of the importance of Latin in the history of English is the fact that – if we include Latin words that entered the language via French – more than half of our modern English vocabulary is of Latin derivation.

We have also taken from Latin many of our prefixes (e.g. *anti–*, *post–*, *pre–*) and suffixes (e.g. *–ate*, *–ic*, *–al*).

Latin words are often quite lengthy, and **Latinate vocabulary** tends to sound weighty and learned. Some examples are shown below:

Words of Latin origin

Ambiguous, colossal, dignified, emotion, exaggerate, history, immense, intellect, magnificent, monopoly, nation, ominous, opponent, quotation, ultimate, vacuum

Grammar and phonology

The **grammar** of Early Modern English reflected the fact that this was a time of transition between Middle English and the English we use today. The language of Shakespeare's plays is still marked by unusual ordering of words, inflections such as *–est* and *–eth* and the pronouns 'thou', 'thee' and 'thy'.

The main development in **phonology** was the **great vowel shift** of the 15th and 16th centuries, when the pronunciation of long vowel sounds was transformed and became similar to the pronunciation we have today.

Specimen texts ●●●

Specimen Middle and Early Modern English texts can be found on pages 148–9.

Take note

Greek was also an influence during the Early Modern English period, though to a lesser extent than Latin.

Examiner's secrets

The presence of Latinate vocabulary in a text you are analysing might be used as evidence that the text is complex or has a high level of formality.

Links

Check pages 158–9 for more on grammatical change and pages 156–7 for more on phonology.

Exam question

In what ways does the language of Text C on page 149 differ from present-day English? Your answer might consider spelling, punctuation, vocabulary and grammar. (60 min)

Examiner's secrets

Try to avoid writing a long list of points. Look for *patterns* in the ways spelling, punctuation, etc. are used.

Specimen texts

This section contains specimen texts from the three periods of English discussed on pages 144–7.

Text A (Old English)

The extract below is from Bede's *Ecclesiastical History of the English Nation*, translated from Latin into Old English in the 9th century. The extract is about Caedmon, a farm labourer who became England's first Christian poet. Beneath each line is a word-by-word translation. At the end of the extract is a translation, which changes the original into more natural modern English.

> wæs he se mon in weoruldhade geseted oð þa tide þe he
> *Was he the man in secular life settled until the time that he*
> wæs gelyfdre ylde; one næfre nænig leoð geleornode, ond he
> *was of infirm age; and never any poem learned, and he*
> for þon oft in gebeorscipe, þonne þær wæs blisse intinga
> *therefore often at banquet, when there was of-joy occasion*
> gedemed, þæt heo ealle sceolden þurh endebyrdnesse be hearpan
> *decided, that they all should by arrangement with harp*
> singan, þonne he geseah þa hearpan him nealecan, þonne aras he
> *to sing, when he saw the harp him approach, then arose he*
> for scome from þæm symble, ond ham eode to his huse.
> *for shame from the feast, and home went to his house.*

Translation

He was a man who was settled into a secular life until he was advanced in years, and had never learned any poems. He was often at banquets when it was decided the occasion should be joyful, and all those present would take it in turns to sing with the harp. When he saw the harp coming towards him, he would arise from the feast in shame, and return home to his house.

Cited in D. Crystal, *The English Language* (Penguin).

Text B (Middle English)

Below is an extract from Chaucer's *Canterbury Tales*, the greatest literary work of the Middle Ages. It was written in the late 14th century. It presents problems for the modern reader but is clearly much closer to today's English than Text A. In the extract, Chaucer describes a yeoman or forester who is travelling on a pilgrimage to Canterbury with his master, a knight.

> A yeman hadde he and servantz namo
> At that tyme, for hym liste ride so,
> And he was clad in cote and hood of grene.
> A sheef of pecok arwes, bright and kene,
> Under his belt he bar ful thriftily
> (Wel koude he dresse his takel yemanly;
> His arwes drouped noght with fetheres lowe),
> And in his hand he baar a myghty bowe.

Translation

At that time he had with him a yeoman but no other servants, for this was how he chose to travel. The yeoman wore a green coat and hood, and attached very carefully to his belt was a sheath of bright, sharp, peacock-feathered arrows. He cared for his equipment as a skilful yeoman should; feathers that did not stick out enough would never cause his arrows to fall short. In his hand he carried a mighty bow.

Text C (Early Modern English) ●●●

The extract below was written by John Donne in 1623. Donne was a poet and was also Dean of St Paul's Cathedral in London.

All *mankinde* is of one *Author*, and is one *volume*; when one man dies, one *Chapter* is not *torne* out of the *booke*, but *translated* into a better *language*; and euery *Chapter* must be so *translated*; *God* imploies seuerall *translators*; some peeces are translated by *age*, some by *sicknes*, some by *war*, some by *iustice*; but *Gods* hand is in euery *translation*; and his hand shall binde vp all our scattered leaues againe, for that *Library* where euery *booke* shall ly open to one another: As therfore the *Bell* that ringes to a *Sermon*, calls not vpon the *Preacher* only, but vpon the *Congregation* to come; so this *Bell* calls vs all; but how much more *mee*, who am brought so neer the *doore* by this *sicknesse*. No Man is an *Iland*, intire of it self; euery man is a piece of the *Coninent*, a part of the *maine*; if a *clod* be washed away by the *Sea*, *Europe* is the lesse, as wel as if a *Promontory* were, as well as if a *Mannor* of thy *friends*, or of *thine owne* were; Any mans *death* diminishes *mee*, because I am inuolued in *mankind*; And therfore neuer send to know for whom the *bell* tols; It tols for *thee*.

Source: David Burnley *The History of the English Language: A Source Book* (Longman, 1992).

Examiner's secrets

You might be able to spot the two well-known English sayings which originated in this text.

Late Modern English

Example

Rules dating from the 18th century include those forbidding double negatives, split infinitives and ending sentences with prepositions. Today, these rules continue to be defended with vigour by supporters of traditional grammar.

Checkpoint 1

What is the difference between **lexical** and **semantic** change?

Checkpoint 2

List some examples of **Americanisms** in common use.

The jargon

A **genre** is a form or type: westerns and thrillers are examples of film genres; novels, letters and advertisements are all genres of written English.

Study of the **Late Modern English** period (which begins in 1700) brings our overview of the development of English up to the present day. The language of the period is much more recognizable to the modern reader than that of earlier times.

Late Modern English

The changes to the language between the beginning of the Late Modern English period and the present day have not been as far-reaching as those that occurred in the centuries before.

Standardization

The movement towards a stable, standardized language continued. Many of the rules of *grammar* that we observe today began life in the 18th century, when several influential textbooks of grammar were written.

The first great dictionary of English, compiled by Samuel Johnson, was published in 1755. This made an important contribution to the standardization of word *meanings* and *spellings*.

During the Late Modern English period, *regional differences* in the way language is used lessened. The growth in education and literacy and improved communications have caused many dialect words and expressions to be replaced by Standard English vocabulary.

Regional slang, however, is still very much alive, and marked differences in *pronunciation* remain between different parts of the country (though the spread of Estuary English has reduced these differences in the south-east).

New words have also continued to pour into the language. The scientific and technological advances of the Industrial Revolution created a huge number of words. New inventions remain one of the main sources of lexical and semantic change.

English as an international language

During this period, English has become an international language, and new varieties (American English, Indian English and so on) have been created. The expansion of the British Empire in the 19th century, and the emergence of the United States as a superpower in the 20th century, have been the driving forces here. These international varieties have in turn had an influence on our own English, as the increasing number of Americanisms in everyday use illustrates.

Specimen texts

Language continues to undergo constant change. Moreover, the styles and conventions of particular genres are always being modified and updated. Texts A and B are both newspaper editorials. Text A is a *Daily Mirror* editorial from 1912 after the sinking of the *Titanic*, and Text B appeared in the *Sun* in 1996, following a fire in the Channel Tunnel.

ONE TOUCH OF NATURE.

DRAUGHTSMEN, expert in floating architecture, sat in their drawing offices and prepared designs for the new great palace of the seas, that was to carry restless comfort-loving people from one world to another. An exquisite little model of the palace was made in wood, with the innumerable plates and rivets marked thereon, from which model, again, a score of detailed plans were made showing each section enlarged. All this employed the well-paid work of scores of clever people: but all this was but a prelude to the real thing.

The real thing, after this relatively abstract preparation, was the concrete battle with resistent matter. Work of the disciplined hand was to follow labour of directing mind.

At once, with formidable din of ringing blow, you may imagine the workshops in the shipyard beginning to hammer upon the hints provided. An army of workmen, a colony of workshops, a population supported upon this! Frames and plates for the gigantic vessel's sides, plates for the keel which must be "sighted" till its evenness is perfect, riveting of steel-frame ribs, staying by cross-girders, a slow building up of the sides of the sea-monster. You see, then, a mighty scaffolding erected by regiments of carefully divided men, each section of them mastering each piece, as the unearthly forest of pine poles rears itself along the length of the building berth. Meanwhile, more men labouring with trained minds and obedient bodies, hour by hour, week by week, proceed with the making of the bulkhead divisions, the deck plates, the deck structures, each in its careful order and situation. Huge hydraulic gantries with electric power assist in the riveting and flattening. Thousands of pounds of electric power, thousands of pounds for the men employed (between three and four thousand of these), thousands of pounds in valuable matter expended, two years or so of unceasing toil in the slow creation of a vessel of many thousand tons—it all amounts at the end to something like a million and a half in money; if, for the moment, you consider money as representative of worth.

And then the launching—the huge building slips, the floating crane, with its enormous pillars, the sense of wonder and triumph on that breezy day with a high tide when the Leviathan leaves workshop to receive her final touches—the bowels of her Vulcanic heat, followed by the dry dock finishings. Next—the inauguration, the proud display of her perfection. Now all is ready and the combined skill, the converging effort of an army of human beings, has resulted at last in this comfortable sea-home for those who buy their passages in it. A permanent population is appointed to live here, with the changing passengers ready to begin the voyage. . . .

There is much in that warning of the philosophers about the grain of sand mightily influential as obstacle in the way of mechanism; or in their thoughts of human endeavour wrecked by some little kink in the brain, some mote in the eye, some stone falling by chance, so that the very philosopher himself, who was to shatter worlds by his speculation, now lies ashes and nothingness. For Nature, in her careless manner, steps in and makes the time and the labour, the constant effort of the many intelligences, void and helpless before a piece of herself, a futile iceberg, left floating in the monster's way. In one second, by a mere touch of this Nature, our stepmother, the striving of an army of men is turned to mockery. The Titanic has met an iceberg on her maiden voyage overseas.

W. M.

Source: The Daily Mirror 16/4/1912

THE SUN SAYS

Black hole

THE one thing everyone feared was a fire in the Channel Tunnel.

But we were assured that the safety measures could cope with anything.

That is clearly not true.

A catalogue of failures and human errors could easily have led to a huge loss of life.

Happily, everyone survived – but it could all have been so different.

The public deserves a full explanation of what went wrong and what will be done to make sure that it never happens again.

WHY did the blazing train stop in the tunnel instead of heading for safety?

Sophisticated

WHY was there almost an hour's delay before Eurotunnel told Kent fire HQ about the blaze?

WHY didn't the driver or the train chief uncouple the blazing wagons and move the train to safety?

WHY did they panic, according to passengers, instead of doing what they were trained to do?

WHY did the train chief open the carriage doors and let in toxic fumes?

WHY didn't the sophisticated ventilation system blow the smoke away?

These are not just quibbles about procedures. They are vital questions of public safety that must be dealt with swiftly.

Eurotunnel have a clear duty to provide answers. Until they do, a lot of people won't go near the Chunnel.

The facts about this near-disaster must not be allowed to disappear down a black hole.

Source: The Sun 25/11/1999

Exam question

answer: pages 166–8

Compare the use of language in the two editorials, considering in particular how far the fact that they were written at different times is reflected in the language of the two texts. (60 min)

Examiner's secrets

You might consider graphological features; content; overall structure; vocabulary and meaning; tone and address to the reader; grammar; and any other linguistic features you consider to be of interest.

Lexical change

The next two sections of this chapter look at changes to the vocabulary that we use. If new words are added to our vocabulary – or if old words fall out of use – this is known as **lexical change**. If words remain in use but change their meaning in some way this is called **semantic change**. In looking at lexical change, we need to examine **word formation** – i.e. the various ways in which new words (or **neologisms**) are formed.

Completely new words

Coinage refers to the creation of words that are completely new and not derived in any way from other words. Very few words enter the language like this, as almost all new words relate in some way to words that already exist.

Words from other languages

Borrowing occurs when words are taken from other languages. Such words are also known as **loan words**. Examples: soprano (Italian), prince (French), lager (German), alcohol (Arabic). Over the centuries, English has absorbed an especially large number of French, Latin and Greek words.

Borrowings sometimes occur when a new idea or product is introduced into English life (the Russian word 'vodka' entered the language in this way). They can also reflect the power or prestige that a language has at a particular time. The political and economic power of the United States, and the influence of American culture, are reflected in our use of an increasing number of Americanisms (e.g. 'gofer', 'off-limits').

Words formed from existing words

Affixing is the most common source of new words. It involves adding **prefixes** or **suffixes** (see page 14) to existing words to form new words. Prefixes often used in this way include *micro-* (as in 'microwave'), *multi-* (as in 'multimedia'), *inter-*, *super-*, *mega-* and so on. The suffix *-ism* is now often used to indicate prejudice (as in 'ageism' and 'sizeism'). Since the Watergate political scandal in the United States in the early 1970s *-gate* has become a suffix denoting scandal (e.g. 'Irangate').

Compounding occurs when words are combined to form a new, larger word or expression. The words 'blackbird' and 'laptop' came about in this way. Compounds are sometimes divided by a hyphen ('blue-eyed') and can also be separate words ('head waiter', 'happy hour').

Blends are similar to compounding, except that only parts of each word are joined together (usually the beginning of one word and the end of another). Examples: 'smog' (smoke + fog), 'motel' (motor + hotel) and the computer term 'bit' (binary + digit).

The jargon

Remember: **lexis** is another word for vocabulary. The collective noun for all of the words in the vocabulary of a language is a **lexicon**.

Checkpoint 1

Do you know any examples of words of French, Latin or Greek origin?

Checkpoint 2

Find more examples by thinking of words that begin with these prefixes.

Take note

The suffix *–ism* can also indicate a philosophy or belief system, as in 'socialism', 'Buddhism', etc.

Watch out!

Make sure you remember the difference between **blends** and **compounds**.

Conversion occurs when the word class of an existing word changes, creating a new use for the word. For example, words might change from noun to verb (to 'bottle'), from verb to noun (a 'contest') and from adjective to verb (to 'open').

Words formed by shortening ●●●

Abbreviation   A new word is formed by shortening an existing word in some way. Examples: 'ad' (vert) (from 'advertisement'), 'bus' (from 'omnibus') and 'burger' (from 'hamburger').

Back formation   A particular kind of shortening in which a word of one type (usually a noun) is shortened to form a word of another type (usually a verb). Examples: 'edit' (from 'editor'), 'donate' (from 'donation') and 'burgle' (from 'burglar').

Acronyms   Words formed from the initial letters of existing words, a process virtually unknown before the 20th century. Examples: 'radar' (from 'radio detection and ranging') and 'scuba' ('self-contained under-water breathing apparatus'). Acronyms often consist of capital letters, as in NATO (North Atlantic Treaty Organisation) and the computer language BASIC (beginner's all-purpose symbolic instruction code).

Initialisms   Here words are abbreviated to their initial letters, but the resulting set of letters is not pronounced as a word: MP (Member of Parliament), BBC (British Broadcasting Corporation). CD-ROM is partly an initialism (CD, short for 'compact disk') and partly an acronym (ROM, from 'read only memory').

Words from names   Some words derive from the names of people or places. 'Sandwich' is named after the fourth Earl of Sandwich, who put food between slices of bread so he could eat while he gambled. 'Denim' was a material originally imported 'de Nimes' (from Nimes, in France). Other words were originally trade names ('yo-yo', 'hoover').

Losing words from the lexicon ●●●

Don't forget that words can also fall out of use. Words and phrases that become obsolete are known as **archaisms**. Shakespeare's plays are full of such archaisms as 'enow' (enough), 'forsooth' (in truth) and 'bark' (ship).

Exam question   answer: page 168

The words and expressions below first appeared in dictionaries of English in the 1990s. Discuss the processes of word formation that they illustrate.

road rage

Blairism

mockney (a fake Cockney accent)

digizine (an internet magazine)

a domestic (a violent family quarrel)

a tamagotchi (a cyber pet)

WLTM and GSOH ('would like to meet' and 'a good sense of humour', both found in lonely hearts columns)

arm candy (a decorative boy or girl friend). (45 min)

The jargon

An alternative term for words formed by abbreviation is **clipping**.

Check the net

The Merriam-Webster New Book of Word Histories has a site that includes some interesting examples of word histories.
www.m-w.com/whist/etyterm.htm

Examiner's secrets

For each word or expression, don't simply name the relevant type of word formation. Explain what it involves and how it has worked in this particular instance.

Semantic change

Semantic changes are changes in the meaning of words. The main types of semantic change are described below.

Broadening (or generalization)

This occurs when the meaning of a word broadens, so that it retains its old meaning but takes on an added meaning as well. Examples:

→ 'Holiday' originally meant 'holy day', a day of religious importance. Now it can mean any day when one does not have to work.
→ 'Dog' originally referred to a particular breed of dog but now includes all breeds.

Examples

Other examples of broadening include 'barn' (which originally referred specifically to a place where barley was stored) and 'aunt' (originally just 'father's sister', now 'father or mother's sister').

Narrowing (or specialization)

The opposite of 'broadening' – here a word becomes more specific in its meaning. Examples:

→ 'Meat' originally denoted food in general, not just animal flesh.
→ 'Girl' in the Middle Ages referred to young people in general, not only females.

Amelioration

This occurs when the change gives the word a meaning that is more pleasant or more positive. Example:

→ 'Pretty' once meant 'sly' or 'cunning' but now means 'attractive'.
→ 'Wicked' still has its older meaning of 'evil' but as a modern slang word can also mean 'superb', 'brilliant'.

Checkpoint 1

Can you think of any other words where the slang meaning is the opposite of the traditional meaning?

Pejoration

This occurs when the change in meaning is in the opposite direction to amelioration, becoming less favourable. Examples:

→ 'Cowboy' is now often used to indicate incompetence or dishonesty (e.g. 'cowboy builders').
→ 'Impertinent' once meant 'irrelevant' (i.e. not pertinent) but now means 'rude'.

Weakening

This refers to words losing over time some of their original force or strength. Example: 'Soon' now means in the near future but used to mean 'immediately'.

Metaphor

Words often acquire new meanings because they begin to be used metaphorically. Examples:

→ 'Hawks' and 'doves' are now not just birds but also politicians favouring war and peace, respectively.
→ 'Onion bag' refers to the net of a goal in football as well as a bag containing onions.

Watch out!

Don't forget that when a word changes its meaning, more than one process is often at work simultaneously – e.g. when words take on a metaphorical meaning this is also **broadening**.

Idioms

Idioms are always formed from previously existing words. Examples:

→ 'In the doghouse', 'under the weather', 'over the moon'.
→ 'Wake up and smell the coffee' is a more recent example, meaning 'Get in touch with the real world'.

Idioms often have interesting and colourful origins. For example, the expression 'raining cats and dogs' may derive from a time when drainage was so inadequate that storms would claim the lives of large numbers of cats and dogs. When the floodwaters subsided, their bodies would litter the streets.

Euphemisms

A **euphemism** is a mild or inoffensive way of describing something distasteful or unpleasant. New euphemisms are constantly being invented. Examples:

→ In the world of business, a lack of money may be described as a 'cashflow problem', and the sacking of employees may be referred to as 'downsizing'.
→ Modern warfare employs many euphemisms: bombing raids are 'surgical strikes', and if civilian casualties occur this is 'collateral damage'.

Political correctness

In modern English, some semantic change has arisen from the desire for political correctness. There has been a drive to replace words and expressions that are considered offensive or demeaning to disadvantaged or minority groups. Examples:

→ 'People with learning difficulties' (in place of 'the mentally handicapped').
→ 'Mixed race' (replacing 'half-caste').
→ Words such as 'actor', 'sculptor', etc. (which now refer to females as well as males).

Checkpoint 2

Can you define the term *idiom*?

Links

For more on euphemisms and political correctness, see pages 108–11.

Exam questions   answers: page 168

1 The words below are cited by Crystal in *The Cambridge Encyclopaedia of the English Language* as examples of semantic change. Each word is followed by its earlier meaning. Explain the modern meanings that these words have and, with reference to these words and to other examples of your own, describe some of the main processes of semantic change. (45 min)

   Lean: thin, emaciated.

   Novice: a member of a religious order who has not yet taken the vows.

   Revolutionary: Someone who favours overthrowing the government.

   Lewd: 'of the laity' – i.e. not occupying an official position within the Church.

2 Consider the influence of euphemisms and political correctness on the language that we use today. (45 min)

Examiner's secrets

Note that, in addition to discussing the words listed, the wording of the question allows you to show your knowledge of processes of semantic change not illustrated by these examples.

Phonological change

Phonological change refers to changes in the pronunciation of words. These are also known as 'sound changes'. Some of the more notable examples of phonological change identified by researchers are outlined below.

The great English vowel shift, 1400–1600

This was a dramatic and important example of sound change. Over a period of approximately 200 years the pronunciation of long vowel sounds changed, replacing them with sounds similar to those we have today. Thousands of words were affected. Some examples of the **great vowel shift** are shown below.

Modern English word	Middle English pronunciation
to	toe
wife	weef
mouse	moos
been	bayn
her	heer

Martha's Vineyard (Labov 1963)

This is a well-known American study of phonological change. William Labov carried out research at Martha's Vineyard, an island off the north-east coast of the United States. The island has a small resident population but is also a popular holiday resort regularly visited by thousands of Americans.

Labov found that the pronunciation of certain vowel sounds was subtly changing, shifting away from the standard American pronunciation.

The source of the change seemed to be the island's fishermen. In fact, the local accent had always differed slightly from that of the mainland, but it appeared that in the speech of the fishermen these differences were now becoming stronger. After the fishermen, the people whose speech was most affected were resident islanders aged 30–45.

Labov believed that the inhabitants of Martha's Vineyard were speaking in this way to distance themselves from the 'outsiders' who holidayed on the island. The fishermen (a tightly knit social group) were especially resentful of the summer influx of visitors, and the 30–45-year-olds imitated their speech in order to show that they too regarded themselves as true, loyal islanders.

Labov found that the islanders were apparently not conscious that their speech was changing. They were not altering their pronunciation deliberately. He refers to this kind of change – change that is unconscious – as change from below (meaning below the level of conscious awareness). Change from above is change that is conscious.

Links

Also check pages 146–7.

Links

Labov's New York research (pages 92–3) is also relevant to this topic.

Checkpoint 1

Why do you think younger islanders were less likely to speak like the fishermen?

Recent British examples ●●●

Kerswill and Williams (1994) studied speech in Milton Keynes (a new town in Buckinghamshire, 50 miles from London). They found that children's speech not only differed from that of their parents (many of whom were not born in Milton Keynes) but also from that of older native inhabitants of the area. The children's speech was closer to that of children in London.

The Milton Keynes findings illustrate the spread of **Estuary English** (see page 98), an accent that is spreading outwards across the country from London and the south-east. Examples of Estuary English pronunciation are 'waaw' (wall), 'cauwt' (caught) and 'auwfuw' (awful).

Aitchison (1991) identified the following additional examples of recent or current change in British pronunciation:

→ Words such as 'mistake', 'astronomy' and 'mosquito' being pronounced 'merstake', 'erstronomy' and 'mersquito'.
→ Replacing *t* in a word such as 'football' with a glottal stop, so that no *t* is heard: ('foo'ball').

Another recent phenomenon is the spread of what has been termed **uptalk** or **upspeak**. This is the tendency to speak with a rising intonation (as if asking a question), even when uttering declaratives. It is a speech habit especially associated with young people, and is thought to be more common among females than males. Its increasing use has been partly attributed to the influence of Australian television soaps such as *Neighbours*.

Why does phonological change happen? ●●●

The reasons for phonological change are not always clear (e.g. no one is quite sure why the great vowel shift occurred). However, in several of the cases referred to above, *social factors* seem to have played an important part: we imitate the speech of people we admire or respect in some way, and in this way language change spreads. Aitchison (1991) has identified four stages to phonological changes of the kind found by Labov on Martha's Vineyard.

→ **Stage 1**   The speech of a particular social group differs in some way from the usual pronunciation of the area in which they live.
→ **Stage 2**   A second social group begins – possibly unconsciously – to imitate the speech of the first group.
→ **Stage 3**   The new pronunciation becomes established among the second group – it is now part of their usual accent.
→ **Stage 4**   A third social group now begins to model itself on the second group, and the process repeats itself.

Checkpoint 2

Do you know the origin of the term **Estuary English**?

Check the net

Visit the Estuary English website at www.phon.ucl.ac.uk /home/estuary/home.htm

The jargon

A **glottal stop** is also present in the Cockney pronunciation of words such as 'better' (be'er) and 'water' (wa'er).

Examiner's secrets

Your answer should have plenty of examples, but try to avoid an answer that reads like a list – arrange your examples into groups.

Exam question   answer: pages 168–9

'Language is always changing'. Discuss this statement with particular reference to phonological change in present-day Britain. (45 min)

Grammatical change

While English grammar has changed considerably since the Old English period, most of these changes occurred before the end of the Middle Ages. In the last few hundred years, the grammar of the language has been relatively stable, though grammatical change can (and does) still happen. In the 18th and 19th centuries, vigorous attempts were made to 'fix' the rules of grammar (see page 150), and this helps to explain why grammar is more resistant to change than vocabulary and phonology.

Inflections

One of the most important developments in the language since Old English has been the loss of **inflections**. Inflections indicate the grammatical form of a word. Most inflections involve the *ends* of words.

Verbs: inflections usually indicate *tense*, *person* or *number*.

Tense	present	he walk*s*
	past	he walk*ed*
Person	first person	I walk
	third person	he walk*s*
Number	singular	he walk*s*
	plural	they walk

Nouns: inflections usually show *number* or *gender*.

Number	singular	actor
	plural	actor*s*
Gender	male	act*or*
	female	act*ress*

Adjectives: inflections are used for *comparatives* and *superlatives*, as in fast, fast*er*, fast*est*.

Although there are still inflections in modern English, there were once many more. Old English was very reliant on them, but most Old English inflections disappeared during the Middle Ages.

Today, the great majority of nouns change from singular to plural by the simple addition of *s* at the end of the word: book/books, pen/pens, etc. In Old English and Middle English the ways of indicating that a noun was a plural were more varied. For example, in Old English the plural of 'hand' was 'handa', and in Middle English the plural of 'eye' was 'eyen'.

In the Early Modern English period, some inflections were still in use that are not found today – e.g. the *–th* and *–st* endings in verbs ('doth', 'dost').

Pronouns

The pronouns 'thou', 'thee' and 'thine' (originally second person singular pronouns) have generally disappeared from English. Interestingly, in some regional dialects a distinction still exists between singular and plural second person pronouns, with the use of 'youse' as a plural word.

Links

For more detail on inflections, check pages 14–15.

Checkpoint 1

Do you think the gender inflections in words such as 'actor/actress', 'sculptor/sculptress', 'author/authoress', etc. will eventually disappear? If so, why?

Checkpoint 2

Plural forms in English are generally regular, but there continue to be some exceptions. Can you think of plural nouns that do not end in –*s*?

Word order

As explained above, in Old English the grammatical functions of words were mainly indicated by inflections. For example, inflections would indicate whether a word was the subject of a sentence or the object. This meant that, compared with modern English, the expression of meaning was less dependent on word order. As a result, the construction of sentences was freer and word order showed more variation.

In modern English word order is less flexible, but there is still some variation. Some English speakers, for example, would say 'She gave me it', while others would say 'She gave it me'. The second of these is the older construction. 'She gave me it' began to be used two or three hundred years ago.

Examiner's secrets

When analysing texts from the past, look for sentences in which the word order differs from modern English.

Negative constructions

Today, multiple negatives (as in the double negative 'I don't want nothing') are considered incorrect grammar. In the past, they were considered quite acceptable and were used for emphasis, as in this line from Chaucer's *Canterbury Tales*, written in the 14th century:

Ther nas no man nowher so vertuous ('Ther nas' = There was not)

An informal negative construction that originated in the United States in the late 19th century is the addition of 'not' at the end of a positive statement, so that the earlier part of the sentence becomes ironic (as in 'That haircut really suits you – not'). The construction became especially popular after it featured in the film *Wayne's World* in 1992.

Take note

Double negatives such as 'I don't know nothing about it' are easy to spot, but other kinds slip into speech unnoticed. 'I shouldn't be surprised if . . .' and 'I shouldn't wonder if . . .' are often followed by an unnecessary second negative: 'I shouldn't be surprised if it didn't rain' should technically be 'I shouldn't be surprised if it rained.'

Who and *Whom*

According to traditional grammar, the personal pronoun 'who' should change to 'whom' when it refers to the object in a clause: *the man who met me yesterday* ('who' refers to the subject, 'the man'); *the man whom I met yesterday* (the subject is now 'I'). In practice however many people would use 'who' in both of these examples. The use of 'whom' is increasingly regarded as excessively formal, though the word may be kept alive by its continued regular use after prepositions ('with whom', 'for whom' etc.).

Exam question   answer: page 169

The following quotations are all from Shakespeare's *King Richard the Third*. In what ways does the grammar of these quotations differ from that of modern English?

a) Saw you the King today, my lord of Derby?

b) A murd'rous villain, and so still thou art.

c) A husband and a son thou ow'st to me;
    And thou a kingdom; all of you, allegiance.

d) What mean'st thou that thou help'st me not?

e) Then say at once what is it thou demand'st. (45 min)

Examiner's secrets

All of the aspects of grammar referred to in this section are relevant to this question.

Causes of language change

Language change usually takes place very slowly, and determining exactly when and where a change began is almost always impossible. This means that it is not easy to say what causes language to change. It seems, however, that a variety of factors – sometimes operating simultaneously – can cause change to occur.

Ease of articulation ●●●

Some words change in ways that make them *physically easier to say*. This helps to explain many of the *phonological changes* that have occurred in English. Usually, such changes involve either **omission** or **assimilation**.

Omission

This occurs when sounds disappear from words. Over the centuries, English has lost many word endings. In Shakespeare's plays, we find characters saying 'hadst' and 'gavest' where we would simply say 'had' and 'gave'. We no longer pronounce the *b* sound at the end of words like 'tomb', 'lamb' and 'thumb'. A similar process was at work when 'God be with you' gradually became shortened to 'goodbye'. In modern English, we usually say 'phone' rather than 'telephone' and 'gym' rather than 'gymnasium' – the longer versions of these words may eventually disappear.

Assimilation

This takes place when the pronunciation of a phoneme is affected by the phoneme that is next to it. Pronunciation of the phoneme is changed so that it becomes easier. The way most people pronounce the word 'sandwich' – 'samwich' – illustrates both omission and assimilation. The *d* is dropped (omission) and the *n* changes to an *m* because the *w* that comes after it makes an *m* sound easier to pronounce (assimilation).

Regularization ●●●

This occurs when we change language in order to make it more consistent. We look (often unconsciously) for rules and patterns in the language that we use and will sometimes change words and constructions if they seem odd or different. This process is also known as **analogy** and can affect all areas of language, including grammar, phonology, lexis and spelling.

An example often cited is the word 'pea'. Originally this was 'pease' (there is still a dish called 'pease pudding'), but over time 'pease/peas' became a plural word and a new singular noun, 'pea', came into use. This brought 'pea/peas' into line with the great majority of other nouns, which only have an –s ending when the word is plural.

An example of regularization in spelling is the word 'delight', which originally was not spelled with the letters 'gh'. Adding these letters made it consistent with such similar sounding words as 'light' and 'night'.

Example

Another example is the omission of *e* from the ends of many words. 'Sweete' and 'roote' are examples. The old word endings reflect earlier pronunciation of the words.

Checkpoint 1

What is a **phoneme**?

Checkpoint 2

Do you know what the word 'analogy' usually means? Can you think why it is used to describe this process?

We see regularization at work when children acquire language. A child might say 'falled over' instead of 'fell over', applying the rule that the past tenses of verbs usually end in –*ed*.

Social influences ●●●

Language change often reflects changes in society:

→ Changing circumstances in society create a need to express new meanings. New inventions, new ideas, etc. all require new words to describe them (see page 142). Words that are no longer needed fall out of use.

→ Some changes are motivated by the desire for novelty, the wish to be different or fashionable. The creation of new **slang** expressions often exemplifies this.

→ Changing attitudes can cause certain words and expressions to become less popular, and others to be favoured in their place. The influence of **political correctness** (see pages 108–9) is an example of this.

→ Changes are more likely to spread if they are considered to have **social prestige**. The work of Labov and others (see pages 92–3) has shown that people sometimes change their language to sound more sophisticated or to claim a higher social status.

→ **Geographical factors** can also be important. The movement of people from one part of the country to another helps changes to spread. The rise of **Estuary English** is partly explained by the movement of Londoners away from the capital (see pages 88–9).

Influence of other languages ●●●

Contact with other languages often brings about language change. This contact can take many different forms: military invasion, immigration, trading links, cultural products such as films and television programmes.

Such contact is especially likely to influence vocabulary. The English language contains many **borrowings** – words taken from other languages (see page 152).

The Viking invasions of the 9th and 10th centuries added many words to the language. The Norman Conquest meant that many French words entered the language during the Middle Ages. Latin and Greek were also important influences. In recent years, the popularity of American culture and the political and economic power of the United States have resulted in an influx of Americanisms.

Links

Overregularization by children is discussed on pages 126–7.

Links

Slang is discussed on pages 100–1.

Exam question   answer: page 169

'At any given time the language of a society reflects the social and economic conditions of the people who use it. We need look no further for the causes of language change'.

Consider this statement with specific reference to English. (45 min)

Examiner's secrets

Often quotations that are included in questions have *some* truth – but you may not want to agree with them in their entirety.

Attitudes to language change

Changes in the language that we use arouse strong emotions, with examples of change often seized upon as confirmation that standards in society are falling. Others argue that change is inevitable, and that we should focus on how language is changing rather than make judgements about how good or how bad these changes are.

Prescriptivist and descriptivist approaches

→ **Prescriptivists** favour rules that identify 'correct' language usage. They disapprove of uses of language that break these rules.
→ **Descriptivists** seek to describe, as accurately and objectively as possible, how language is actually used. They do not label particular uses of language 'correct' or 'incorrect'.

Origins of prescriptivism

Hostility to language change is not surprising. Each generation tends to regards its tastes, habits and values as superior to those of succeeding generations. There is a long tradition of such hostility: 2 000 years ago in ancient Rome, writers were railing against the way their younger contemporaries were speaking Latin.

Prescriptivism in England became firmly established in the 18th century, when there were strenuous efforts to standardize the language. Books of grammar set out numerous rules and sought to define correct and incorrect usage. Their authors were partly attempting to model English on the revered ancient languages of Latin and Greek, but personal likes, dislikes and prejudices also influenced what they wrote.

The rules of the 18th-century grammarians found their way into school textbooks, and many are still taught today. In fact, many of the complaints about declining standards of grammar in present-day English (see below) are concerned with breaches of these same rules.

During the 19th century, language became linked with general standards of behaviour. Just as there were 'proper' ways to act, so there was a proper way to speak. This association of language and morality is still with us: language is seen as a reflection of character, and those who deviate from the old standards of 'correctness' are condemned as 'uncouth' and 'slovenly'.

Examples of prescriptivism

Grammar

→ **Double negatives**, e.g. 'I don't know nothing about that'. These are often condemned on the grounds that in mathematics two negatives make a positive, so that the speaker is actually saying the opposite of what he or she intended. Double negatives were once perfectly acceptable in English (they can be found in Chaucer and Shakespeare), and sentences containing them are not likely to be misunderstood. Many other languages employ multiple negatives.

- → **Ending a sentence with a preposition.** According to traditional rules of grammar, this is to be avoided: instead of asking 'Who will you be coming with?' we should say 'With whom will you be coming?' The rule is widely ignored but if obeyed can result in clumsy, tortuous sentences (compare 'People worth talking to' with 'People with whom it is worthwhile to talk').
- → **Split infinitives,** as in the example made famous by *Star Trek*: 'to boldly go'. Some prescriptivists would argue that this should be corrected to 'boldly to go' (or 'to go boldly'). Again there is no logic to this rule, and following it can lead to awkward, unnatural constructions.

Vocabulary

There is often hostility to **borrowings**, especially if they seem likely to replace existing English words. People who wish to conserve English and protect it from foreign influences are known as *purists*.

In recent years, American English has been an especially strong influence on our language (as it has on other world languages), and objections are often raised to our increasing use of **Americanisms**.

Opposition to loanwords (another term for borrowings) is not confined to England. In France, the Académie Française is an institution which has tried to stem the flow of foreign words into the language, and which exercises some control over the vocabulary that is used in advertising, broadcasting and official documents. It appears though to have had little influence over the spoken language of French people, who happily refer to *un bestseller*, *le parking*, *le hotdog* and so on.

Phonology

The spread of **Estuary English** is often condemned, with broadcasters using an Estuary accent perceived as loutish and ignorant.

Language change – progress or decay? ●●●

In the 19th century, it was often suggested that English, with other European languages, was experiencing a slow and inevitable decline. An alternative theory is that languages improve over time, steadily becoming more accurate and efficient.

The view most favoured today is that English is neither progressing nor decaying – it is simply changing. Languages adapt themselves to the differing needs of each generation.

If language change is inevitable, those who oppose it are essentially fighting a losing battle. But they do have some influence on the language: it has been said that the *h* sound would have disappeared from English long ago if it were not considered socially undesirable to drop one's aitches.

Example

Winston Churchill once famously ridiculed this rule by remarking, 'This is the sort of English up with which I will not put!'

The jargon

Borrowings are words that enter English from other languages.

Take note

This objection overlooks the fact that English has absorbed many Americanisms that are now accepted as standard usage (e.g. 'lengthy', 'belittle', 'bite the dust', 'strike it rich').

Examiner's secrets

While you should certainly express your opinion, you should also show that you have knowledge and understanding of both sides of the argument.

Exam question   answer: page 169

Would you agree that the English language has changed for the worse? (45 min)

The future of English

Checkpoint

Give examples of countries where English is (a) the national language and (b) the second language.

The jargon

These international varieties of English are sometimes known as **New Englishes** or **World Englishes**.

We have seen in this chapter some of the ways in which English has changed in the past. In the future there will inevitably be further change, but the likely nature of this change is a matter of great debate.

English – a world language

English is today *the* global language and is more widely used than any other language. It is the recognized international language of business, technology, politics and popular culture.

As the table shows, over 300 million people speak English as their native language. To these can be added approximately 300 million more who use English regularly as a second language.

Languages of the world: top ten

Language	No. of speakers	Language	No. of speakers
1. Chinese	700 m	6. Bengali	140 m
2. English	320 m	7. Portuguese	130 m
3. Hindi	220 m	8. Japanese	115 m
4. Spanish	200 m	9. Arabic	110 m
5. Russian	150 m	10. German	100 m

(Source: *The Sunday Times* 1995)

The number of speakers of Mandarin Chinese is actually greater than the combined total of native English speakers and speakers of English as a second language. However, the great majority of Chinese speakers live in China itself, whereas English is spoken as a first language on every continent except South America. It is used in over 70 countries as an official or semi-official language. It has also been estimated that 75% of the world's electronically stored information is in English.

The supremacy of English as a world language can be traced back to the rise of the British Empire in the 18th and 19th centuries. As Britain established colonies around the world, so the use of English grew. In the 20th century, the economic and political strength of Britain has declined, but the emergence of the United States as a world power has meant the continued spread of English.

The future: disintegration?

Although English is spoken in many different countries of the world, each of these countries has its own **variety** of English. Important differences (especially in relation to phonology and lexis) exist between British English, American English, Indian English, etc.

There are several reasons for this. Over time, the English that is used in each country is influenced by the pre-existing languages of the country, and by the language of neighbouring territories. The language also adapts itself to local needs and conditions, and the desire for an independent national identity encourages countries to develop their own distinct versions of English.

This has led some to speculate that eventually the English language will disintegrate into a collection of related but largely separate dialects. In 1978, Robert Burchfield (then editor of the *Oxford English*

Dictionary) predicted that within a few centuries the speakers of British and American English would be unable to understand each other.

A comparison is sometimes made with Latin, now a 'dead' language but once the dominant language of Western Europe. French, Italian and Spanish, now three clearly distinct languages, all developed from Latin.

The future: uniformity? ⦿⦿⦿

A contrasting vision predicts development in the opposite direction. A **World Standard English** is said to be emerging, with the different varieties of English growing closer together – e.g. differences between British English and American English seem to be decreasing rather than increasing.

The main reason for this trend towards uniformity is the amount of communication that takes place between speakers of different varieties. Contact occasionally occurs at a personal level but is more usually by means of television, the internet, films, popular music and so on. A common culture encourages the growth of a common language.

The high level of literacy in most English-speaking countries is another factor. The people of these countries are taught to read and use a similar written language.

The number of languages in the world is diminishing, and the global spread of English is sometimes viewed as destructive. The languages of many minority races and cultures have disappeared (e.g. in Australia it has been estimated that more than 200 languages have been lost).

In England, the loss of much regional dialect vocabulary points to the development of a common variety of English. Accents appear more resistant to change, but the rise of Estuary English suggests that there is also growing phonological uniformity.

The future: bidialectalism? ⦿⦿⦿

David Crystal and others believe that the future of English is most likely to entail neither disintegration nor absolute uniformity, but a kind of compromise between the two. This view holds that **bidialectalism** – the ability to use two dialects of the same language – will persist and develop, with people able to adapt their language to meet the needs of different situations. They will use a local variety of English in their own community but a different, more international, variety when communicating with speakers from other communities.

In many areas of life (international commerce, the use of email and the Internet) we already see this happening. It is an extension of the idea that every individual has a **repertoire** of language varieties at his or her disposal.

> *"If we should be worrying about anything to do with the future of English, it should be not that the various strands will drift apart but that they will grow indistinguishable. And what a sad, sad loss that would be"*
>
> Bill Bryson, 1990

The jargon

When an individual changes from one language or language variety to another, this is known as **code-switching**. For example, people may move between regional and standard forms of English according to situation and audience.

Examiner's secrets

Don't just consider the future of English. Examine what the quotation says about English today as well.

Exam question   answer: page 169

'Today it rules the world, but tomorrow it faces inevitable extinction'. How far do you agree with this view of English? (45 min)

Answers
Language change

Origins of English; Old English

Checkpoints

1 Altogether there are about a hundred Indo-European languages, including German, Dutch, Danish, Swedish, Italian, Spanish, French, Russian, Hindi, Urdu and Bengali.
2 A dialect is a variety of language with distinctive features of vocabulary, grammar and accent. The term is most commonly used when referring to regional dialects.

Middle English; Early Modern English

Checkpoints

1 Words taken from other languages are also known as *borrowings.*
2 The following words are derived from Old English: 'great', 'small', 'good', 'roof'. The remaining words are of French origin: 'remember', 'romance', 'purchase', 'renaissance'. These words are typical in that the Old English words are shorter and more direct.

Specimen texts

Exam question

This celebrated passage by John Donne is the source of two quotations still common in English: 'no man is an island' and 'for whom the bell tolls'. The passage is notable for its development of two extended metaphors, both of which stress the unity of human life: mankind is compared to a vast 'continent', and to a 'volume' in which individual human lives are chapters.

In responding to this question, an introduction might explain that the text is from the Early Modern English period and exhibits may be of the characteristics of the English of that time. After that, the question offers a ready-made structure for an answer.

In considering the *spelling*, try to avoid a simple list of words that are spelled differently from modern English. Try to identify patterns in the spelling that is used. If you know why these differences exist, this could also be mentioned. Here are some points about the spelling of the text:

- The spelling is generally consistent, and much of it is similar to present-day English. However, there are occasional inconsistencies – 'wel' and 'well', 'sicknes' and 'sicknesse' – reflecting the fact that a completely standardized system of spelling had yet to emerge.
- Many words have an extra –*e* ending: 'mankinde', 'torne', 'booke' and so on. These endings were common in the English of the time and existed for a variety of reasons. In many cases, they were inflectional endings that had survived from Old English, though they had ceased to serve any grammatical function. In some instances, they also reflected earlier pronunciation of the words. A third reason was that early printers often added –*e* endings to words in order to justify the text (i.e. make line lengths regular). They also frequently doubled consonants for the same reason (see next point).

- Doubling of consonants is evident in 'seuerall' and 'mannor'.
- The letter *u* is often used where now there would be *v*: 'leaues', 'euery'. At the same time, there is a reverse pattern in the spelling of the time, with *v* instead of *u* at the beginning of words: 'vpon'.
- Use of *I* and *y* had not yet settled into the modern English pattern, and this is reflected in the spelling of 'imploies'.

The most notable feature of the *punctuation* is that there are very few full stops (in the original text there are just two – at the end and after 'by this sicknesse'). Instead, there is much more extensive use of semicolons than in modern English, used where we would have full stops or commas. Capital letters follow some but not all of these semicolons. At this time, capital letters were used not only for proper nouns and at the beginnings of sentences but also for important common nouns (e.g. 'Iland', 'Chapter', 'Sea') and to indicate emphasized words and phrases. It was not until the late 18th century that they began to be used more sparingly. Another feature of the punctuation is that an apostrophe followed by an *s* ('*s*) is not used to show possession ('Gods hand', 'Any mans death').

The *vocabulary* of the text includes a few archaisms, such as 'leaues' (meaning pages), 'the maine' (the mainland) and 'Mannor' (house, as in 'manor house').

An aspect of the *grammar* of the text noted earlier is that it is not constructed in conventional modern sentences. The second person singular pronouns 'thee', 'thy' and 'thine' are used, together with 'it self' for the modern English 'itself'. The preposition 'of' was more widely used at the time of the text than now, resulting in such constructions as 'intire of it self' and 'All mankinde is of one Author'. The word order of some constructions is also different from modern English, as in 'calls not upon the Preacher only'.

Examiner's secrets

> Above all, in answering questions such as this try to be analytical. Do not simply say what the differences are: comment on them, look for links between them and try to explain why they are there.

Late Modern English

Checkpoints

1 Lexical change occurs when new words enter the language and others disappear. Semantic change refers to changes in the meanings of words.
2 The many Americanisms in everyday use include 'radio', 'airline', 'soap opera', 'junk food', 'face the music', 'strike it rich', 'make the grade'.

Exam question

Candidates tend to approach comparison questions of this kind in one of two ways. The first approach is to analyse each text in turn. The second text is analysed in the light of what has been said about the first, so it is the second part of the answer that actually compares the texts. The other approach is to devote a paragraph each to graphological features, content, overall structure and so on. In each of these paragraphs there is discussion and comparison of both texts. Both these approaches can work well, though a danger of the first is that too much time may be spent on the first text, with the result that the answer does not contain enough *comparison* of the texts. Some suggested points are listed below.

Graphological features
Text A

Little attempt to make the text visually appealing or accessible. Mostly dense text. Has a headline plus larger type size for the opening of the article, with use of a dropped capital at the beginning of the first word ('DRAUGHTSMEN'), which is also capitalized.

Text B

More extensive use of graphological features, as is typical of modern tabloids. Variety of type sizes; extensive use of bold face, underlining, and italics; text broken up by inclusion of crosshead ('Sophisticated').

Content
Text A

Devotes much of the editorial to a detailed account of the different stages in the construction of the *Titanic*. Then ends by describing how the product of all this human endeavour was destroyed in an instant. Sees a lesson in this – a reminder of the power of nature. Doesn't seek to attribute blame for the accident or call anyone to account.

Text B

Believes the accident in the tunnel was the result of human failure and error. Emphasizes that Eurotunnel has a responsibility to the public and demands that it answer a series of questions.

Overall structure
Text A

Paragraphs generally much longer than in Text B. Four of the five paragraphs trace the construction of the *Titanic*. First paragraph – the design of the ship. Second paragraph – a short paragraph that serves as a transition between the 'abstract' design work described in the first paragraph and the 'concrete' construction work that is then described in the third paragraph. Fourth paragraph – the launching. Final paragraph – more abstract, philosophical; a reflection on the significance of the accident.

Text B

A series of very short paragraphs, again characteristic of modern tabloids. All but two are single-sentence paragraphs. After a few introductory paragraphs about the fire – an event everyone feared but had been assured would present no danger – main body of the article is set of questions the newspaper insists Eurotunnel must answer. Concluding three paragraphs are a series of repeated demands for a response from Eurotunnel.

Vocabulary and meaning
Text A

- Occasional archaisms: 'thereon', 'a score', 'electric power', 'draughtsmen', 'mechanism', 'buy their passages'.
- Often formal: 'relatively abstract preparation', 'concrete battle with resistant matter', 'work of the disciplined hand', 'labour of directing mind', 'expended', 'unceasing toil', 'proceed'.

- Detailed account of how ships were constructed at the time gives rise to much field-specific lexis, often quite technical: 'plates', 'rivets', 'frames', 'staying by cross-girders', 'building berth', 'bulkhead divisions', 'dry dock finishings'.
- More extensive use of metaphor than text B: 'great palace of the seas', 'comfortable sea-home', 'sea-monster', 'army of workmen', 'colony of workshops', 'unearthly forest of pine poles'.

Text B

- Less complex. Train-related field-specific lexis is simple, uncomplicated: 'trains', 'wagons', 'carriage', 'doors', 'ventilation system'.
- Less formal. Occasional contractions ('won't', 'didn't'). 'Chunnel' – informal blend. 'Kent fire HQ' – abbreviation.
- Use of journalese: 'blaze', 'blazing'. Also typical of the tabloids is the play on words in 'black hole' – used metaphorically at the end of article but also refers literally to the tunnel.

Tone and address to reader
Text A

- More restrained than Text B. But does emphasize the scale of the construction work: 'Innumerable plates and rivets', 'scores of clever people', 'regiments of carefully divided men', 'many thousand tons'. Also stresses the impressiveness of the ship: 'palace', 'exquisite', 'huge', 'gigantic', 'enormous', 'wonder', 'triumph'.
- Occasionally addresses the reader directly – 'you may imagine'; 'if, for the moment, you consider' – but generally more impersonal than text B.
- Also more formal than Text B, though there are occasional informalities: 'something like', 'for the moment', 'the real thing'.

Text B

- Tone is much more direct and aggressive than Text A. Much of the editorial is a series of challenging questions- forceful tone of these is emphasized by the bold face of the repeated, capitalized 'WHY'.
- Often emphatic: '*must* not be', 'a *full* explanation', '*vital* questions', 'That is clearly not true'.
- Use of 'we' and 'everyone' early in the article establishes an immediate sense of solidarity between writer and reader. The *Sun* presents itself as speaking up on behalf of its readers.

Grammar
Text A:

- Sentences are longer than in Text B and are mostly complex sentences.
- Constructions and word order often enhance the formality of the piece: 'from which model', 'thousands of pounds in valuable matter expended', 'the grain of sand mightily influential as obstacle in the way of mechanism'.
- Sentences appear more obviously crafted than those in Text B and make use of such literary techniques as antithesis ('abstract/concrete, permanent/changing') and parallel structures ('Work of the disciplined hand was to follow labour of directing mind'; 'some little kink in the brain, some mote in the eye', 'some stone falling by chance').

Text B
- Sentences often simple or compound.
- Material has been deliberately divided into short sentences – e.g. the following could have been one sentence, with a comma replacing the full stop: 'The one thing everyone feared was a fire in the Channel Tunnel. But we were assured that the safety measures could cope with anything'.
- Short sentences are a stylistic feature of contemporary tabloids and help to create the vigorous, assertive tone.

Lexical change

Checkpoints

1 Some examples of words of French and Latin origin are listed on pages 146 and 147. Words of Greek origin include 'telescope', 'photograph', 'skeleton' and many others.
2 There are many possible answers, including 'microchip', 'multiracial', 'interact', 'supernatural', 'megaton'.

Exam question

The words and expressions illustrate a variety of word-formation processes. 'Road rage' and 'arm candy' are compounds. 'Mockney' (Mock + Cockney) and 'digizine' (digital + magazine) are blends. 'Domestic' used as a noun is a conversion (because the word is usually an adjective). WLTM and GSOH are abbreviations (or initialisms). 'Blairism' is an example of affixing (adding the suffix –ism to 'Blair') and is also a word formed from a person's name. 'Tamagotchi' is another word deriving from a name and is a borrowing (from Japanese). Note that questions about the origins of new words will also often ask you to consider what social or other factors may have led to the words being created. 'Blairism', for example, arose because of the need for a word to describe the style of politics associated with Tony Blair (previously there were 'Thatcherism' and 'Majorism'). This aspect of word formation is referred to in the section 'Causes of language change'.

Semantic change

Checkpoints

1 Another example is 'bad' used to mean 'good'.
2 An idiom is an expression that has a meaning that cannot be understood from the meanings of the individual words that make up the expression. See page 18.

Exam questions

1 The words cited in the question illustrate different processes of semantic change. After a brief introduction in which you explain what is meant by semantic change, you could devote a paragraph to each of the words, explaining the modern meanings that they have and the processes involved in these changes in meaning. In each paragraph, you should also give your own examples of other words that have changed in similar ways.

Lean This is an example of amelioration. Applied to human beings, it tends to imply fit, trim and healthy rather than undernourished.

Revolutionary This again illustrates amelioration and is also a good example of broadening. The word now applies not just to politics and can describe someone in almost any field who is associated with pioneering, ground-breaking achievements.

Novice Another example of broadening. Use of the word has been extended far beyond the religious sphere.

Lewd An illustration of pejoration. The word now tends to mean 'obscene' or 'indecent'.

Examiner's secrets

Before finishing your answer, you can show your knowledge of other processes of semantic change by describing (with examples) such processes as narrowing, weakening and the development of metaphorical meanings. The wording of the question allows you to do this.

2 You should cover both parts of the question, but it is likely that you will have more to say about political correctness. This part of the answer could look in turn at different disadvantaged or minority groups – e.g. at attempts when using language to avoid racism, sexism and prejudice against people with disabilities. It would also be interesting to note that there is some resistance within society to political correctness, and as a result not all politically correct words and expressions have been generally adopted or accepted.

Phonological change

Checkpoints

1 A possible explanation is that, compared with the older islanders, the younger islanders identified less strongly with the island, and their loyalty towards it was not so great.
2 The estuary referred to in 'Estuary English' is the Thames Estuary – the area where the accent is thought to have originated.

Exam question

Although the focus of this question is clearly present-day Britain, it would nevertheless still be relevant to include some mention of Labov's research in Martha's Vineyard and New York. This is because the *conclusions* that Labov draws are relevant to language change anywhere – e.g. his concepts of change from above and change from below, and his emphasis on the part that social factors play in language change. You should be careful though to keep your discussion of Labov relatively brief and should certainly not give a detailed account of his research findings.

In the same way, it would be relevant to mention the four stages of phonological change identified by Aitchison – provided you stress that this model is applicable to language change currently taking place in the UK.

The main body of the answer should be directly devoted to what is happening in Britain today. You can draw upon your own first-hand knowledge and experience of how language is being used, but you should also refer to recent research findings, such as those of Kerswill and Williams in Milton Keynes.

Grammatical change

Checkpoints

1 In some cases they have already virtually disappeared – 'authoress', for example, is almost never used today. Words such as 'sculptor' and (though to a lesser extent) 'actor' are increasingly used as gender-neutral terms; the use of 'sculptress' and 'actress' is considered sexist.
2 Examples include 'children', 'mice' and 'geese'.

Exam question

A sensible approach would be to look for *patterns* in the grammar of the quotations and group the sentences together accordingly. Here are some points that might be made:
Word order: Older word orders are evident in several of the quotations. (a) 'Saw you the King' instead of 'Did you see/Have you seen the King'. (b) 'So still thou art' instead of 'So you are still'. (c) 'What mean'st thou' instead of 'What do you mean'. (e) 'What is it' instead of 'What it is'.
Verb forms/inflections: The inflection –*st*, which has now disappeared from the language, is evident in quotations (c), (d) and (e): 'ow'st', 'help'st' and 'demand'st'. The older verb form 'art' (for 'are') is also present in quotation (b).
Pronouns: The second person singular 'thou' is used in several of the quotations – (b), (c), (d), (e). The second line of (c) illustrates how 'thou' was a singular pronoun and 'you' a plural pronoun: 'And thou a kingdom; all of you, allegiance'.

Causes of language change

Checkpoints

1 A phoneme is the smallest unit of sound in a language. The word 'dog', for example, has three phonemes: *d-o-g*.
2 An analogy is a likeness or resemblance between things; often it is used to refer to situations that are in some way similar. It is an appropriate term here because regularization arises from the wish to make aspects of language use more consistent with each other.

Exam question

When candidates are given an option to discuss, they are often tempted to agree with it and construct an answer that supports their case. Remember, however, that there are two sides to an argument and that in many instances you will gain credit by showing that you are aware of the weaknesses

as well as the strengths of a point of view. In the case of this question, it is certainly true that 'social and economic conditions' are an important cause of language change, and much of an answer could be devoted to supporting and illustrating this idea. However, the assertion that 'We need look no further for the causes of language change' is more questionable, and a sensible answer would also identify and discuss *other* causes (e.g. ease of articulation, regularization and the influence of other languages).

Attitudes to language change

Checkpoint

Two of the most prominent were Robert Lowth and Lindley Murray.

Exam question

This is a broad question that offers the opportunity to consider a range of current linguistic controversies. It is important to include plenty of specific examples, and you also need to organize these in some way. One approach would be to devote a paragraph each to vocabulary, grammar and phonology. It would also be useful to show an awareness of the contrasts between prescriptivist and descriptivist attitudes to language change. Most linguists today would favour a descriptivist approach and would see language change as an inevitable response to the changing needs of society rather than a change for the better or the worse.

The future of English

Checkpoint

(a) Examples of countries where English is the national language: United Kingdom, United States, Australia, Canada, New Zealand.
(b) Examples of countries where English is regularly used as a second language: India, Pakistan, Singapore, Hong Kong, the Philippines.

Exam question

This is another question where a sensible answer would consider both the strengths and the weaknesses of the viewpoint expressed in the statement. It is also important to note that the statement makes *two* distinct (if related) points – about English today and English tomorrow – and both of these should be discussed. The first part of an answer might describe the present-day supremacy of English. The rest of the answer could then consider a range of contrasting views about the future of English, including views that tend to support the statement (e.g. the idea that English faces disintegration) and views that do not (e.g. the predictions of uniformity or bidialectalism).

This closing chapter is about the skills and techniques you will need to complete your course successfully. The first three sections offer advice on coursework. Original writing assignments are usually completed as part of the AS course and language investigation assignments in the second A-level year. The rest of the chapter is concerned with tackling different types of examination question: analysis of texts (written and spoken); essay writing; and editorial writing (also known as textual recasting).

Exam boards

In order to organize your notes and revision you will need a copy of your exam board's syllabus specification. You can obtain a copy by contacting the board or by downloading the syllabus from the board's website.

AQA (Assessment and Qualifications Alliance)
Publications Department, Stag Hill House, Guildford, Surrey GU2 5XJ – www.aqa.org.uk

EDEXCEL
Stewart House, 32 Russell Square, London WC1B 5DN – www.edexcel.org.uk

OCR (Oxford, Cambridge and Royal Society of Arts)
1 Hills Road, Cambridge CB2 1GG – www.ocr.org.uk

WJEC (Welsh Joint Education Committee)
245 Western Avenue, Cardiff CF5 2YX – www.wjec.co.uk

Topic checklist

O AS ● A2

	AQA/A	AQA/B	EDEXCEL	OCR	WJE
Language investigation 1	●	●	O●	●	O●
Language investigation 2	●	●	O●	●	O●
Original writing (language production)	●	O		O	O
Exam technique: written texts 1	O●	O●	O●	O●	O●
Exam technique: written texts 2	O●	O●	O●	O●	O●
Exam technique: spoken texts and essays	O●	O●	O●	O●	O●
Exam technique: editorial writing	●	O●	O●	●	O●

Language investigation 1

Most syllabuses include one or more language investigations, usually completed as a coursework component in the second year of A level. This first section on language investigations includes advice on choosing a topic and collecting the raw data for an investigation.

What is a language investigation?

A language investigation is a piece of original research on a topic connected with the study of language. The length of the investigation varies from syllabus to syllabus, and you should check carefully the requirements of the specification you are taking. The different examining boards stipulate lengths ranging from 1 500 to 4 000 words (excluding data).

What should I investigate?

Some syllabuses allow you considerable freedom in your choice of topic. Others limit your choice a little more – specifying, for example, that your topic must be related to the mass media, or based on spoken language or on written texts. Again, you need to be sure that you know what your syllabus requires.

Your investigation needs to have a very specific focus. 'The language of slang', for example, is much too broad a topic. It would be far better to investigate the slang associated with a particular activity (e.g. skateboarding) or social group (e.g. fans of heavy metal). You also need to choose a topic that will interest you and give you the opportunity to carry out some original research. Your teacher will help you to make a suitable choice.

To give you an idea of the kind of topic that might be studied, some examples are listed below. The list includes specimen titles from the examining boards and topics that have actually been investigated by students in the past.

Media-related

→ A study of how a range of newspapers covered a particular news story.
→ The language of newspaper horoscopes.
→ The language of job advertisements.
→ A study of advertisements for a particular type of product.
→ The language of phone-in radio programmes.
→ An analysis of a television or radio sports commentary.
→ A study of magazine names.
→ A comparison of album reviews in rock and classical music magazines.

Spoken language

→ A comparison of male and female conversational behaviour (based on the study of transcripts).
→ Children's conversational behaviour (based on transcripts).

Watch out!

The word 'specification' is now often used instead of syllabus.

Checkpoint

Which parts of the English Language course have most interested you? This might help you to think of a topic.

Watch out!

Before settling on a topic, make sure you will have access to the people or the material you plan to investigate.

- → Variations in accent and dialect across different generations in the same family.
- → Attitudes to accents.
- → A study of the slang used by people of different ages.
- → The development of specific language skills (e.g. semantic or pragmatic) in a child.
- → An analysis of a politician's speech.
- → The language of stand-up comedians.

Written language

- → The language of health information leaflets.
- → The language of holiday brochures.
- → The language of death (looking at tombstones, obituaries, etc.).
- → The language of school or college reports.
- → Email language.
- → The language of internet chatrooms.
- → The language of children's story books.
- → The language of menus.

Collecting data

If you need to record people speaking, remember that speakers tend to feel inhibited when they know they are being taped. This self-consciousness usually wears off after a few minutes, so it is a good idea to leave the tape recorder running for some time. (When you make the transcription you can simply ignore the material at the beginning.) Students sometimes try to capture people speaking naturally by recording them without their knowledge, but if you do this you should tell them about it afterwards and ask for their permission to use what you have recorded in your investigation.

You need to avoid having *too much* or *too little* data:

- → If you are comparing newspapers or magazines, it is usually preferable to concentrate on specific articles or sections.
- → Transcripts of spoken language should not be too lengthy (one of the examining boards stipulates that transcripts should be based on two and a half minutes of recorded speech).
- → Having the right amount of data means that your analysis of it can be detailed and thorough. Remember though that too little data will mean that you don't have enough material to analyse. A single magazine advertisement, for example, is unlikely to be sufficient for a substantial, developed analysis.

Take good care of your data and try not to lose it or damage it. Tapes can be accidentally erased and newspapers or magazines thrown away. Remember you will need to give in your data with the results of your investigation so it is important to keep hold of it. With printed data (e.g. magazine articles or advertisements) it is a good idea to make photocopies which you can then annotate as you're working on the investigation.

Examiner's secrets

Try not to spend too much time deciding your topic and collecting data. Occasionally students spend too long on this and then find they have very little time to carry out the actual investigation.

Link

The next section (pages 174–5) includes advice on setting out transcripts.

The jargon

Data refers to the material that you investigate.

Language investigation 2

In this second section on language investigations, we consider how your investigation should be organized and presented.

Elements in the investigation

The precise arrangement of your investigation will depend on how long it is and also on the topic you have chosen. In addition, some of the specifications recommend particular formats, and you should check whether this is the case with your syllabus. AQA's Specification A, for example, offers the following helpful breakdown of the key elements in a language investigation: *Introduction*; *Description of data*; *Aims*; *Methodology*; *Analysis*; *Conclusions*; *Evaluation*; *Data*; *Bibliography*.

Introduction

First, you explain what you have chosen to investigate, and why. You may also want to refer here to any language theory that is relevant to your area of investigation. If you are investigating gender differences in conversational behaviour, for example, you might mention previous research findings and the conclusions that have been drawn from these. Remember though that the bulk of the investigation must focus on your own research, so you shouldn't describe background theory in too much detail.

Description of data

Here you give factual information about the data you will be analysing. If you are comparing newspaper stories, for example, clearly identify each article by giving the name of the newspaper, the date it was published and the subject of the story. If you will be analysing a transcript of spoken language, explain when and where the recording was made and who is speaking.

Aims

Give a broad explanation of what you are hoping to find out. You may want to base your investigation on a *hypothesis*. This means that you begin with a proposition and then test how accurate it is. An example of a hypothesis is: 'There are significant differences in the ways that men and women behave in conversation'.

Methodology

Explain the design of your investigation, and why these methods were chosen. For example, if you distributed a questionnaire (e.g. surveying people's attitudes to accents), explain how many questionnaires you distributed, who you gave them to and how you intend to analyse the results. If you are analysing spoken or written language, explain which aspects of the language you will be looking at. A comparison of magazine articles, for example, might consider graphology, address to reader, vocabulary and grammar.

Links

You might find there is an outline of the theory elsewhere in this book.

Analysis

This will be the largest section of the investigation and should be divided into sub-sections. The headings for these sub-sections will depend on the topic being investigated. An analysis of conversation, for example, might look at turn taking, interruptions, feedback and changes of topic. The headings will usually have been identified and explained in the preceding 'Methodology' section.

In this section, you carry out a detailed, systematic analysis of the language being studied. Use appropriate linguistic terminology and concentrate on those aspects of the language that are relevant to your aims.

Watch out!

This section should be the heart of your investigation. Make sure it is detailed and thorough.

Conclusions

Explain the conclusions that you draw from your analysis. Has your hypothesis been proved or disproved? It might be appropriate to summarize the main features of the language you have studied, and to consider why these features exist.

Evaluation

Evaluate the success of the methodology employed and the validity of the conclusions you have reached. You might, for example, acknowledge that your analysis was based on a relatively small amount of data and that more extensive research would be needed to confirm your conclusions.

Data

The data you have analysed should be included with the investigation, usually as an appendix. This might comprise transcripts, newspaper or magazine articles, completed questionnaires, etc. If speech has been recorded, you are usually also expected to include the tape.

Conventions in common use when transcribing speech include the following:

Link

Looking at transcripts you have studied (or at those on pages 56–7) will give you an idea of how transcripts should be presented.

→ Do not include any punctuation marks, and only use capital letters for proper nouns or to indicate that a word is emphasized or said loudly.

→ A full stop in round brackets indicates a pause of half a second or less. Numbers in brackets are used to indicate the length in seconds of longer pauses.

→ There are various ways of indicating overlapping speech. One is to underline those words that are spoken simultaneously.

Take note

Symbols in common use to indicate additional features include:

[ ] square brackets around non-verbal features
/   rising tone
\   falling tone

You may also want to make use of the International Phonetic Alphabet (see page 21) to indicate pronunciation.

Bibliography

List any books, articles, etc. used in your investigation. This includes material that was analysed and texts that were consulted (e.g. for background theory).

Original writing (language production)

The name of this component varies from specification to specification. You may find it is called 'original writing', 'own writing', 'language production' or 'experiments in writing'. The component usually forms part of the AS syllabus, and there are strong similarities in the requirements of the various boards.

What will I have to do?

As ever, you should check the precise requirements of the syllabus you are taking and discuss them with your teacher. You are likely to find that you need to produce one or (more commonly) two pieces of original writing. Word lengths vary, but the total for the two pieces is often in the region of 1 500 to 2 000 words. In addition, you are usually asked to write an accompanying commentary of approximately 1 000 words.

What could I write?

The syllabuses generally give you a great deal of freedom of choice, and the opportunity to write creatively about topics that interest you.

It is important, however, that you do not begin writing until you have a very clear idea of the following:

→ Your *audience* (who exactly are your intended readers?).
→ Your *purpose*.
→ The *form* or *genre* you will be writing within (what *type* of writing is it? A broadsheet newspaper article, a radio talk, an educational text for children?).

Watch out!

As you write, keep these three factors constantly in mind.

Listed below are specimen topics, including some suggested by the examining boards:

→ a film, theatre or concert review
→ a magazine or newspaper feature article
→ a guide to a local amenity
→ a short story
→ a beginner's guide to . . .
→ an advertisement (or set of advertisements)
→ a play script for radio or TV
→ a script for a radio or TV documentary
→ a piece of travel journalism
→ educational texts (e.g. study guides, study packs)
→ publicity material for a drama group, sports club, etc.
→ a handbook for new employees of a business or organization
→ a leaflet giving health advice or information
→ a programme for a school or college play.

Watch out!

Remember that your writing must be *original*. Don't duplicate something that already exists.

Important considerations

As mentioned above, you need a clear idea of your audience. You should be able to define it with reference to such characteristics as age, experience, knowledge, education, interests, attitudes, values, etc.

You also need a clear sense of purpose. Your purpose might, for example, be to persuade, inform, entertain, instruct or argue (or a combination of these).

You will need to be familiar with the conventions and characteristics of your chosen genre. This is likely to involve you in research and can be discussed in your commentary (see below).

You need to adopt a register and a style of writing appropriate to your audience, purpose and genre. Vocabulary and sentence construction, for example, should be given careful consideration. How formal, informal, technical, non-specialist, etc. should your vocabulary be? Is there a particular need at any point in your text for short, simple sentences?

If you are obtaining information from other sources, you need to think about how it should be re-presented. In what ways should the language of the original sources be altered to make it more suitable to your audience?

You may well write a rough draft first and then a final draft later. You might test your initial draft on one or more members of your audience, or discuss it with your teacher.

You may want to make use of computer software in order to give your text an authentic, professional appearance, but remember that your first priority is the language that you use in the text.

Links

Register is discussed on pages 36–7.

Writing a commentary

Most syllabuses specify that original writing pieces should be accompanied by a commentary. In the commentary you analyse your own work, explaining the linguistic choices you have made. Most of the important considerations referred to above can be discussed. You should make sure that you include detailed points about the language you have used, and why it is appropriate for your genre, audience and purpose. Aspects of language you might address include:

Links

The skills you use in analysing texts (see pages 178–81) should help you here.

Lexis (e.g. use of formal or informal lexis, field-specific lexis, words with particular connotations etc.)

Grammar (e.g. use of different types of sentence, first or second person, tenses, non-standard grammar etc.)

Phonology (e.g. techniques such as onomatopoeia and alliteration; in a spoken text, features such as stress and intonation)

Discourse structure (e.g. how you have organised the text, use of paragraphs, how cohesion was achieved etc.)

Graphology (any layout/visual features – why they were included and the effects they are intended to have)

Examiner's secrets

When you identify language features you have used, quote examples and explain the effects you were trying to achieve.

Exam technique: written texts 1

The analysis of written texts is one of the main features of both the AS and A2 specifications. The next two sections offer advice on tackling questions of this type.

The GASP formula

Applying the GASP formula is a good way to begin work on analysing a text. You shouldn't begin writing until you have a clear idea of the following:

Genre; **A**udience; **S**ubject; **P**urpose

Understanding these four elements will give you a good overview of the text. In addition, all of these elements are likely to have an important influence on the language that is used. This means you will find it easier to identify the language features that the text contains, and to explain why they are present. So as you read the text, think about the following:

Genre What *type* of writing is it? For example, is it a tabloid or broadsheet newspaper article, an advertisement, a diary, an information leaflet? Every genre has its own conventions and characteristics with regard to language (e.g. we associate tabloid and broadsheet newspapers with different kinds of language use), and you can look for these in the example you are analysing.

Audience Who is the text aimed at? This may be obvious, and may be explained to you in the question. If you are given an extract from an educational text aimed at 13–14-year-olds, there will be no problem identifying who the audience is. Often, however, texts have an *implied* audience and you need to study the text carefully to work out who this is. You will need to consider in your answer how the language of the text reflects its intended audience, and how language is used to address the intended readers.

Subject What is the text about? On a superficial level, this is likely to be obvious but you should think more deeply about the text's *meaning*. What ideas, attitudes and opinions are expressed? One of the most common failings of text analysis answers is for students to spend almost all of their time identifying language features, without ever giving a clear explanation of the meanings these features are being used to express.

Purpose What is the author's purpose in writing the text? The most common purposes are to persuade, inform, entertain, instruct and educate. Try to be precise about the specific purpose of the text you are analysing. If the purpose is to persuade, what exactly is it trying to persuade the reader to do or think? Remember that texts can have more than one purpose: an educational text for children, for instance, may seek to entertain as well as to educate. Think about how language is used to achieve purposes. If an advertisement tries to persuade readers to buy a product, for example, how does the language of the advertisement make the product appear attractive or desirable?

Links

The characteristics of different types of written text are discussed on pages 65–84.

Examiner's secrets

Audiences can be defined with reference to such characteristics as the following (not all will be relevant to every text): age, gender, socio-economic class, occupation, education, knowledge, experience, interests, attitudes and values.

Take note

The subject matter of the text is likely to have a particular influence on the vocabulary that is used (e.g. field-specific lexis may be present).

Planning an answer

As you read the question, it is a good idea to underline or highlight key words, making sure you have a clear understanding of what you are being asked to do.

As you read the text, you can similarly underline or highlight words and sentences that you might want to comment on. You can also make brief notes in the margins.

You should plan your answer by working out the sequence of paragraphs that it will contain. Sometimes questions contain a ready-made plan. Imagine, for instance, that you have been asked to study a magazine article and answer the following question:

> 'What views are expressed in this article and how does the writer use language to persuade the reader to share these views? In your answer, you might like to consider tone, vocabulary, grammar and any other linguistic features you consider relevant'.

This question immediately suggests five paragraphs that an answer could contain:

→ an explanation/summary of the writer's views
→ an analysis of tone
→ an analysis of vocabulary
→ an analysis of grammar
→ an analysis of any additional linguistic features.

It might be sensible to add to this an *introduction* and a *conclusion*. In the introduction, you could give an overview of the text by outlining the four GASP elements referred to above (this is often an effective way to begin a text analysis). The conclusion can be a good place to discuss how successful you consider the text to be. Have the writer's purposes been achieved? Which aspects of the text are especially effective/unsuccessful?

In the absence of a ready-made plan in the question, devise your own sequence of paragraphs. Note that it is best to avoid a line-by-line commentary on the text. This approach has two main weaknesses:

→ Answers often contain a lot of repetition because the same linguistic features recur in different parts of the text.
→ Students run out of time and say very little about later parts of the text.

You need to decide what the *topic* of each paragraph in your answer will be. An approach that usually works well is to devote a separate paragraph to each of the main aspects of the text's language (vocabulary, grammar, tone and so on). The aspects of language you might focus on are discussed in the next section (pages 180–1). It might also be appropriate to add an introduction and a conclusion of the type suggested above.

Examiner's secrets

You will probably need to read the text at least twice: once fairly quickly to get a general idea of it, followed by a slower, more careful reading.

Watch out!

Resist the temptation to start writing before you have devised a plan.

Watch out!

Don't be afraid to express your opinion – but try to give *reasons* for your point of view.

Examiner's secrets

An alternative approach is to divide the text into sections or stages (usually no more than three or four) and analyse each in turn. Another is to single out key aspects of the text's meaning or purpose and devote a separate paragraph to each, commenting in each case on relevant language features.

Exam technique: written texts 2

This second section looks in more detail at what answers to text analysis questions should contain.

Writing an answer

When you are analysing a text, a typical point is likely to contain the following elements:

→ Identification of a *linguistic feature*.
→ One or more *examples* from the text.
→ Comment on the *effect* that the feature has.

Sometimes all three elements can be combined in a single sentence:

> The powerful verbs used to describe the politician's delivery of his speech ('stormed', 'raged', 'blasted') contribute to the impression of a violent confrontation.

Failure to include all three elements is a common weakness in text analysis answers:

> Students often do not show enough knowledge of *terminology* in their answers, failing to use appropriate terms to identify language features.

> Many students do not *quote* enough from the text. Always support your points with plenty of examples. Most quotations are unlikely to be more than one or two words long. In longer quotations, it is a good idea to underline those words that are especially significant, or relevant to the point you are making.

> Often students identify a linguistic feature but say nothing about the *effect* that it has. Never lose sight of the meaning and purpose of the text and always try to explain how the language that is used relates to these aspects. Try to avoid vague descriptions of effect ('helps to get the meaning across', 'helps the passage to flow', 'has a good effect', etc.).

Using paragraphs

As was explained in the previous section (page 179), you may well find that the question mentions specific aspects of language that you should discuss. As was also mentioned, an approach to analysis questions that often works well is to devote a separate paragraph to each of these aspects. If you do this, it is a good idea to begin each paragraph with a *topic sentence*. This is a sentence that tells the reader the theme of the paragraph. Here is an example:

> The vocabulary of the text is also very appropriate for the target audience.

This sentence make it very clear that the paragraph that follows will be about vocabulary. It also makes an immediate point about the vocabulary, a point that the next few sentences can develop. Topic sentences such as this are better than bald statements such as 'I am now going to discuss vocabulary'.

Action point

Try to develop the habit of always including all three of these elements when you make a point.

Watch out!

Avoid quoting long, unbroken chunks of text.

Examiner's secrets

It is important to get into the habit of analysing texts in a structured, systematic way.

180

Linguistic features: what to look for

Graphology

This refers to the *visual* aspects of a text: layout and the use of particular fonts, bold face, italics, upper and lower case letters, bullet points and so on. Consider how the text is arranged on the page: is it broken up by the use of headings, sub-headings, spacing? Always explain the *effects* of graphological features – e.g. *why* are certain words in bold face? Be careful not to devote too much of an answer to graphology. Remember that the written language of the text should be your main focus.

Links

Most of these aspects of language are explored in more detail elsewhere in the book. Use the index to find the relevant sections.

Discourse structure

How is the text as a whole organized, and why is it structured in this way? If paragraphs are used, what are the differences between them? Do the paragraphs correspond to different stages in an argument, or do they deal with different topics? Do any of the paragraphs contrast with each other? Does the text *develop* in any way – e.g. does it build to a climax? How is *cohesion* achieved in the text?

Vocabulary

You can comment on *groups* of words and also on *individual* words. Are there several words with similar connotations? Are there several verbs that have similar effects, or nouns or adjectives? Are certain words especially associated with a particular topic or subject (field-specific lexis)? Are there examples of colloquial vocabulary, or slang? Look also at the impact that particular words have, and how this contributes to the meaning of the text.

The jargon

The **connotations** of a word are its associations (see page 16).

Address to reader

Does the text address the reader directly, using the second person pronoun 'you'? Does the text address the reader in a familiar, friendly way? Does the text try to create solidarity between writer and reader by using the first person plural pronoun 'we'?

Tone

How would you describe the tone? Formal? Informal? Serious? Lighthearted? Ironic? Angry? Quote examples to illustrate your arguments. Is the tone consistent throughout the text?

Grammar

Consider sentence lengths and sentence structure. Are any or all of the sentences noticeably long or short? Are sentences generally simple, compound or complex? Is there any non-standard grammar? Are there any grammatically incomplete sentences? Is word order ever used to emphasize part of a sentence (*foregrounding*)?

The jargon

Foregrounding occurs when the arrangement of a sentence places emphasis on a particular word or phrase (often by placing it at the beginning of the sentence).

Phonology

This is the use of *sound*. Look for such devices as onomatopoeia, alliteration and rhyme and the effects that these have.

Exam technique: spoken texts and essays

This section offers advice on two more types of exam question. The analysis of spoken texts is an important element in both AS and A2 exams. Conventional essay questions are now less common than they once were but are still a feature of some syllabuses.

Analysing spoken texts

Studying the question

Usually, the question on a spoken text will ask you to approach it from a particular angle. Often you will be asked one or more of the following:

→ How typical the text is of spoken language/conversational interaction.
→ How speakers use language to express ideas, attitudes and emotions.
→ How particular speakers interact with each other in a conversation, which may be informal or formal (e.g. a job interview).

In addition, you may be directed towards specific language features, such as vocabulary, grammar and non-fluency features.

When you read the question, you should underline the key words and then make sure you focus on these elements of the text in your answer.

What to look for

As explained above, the question may require you to concentrate on certain specific features of the text. The following aspects can often be discussed:

→ The *type* of discourse; e.g. is it a monologue, or dialogue? Is it a prepared speech, an informal conversation or a formal interview?
→ The *functions* of the discourse; e.g. if it is a conversation, is it interactional or transactional?
→ Features that are characteristics of spoken English. Certain lexical and grammatical features are especially associated with spoken English, and speech is also often characterized by non-fluency features.
→ Non-verbal aspects of speech (pauses, stress, etc.).
→ Structural features of conversation; e.g. openings and closings, turn taking, adjacency pairs, changes of topic, feedback.
→ Conversational theory, such as Grice's cooperative principle and theories relating to differences in male and female conversational behaviour. Remember though that your answer must be firmly rooted in the text. Unless the question indicates otherwise, keep references to theory relatively brief and only include them in order to clarify aspects of the text.

Writing the answer

If the question lists aspects of the text that you should examine, this can provide you with a ready-made plan: look at each aspect in turn, allocating a separate paragraph to each.

Alternatively, devise your own plan. One approach is to decide the main linguistic features you wish to consider and then discuss each of these in a separate paragraph.

If you are analysing a piece of dialogue, it can sometimes make sense to write a commentary that follows the course of the conversation, discussing how it opens, develops and closes. Another approach is to consider each speaker's role in the conversation separately.

Remember to include plenty of quotations from the text to support your points.

Writing essays

Studying the question

Underline the key words in the question. Try to break the question down into smaller units; often essay questions have two or more parts to them, as in the following example:

What are the main characteristics of slang, and why do people use it? Do you consider slang to be a good use of English?

This question has three parts to it: the main characteristics of slang; why people use it; whether or not it is a good use of English. In your answer, you must take care to cover all parts of the question.

Writing the essay

Again, the question may offer a ready-made plan. The above question on slang is an example of this.

If the question doesn't suggest an obvious plan, you should work out one of your own. You need to decide how many paragraphs to include, what they will be about and what their sequence will be. Remember that a single paragraph should have a single topic or theme. It is also a good idea to begin each paragraph with a *topic sentence*, which identifies the topic of the paragraph (see page 180). Avoid using a large number of paragraphs. Usually, the main body of an exam essay should contain about three or four paragraphs, with additional paragraphs for the introduction and conclusion.

The introduction might give a broad overview of the subject, define terms that are used in the title and give an indication of what the rest of the essay is going to contain. In the conclusion, you should avoid merely repeating what you have already said. The concluding paragraph might be where you express your own opinion, or where you speculate on future developments in English.

In your answer, you should show your knowledge of relevant theory but should make sure you relate the theory discussed to the question. You should also support your arguments with *examples* of language use. Many language issues are controversial, and you should try to show an awareness of contrasting viewpoints, and of their respective strengths and weaknesses.

Examiner's secrets

If the text is *prepared* speech, it may resemble a written text (e.g. it is likely to have sentences and paragraphs). However, it is important to show in your analysis that you are aware the text was written to be *heard* rather than read. Look for aspects of language which reflect this.

Watch out!

Try to ensure that both your introduction and conclusion have something of substance to say.

Action point

Debates about language often make the news; try to keep yourself informed about language issues.

183

Exam technique: editorial writing

As explained below, editorial writing questions require you to produce new texts from source materials that you are given. They are a feature of all A2 syllabuses and also of most AS syllabuses.

What will I be asked to do?

Make sure you find out the precise format of the textual recasting questions set by your particular specification. You will probably find that they broadly correspond to the following pattern:

→ You will be given a collection of texts. The texts may be of different types and of varying lengths (see below), but they will relate to a common topic. Depending on your syllabus, you may receive these texts a few days before the exam or in the exam itself. If you are given them in advance of the exam, you will be able to study the texts and make brief annotations, but you will not find out the actual question you have to answer until you take the exam.

→ In the exam, you will be asked to produce a new text, based on the material you have been given. The question will usually specify the *audience* you are writing for, the *purpose* of your text, the type (or *genre*) of writing you should produce and *how much* you should write.

→ Some syllabuses also require you to write a commentary to accompany your answer, explaining the changes you have made to the material and justifying the approach you have taken.

Types of texts

The source materials you are asked to study may take many forms: magazine and newspaper articles, diaries, letters, leaflets, extracts from books, charts, graphs, etc.

Similarly, the question you are set may ask you to write in any one of a number of forms. What you will *not* be asked to write is a conventional exam essay. Instead, you will be asked to produce a practical text, aimed at a specific audience. In producing the new text you will probably have to make substantial alterations to the original materials, which are unlikely to have been aimed at the audience you will be addressing.

Using the preparation time

As explained earlier, you may be allowed a few days to study the source materials, or you may not see them until the actual exam. Either way, you will need to read the materials carefully, and you should annotate them as you do so. If you know the question, you can focus on those parts of the texts that are of most relevance. If not, you should still make sure you read the texts in a productive way. Whether you know the question or not, you will find it helpful to look for the following:

→ The *main points* made in each text. Underline or highlight key passages and try to summarize the meaning of each text in a few words or sentences.
→ *Connections* between the texts. Do certain texts deal with similar aspects of the topic?
→ *Contrasts* between the texts. Are opposing points of view expressed, or are there contrasting interpretations of the same information?
→ *Factual information* (statistics, dates, etc.) that might be of use to you.

Writing an answer

Here are some important considerations for you to bear in mind when writing an answer:

→ You do not need to use *all* the source material. On the contrary, you will be given credit if you are selective and show discrimination in your use of the texts. At the same time, if you are given several texts, do not rely too heavily on just one or two of them.
→ Don't copy out long passages from the source materials. Use your own words as much as possible. You are expected to transform the materials into a new text. This might, for example, mean that you have to simplify or condense parts of the original texts.
→ Don't simply use the texts in the order in which they are presented to you. You will almost certainly need to reorganize the material.
→ You will need to think about how to *link* ideas and information taken from different texts. Ideally, the reader shouldn't be able to see the 'joins'. The new piece should have a single consistent 'voice' – unlike the original source materials, which will be a collection of different voices.
→ In creating a voice for your piece, you need to decide on an appropriate tone and register. Your approach should be suited to the audience and purpose specified in the question.
→ Think about the conventions of the *type* of writing you have been asked to produce. If you are asked to write a magazine article, information leaflet, etc., try to produce a realistic text.
→ If you are a little above or a little below the word limit you are not likely to be penalized, but don't go way above or way under. Too few words probably means the content of your answer is inadequate, too many will mean you have not been concise enough.

Writing a commentary

This is not a requirement of every syllabus. Much of the advice on commentaries given in the section 'Original writing' (pages 176–7) is also relevant to textual recasting commentaries. Essentially, you need to explain how the language you have used is appropriate for your genre, audience and purpose.

Watch out!

If your syllabus requires you to write a commentary (see below), you will also find it useful to note the main linguistic features (vocabulary, grammar, etc.) of the source materials.

Examiner's secrets

The examiner's main concern will be whether you have *changed* the original material in appropriate ways.

Examiner's secrets

If you are required to write a commentary, bear this in mind when you complete the initial writing task. Try to 'build in' features you will later be able to comment on.

Glossary

accent

The pronunciation of words. *Regional* accents include Cockney and Geordie.

accommodation

A theory suggesting that we adjust our speech to 'accommodate' the person we are addressing.

acronym

A word formed from the initial letters of other words (e.g. 'radar', from 'radio detection and ranging').

active voice

When the subject of a verb is the agent performing the action (e.g. 'The police caught the burglar').

adjacency pair

Two-part exchanges following a predictable pattern and found in conversation (e.g. question followed by answer).

adjective

A word that can be used to describe a noun.

adverb

A word that tells us more about a verb, adverb or adjective.

adverbial

A word or group of words working as an adverb, usually giving information about time, place or manner.

affix

A group of letters forming part of a word, usually a prefix or a suffix.

alliteration

When two or more words begin with the same sound.

amelioration

A change in the meaning of a word that gives the word a meaning that is more positive.

anaphoric reference

A word or expression in a text that refers back to another part of the text.

antonym

A word that is opposite in meaning to another word.

assonance

When the vowel sounds in the middle of two or more words are similar.

asyndetic listing

Listing which does not involve the use of conjunctions.

auxiliary verb

A verb placed in front of a main verb (e.g. 'is', 'have', 'can').

blend

A word formed by combining parts of other words (e.g. 'smog' from 'smoke' and 'fog').

borrowing

A word or expression taken from another language.

broadening

Occurs when the meaning of a word is extended; the word retains its old meaning but takes on one or more added meanings as well.

cataphoric reference

A word or expression in a text that refers forward to another part of the text.

clause

A group of words forming a unit within a sentence, usually containing a subject and a verb.

clipping

A word formed by shortening an existing word (e.g. 'phone' from 'telephone').

cohesion

The techniques and devices used to connect different parts of a text with each other.

coinage

The creation of a completely new word.

collocation

Groups (usually pairs) of words that are commonly found alongside each other (e.g. 'driving rain').

comparative

An adjective that makes a comparison, usually ending in –*er* (e.g. 'colder', 'faster').

complement

A part of a sentence that describes a subject or an object.

complex sentence

A sentence containing a main clause and one or more clauses of lesser importance.

compound

A word or expression formed from the combination of other words (e.g. 'blackbird', 'head waiter').

compound sentence

Two or more simple sentences joined together by a coordinating conjunction ('and', 'but' or 'so').

conjunction

A word which joins together the different parts of a sentence (e.g. 'and', 'or', 'but').

connotation

The associations that a word has.

contraction

Occurs when words are combined to form a single, shortened word (e.g. 'we've' from 'we have' or 'don't' from 'do not').

convergence

When the speech styles of two or more people move closer to each other.

creole

A pidgin language that has developed and become the first language of new generations of speakers.

declarative sentence

A sentence that makes a statement.

deixis

Deictic expressions cannot be understood unless the context of the utterance is known (e.g. 'here', 'there').

denotation

The straightforward, objective meaning of a word (i.e. its dictionary definition).

descriptivism

An approach to the study of language that describes how language is used but does not judge language use as correct or incorrect.

determiner

A word used before a noun to indicate quantity, identity or significance (e.g. 'a', 'the', 'some').

dialect

A variety of language with distinctive features of vocabulary, grammar and accent (e.g. regional dialects).

divergence

When the speech styles of two or more people move away from each other.

ellipsis

The omission of one or more grammatical elements from a sentence.

end-focus

Placing emphasis upon the closing part of a sentence.

Estuary English

An accent that originated in London and the south-east and that has spread outwards to other parts of the country.

euphemism

A mild or indirect expression used instead of one that is considered in some way offensive, painful or unpleasant.

exclamatory sentence

A sentence that ends with an exclamation mark.

field-specific lexis

Vocabulary associated with a particular topic or field.

filled pause

A hesitation such as 'um' or 'er'.

filler

A word or expression of little meaning commonly inserted into speech (e.g. 'you know', 'like').

genre

A type or form (e.g. novel, short story, magazine article, etc.).

graphology

The visual aspects of a text (layout, headings, etc.).

head word

The main word in a phrase.

hypernym, hyponym

A *hypernym* is a general word linked in meaning to more specific words, known as *hyponyms* (e.g. 'furniture' is a hypernym, 'desk' a hyponym).

idiolect

The form of language used by, and unique to, a single individual.

idiom

An expression whose meaning cannot be understood from the meanings of the individual words that make up the expression.

imperative sentence

A sentence that is a command.

infinitive

A form of a verb that does not specify person or number (e.g. 'to run', 'to lift', 'to write' are infinitives).

inflection

A letter or group of letters at the end of a word serving a grammatical function. Also known as an **inflectional affix**.

interrogative sentence

A sentence that is a question.

intertextuality

When a text makes reference to, or incorporates elements of, another text.

intransitive verbs

Verbs which do not require an object.

jargon

The specialist vocabulary associated with a particular occupation or activity.

lexical field

A group of words with associated meanings and uses.

lexis

Another term for vocabulary.

loan word

A word that has been taken from another language.

metaphor

A comparison that describes a person, object or situation as if it actually were something else.

modal auxiliary

Auxiliary verbs which are only ever used in conjunction with a main verb (e.g. 'can', 'must').

modifier

A word that gives more information about a head word.

monosyllabic words

Words of one syllable.

morpheme

The smallest unit of language that expresses meaning or serves a grammatical function; always a letter or group of letters.

morphology

The study of the structure of words.

narrowing

When the meaning of a word narrows so that it becomes more limited and specific.

non-fluency features

Features that interrupt the flow of a person's speech (e.g. hesitations, repetitions).

noun

A word that indicates the name given to a person, place, object, feeling, etc.

onomatopoeia

When the sound of a word echoes its meaning (e.g. 'buzz', 'splash').

parallelism

Occurs when phrases or sentences have a similar pattern or structure (also known as 'parallel structures').

passive voice

When the subject of a verb is the element affected by the action (e.g. 'The burglar was caught by the police').

pejoration

A shift in the meaning of a word so that its meaning becomes less positive.

phoneme

The smallest unit of sound in a language.

phonetics

The study of the sounds of speech.

phonology

The study of the patterns and systems of sounds in particular languages.

phrase

A word or group of words that functions as a unit in a sentence.

pidgin

A language that combines two or more other languages, enabling the members of different speech communities to communicate.

polysyllabic

Words with three or more syllables.

pragmatics

The study of the part that language plays in social situations and social relationships.

prefix

A group of letters commonly found at the beginnings of words (e.g. *re–*, *un–*).

preposition

A word that relates one word to another (e.g. 'in', 'at', 'under').

prescriptivism

An approach to the study of language that favours rules identifying correct and incorrect language use.

pronoun

A word that takes the place of a noun (e.g. 'he', 'she', 'it').

prosody

Non-verbal aspects of speech such as volume, intonation and pitch.

Received Pronunciation

The accent associated with upper-class speakers of English.

register

A form of language appropriate to a particular situation.

repair

In conversation, a repair resolves a problem that has arisen – e.g. speakers may correct themselves if something has been said in error.

semantics

The study of word meanings.

simile

A comparison that includes the words 'like' or 'as'.

simple sentence

A sentence that contains only one clause.

sociolect

A variety of language (or dialect) used by a particular social group.

Standard English

The vocabulary and grammar associated with educated users of the language.

subordinate clause

A clause within a sentence that is less important than the main clause.

suffix

A group of letters commonly found at the ends of words (e.g. *–able*, *–ly*).

superlative

An adjective indicating the highest degree, usually ending *–est* (e.g. 'coldest', 'fastest').

syllable

A single unit of speech or a sub-division of a word (e.g. *ma-gic* has two syllables, *af-ter-wards* has three).

syndetic listing

Listing which involves the use of conjunctions.

synonym

A word similar in meaning to another word.

taboo language

Words that are avoided because they are considered offensive, embarrassing, obscene or unpleasant.

tag question

A question attached to the end of a statement (e.g. 'It's cold, *isn't it*?').

topic loop

Occurs when a conversation returns to an earlier topic.

topic marker

An utterance which establishes the topic of a conversation.

topic shifter

An utterance that moves a conversation on to another topic.

transitive verbs

Verbs which require an object.

unvoiced pause

A silent pause in speech.

verb

A word that indicates doing or being, i.e. actions ('write', 'give') or states ('is', 'seems').

word class

Words are grouped into word classes according to their grammatical function. Nouns, verbs, adjectives etc. are examples of word classes. Also known as **parts of speech**.

Index

abbreviations 153
abstract nouns 4
accent 32, 61, 86–9
accommodation theory 50
acronyms 153
active voice 7
address forms 102–3
adjacency pairs 48
adjectives 5
adverbial 11
adverbs 7
advertisements 72–5
affixes 14–15
affixing 152
Aitchision, Jean 123, 157
alliteration 20
amelioration 154
anaphoric reference 22
Anglo-Saxon 144
antonym 17
archaisms 153
assimilation 160
assonance 21
auxiliary verb 6

babbling 118–19
back-channel noises 49
back formation 153
Bernstein, Basil 112–13
blends 152
body language 58–9
borrowing 152
British Black English 91
broadening 154
broadsheet newspapers 66–71

cataphoric reference 22
Chall, Jeanne S. 136
Cheshire, Jenny 94–95
child-directed speech 134–5
Chomsky, N. 131
class and language 92–3, 112–13
clauses 10
clippings 153
cognition 132
cohesion 22–3
coinage 152
collective nouns 4
collocations 19, 23
common nouns 4
comparative adjectives 5
complement 10
complex sentence 12
compound sentence 12
compounding 152
concrete nouns 4
conjunctions 9, 23

connotation 16
contractions 37
convergence 43, 50, 87
conversation 46–55
conversion 153
cooperative principle 50
coordinating conjunctions 9
covert prestige 95
creoles 90–1
Crystal, David 37, 165

dead metaphors 18
declarative sentences 13
definite article 9
deictic expressions 44
demonstrative pronouns 8
denotation 16
descriptivism 162
determiners 9
dialects 32–3, 86–9
dialogue 42
digressions 45
diphthongs 21
divergence 43, 50

Early Modern English 146
education and language 112–13
elaborated code 112–13
ellipsis 12, 22, 67
email 80–1
Estuary English 88–9, 157, 163, 165
euphemisms 110–11, 155
exclamatory sentences 13
extended metaphors 18

face 52
false starts 45
feedback 49
field 36
field-specific lexis 16
filled pauses 45
fillers 45
formal language 19

GASP formula 178
gender and language 54–5, 94–5, 105, 106–7
generalization 154
Giles, Howard 50
Goffman, Irving 52
graphology 24–5, 66
great English vowel shift 156
Grice, H. P. 50

Halliday, Michael 36, 128
head word 10

headlines 67
Honey, John 113
hook 72
hypernym 16–17
hypertext 81
hyponym 16–17

identification 22
idiolects 33
idioms 18, 155
imitation and reinforcement 130
imperative sentences 13
indefinite article 9
indefinite pronouns 8
Indo-European languages 144
infinitive 6
inflectional affixes (inflections) 14–15
informal language 19
information texts 76–7
innateness 131
input 132
instruction texts 76–7
interactional exchanges 42
International Phonetic Alphabet (IPA) 21
interrogative pronouns 8
interrogative sentences 13
intertextuality 73
intonation 60

jargon 98–9
journalese 37, 67

Kroll, B. M. 137

Labove, William 92, 156
Lakoff, Robin 53, 55, 95
language acquisition device 131
Late Modern English 150
legal language 97, 99
levels of formality 19
lexical change 152
lexical field 16
literary texts 78–9

main verb 6
manner 36
Martha's Vineyard 156
metaphor 18, 154
Middle English 146
Milroy, Lesley 93
modal auxiliary 6
mode 36
modifiers 10
monologue 42
morphemes 14
morphology 14

narrowing   154
new technology   80–1
newspapers   66–71
non-fluency features   45
non-verbal communication
   58–61
noun phrase   10
nouns   4

object   10
occupational dialects   32, 96–7
Old English   144
omission   160
one-word stage   124
onomatopoeia   20
overextension   123
overgeneralization   126–7
overregularizaton   126–7
overt prestige   95

pace   60–1
passive voice   7
pauses   61
pejoration   154
personal pronouns   8
phatic communication   42–3
phonemes   20
phonemic expansion and
   contraction   119
phonetics   20
phonology   20–1
phrases   10
Piaget, J.   132
pidgins   90–1
pitch   60
Plain English Campaign   99

politeness   52–3
political correctness   108–9, 111,
   155
possessive pronouns   8
power and language   102–3
prefixes   14–15
prepositions   9
prescriptivism   160
primary verb   6
pronouns   8
proper nouns   4
prosody   20, 60–1

racism   105
Received Pronunciation   34–5,
   86–7
reflexive pronouns   8
register   36–7
relative pronouns   8
repairs   48–9
representation   104–5
restricted code   112–13
rhetorical techniques   78
rhyme   20

Sapir–Whorf hypothesis   104–5
semantic change   154
semantic field   16
semantics   16
sentences   12
sexism   105, 106–7
signature line   72
simile   18
simple sentence   12
Skinner, B. F.   130
slang   100–1

social class and language   92–3,
   112–13
sociolects   32–3
specialization   154
speech and writing (differences)
   30–1
split infinitive   163
Standard English   32, 34–5, 86,
   113, 150
stress   61
subject   10
subordinate clauses   12–13
subordinating conjunctions   9
suffixes   14–15
superlative adjectives   5
suprasegmental features   20
syllables   20
synonym   17

tabloid newspapers   66–71
taboo language   110–11
telegraphic stage   125
tense   7
Tok Pisin   90
transactional exchanges   42
Trudgill, Peter   92–3, 94–5
turn taking   46–7
two-word stage   124–5

underextension   122–3

verb phrase   10
verbs   6
volume   61

weakening   154
word classes   4–9